# DATE DUE

| | | | |
|---|---|---|---|
| ~~MY17'00~~ | | | |
| ~~DE2 0'00~~ | | | |
| FE 7'06 | | | |
| | | | |
| | | | |
| | | | |
| | | | |
| | | | |
| | | | |
| | | | |
| | | | |
| | | | |
| | | | |
| | | | |
| | | | |

DEMCO 38-296

PHILIP MARSDEN

# The Crossing Place

A Journey among the Armenians
With a new Introduction by Peter Sourian

KODANSHA INTERNATIONAL
New York • Tokyo • London

The wind is singing, the leaves of the mulberry-tree are shuffling.
Eternal song; eternal life; eternal death; eternal sorrow; and eternal joy . . .

Vahan Totovents, *Scenes from an Armenian Childhood*,
(Trans. Mischa Kudian)

Kodansha America, Inc.
114 Fifth Avenue, New York, New York 10011, U.S.A.

Kodansha International Ltd.
17-14 Otowa 1-chome, Bunkyo-ku, Tokyo 112, Japan

Published in 1995 by Kodansha America, Inc.
by arrangement with HarperCollins Publishers.

First published in 1993 by HarperCollins Publishers, London, England.

First American edition

This is a Kodansha Globe book.

Library of Congress Cataloging-in-Publication Data

Marsden, Philip, 1961–
The crossing place : a journey among the Armenians / Philip
Marsden ; introduction by Peter Sourian.
p.    cm. — (Kodansha globe)
Includes bibliographical references (p.     ) and index.
ISBN 1-56836-052-5
1. Armenia—Description and travel.  2. Armenians.  I. Title.
II. Series.
DS165.M37    1995
909'.0491992082—dc20                                    94-42114

Printed in the United States of America

95  96  97  98  99  RRD/H  10  9  8  7  6  5  4  3  2  1

# CONTENTS

# LIST OF ILLUSTRATIONS

# ACKNOWLEDGEMENTS

To all the priests and community leaders of the Armenian diaspora, to the taxi-drivers and villagers, to the short-fused visa officials and long-suffering librarians, to those I cannot mention and those whose names I've had to change, to all who harboured and helped me in a hundred ways to reach Armenia and its troubled corners – thank you.

But particular thanks are due:

To His Beattitude Archbishop Torkom Manoogian, Armenian Patriarch of Jerusalem, George Hintlian and Father Anooshavan and members of Jerusalem's Armenian community.

To Father Levon Zekiyan, Chair of Armenian Studies, University of Venice.

To His Holiness Karekin II, Catholicos of Cilicia and members of Beirut's Armenian community.

To Ivo Hadjimishev of Sofia.

To staff of the *Ararat* and *Nor Gyank* Armenian newspapers in Bucharest.

To Ashot and Sylvie Shaboian of Yerevan.

To Father Nerses Nersessian, Curator of Armenian manuscripts, British Library, London.

To Christopher J. Walker, Garo Keheyan, Nouritza Matossian, Terence Rodrigues and Will Self.

To the late Dieter Klein and Mike Fishwick for marshalling the idea.

To Bridget and Francis Hoare for a suitably remote cottage in Sutherland.

And to Laura, to whom this book is dedicated.

# INTRODUCTION

## BY PETER SOURIAN

Please imagine, if you will, that the following newspaper excerpts and government memo had been published during the past twelve years. An excerpt from a *New York Times* article of July 31, 1983: *Many of the Jews . . . had fled Germany while hundreds of thousands of their relatives, they say, were being massacred.* And another, of December 1, 1983: *"I understand what this means, because of my own background as a Jew,"* he said, *referring to a massacre of Jews in the 1940s.* From the *Boston Globe* of April 25, 1988, in an article by Professor Justin McCarthy: *Europe was the scene of horrible acts of inhumanity between Jews and Germans.* An editorial in the *Wall Street Journal* on October 19, 1990, states: *Germany has been fighting its past for years and has been only partly successful. Must it now accept the possibility that one of its strongest allies, the United States, blames it for the genocide of another people?* And, finally, from a box accompanying an article by Andrew Corsun in the *Department of State Bulletin*, official monthly record of United States Foreign Policy, volume 82, number 2605, August 1982: *Because the historical record of events in Europe during World War II is ambiguous, the United States Department of State does not endorse allegations that the German government committed a genocide against the Jewish people.*

Even though there has been evidence of some tendency in recent years toward a deplorable revisionism regarding the Jewish Holocaust, the idea that it could be characterized as above and in such reputable publications would seem implausible. In fact, it has not actually been thus characterized; if it were, the outcry would properly be massive and instantaneous. The passages in question have indeed been cited verbatim here—*except* that I have substituted the word *Jew* for the word *Armenian*, the word *German* for the word *Turk*, and World War II for World War I.

I have played this rather shabby little trick in an attempt to put

ix

readers of Philip Marsden's remarkable book, *The Crossing Place: A Journey Among the Armenians*, in the shoes of that relatively little-known ancient people, the Armenians, who, unlike the Babylonians, the Hittites, the Parthians, have survived as an identifiable entity, but who have not yet managed to bury their dead, whose ghosts still wander restlessly abroad. Some people, often by reason of their own historical experience, will comprehend the ongoing pain of this more deeply than others. Marsden is one who does, and there are those of Armenian background, like myself, who are grateful for the attestations of such non-Armenians, as being less susceptible to the charge of special pleading.

In 1929, long before the term *genocide* was coined by Raphael Lemkin in reference to the mass murder of Jews because they were Jews by the Nazis, Winston Churchill wrote that "the clearance of this race from Asia Minor [where the Armenians, known to Herodotus and Xenophon, had been living continuously for 3,000 years] was about as complete as such an act, on a scale so great, could be." In 1994, Cornell University professor Stephen T. Katz, scrupulously examining the ample record, concludes that "the percentage of the Armenian people in Turkey destroyed by Turks in World War I is generally held to be in the region of 35 to 60 percent."

Turks generally continue to refuse to acknowledge the genocide. Among the reasons are pride, fear of possible territorial and reparations claims, and more or less willful ignorance. Their version of what happened goes something like this: Both sides suffered under terrible wartime conditions; Armenians killed many Turks; the Armenian Christian minority was legitimately suspected of dangerous disloyalty and had to be forcibly, yet with all possible consideration, removed from the sensitive eastern provinces bordering the Russian Empire. They claim that what may have occurred was thus, if regrettable, normal under the circumstances, more than anything else the fault of the Armenians themselves, and certainly no genocide.

In recent years the movement toward denial has intensified, for a variety of reasons, notably geopolitical, involving what are classically termed *raisons d'état*. Although I cannot imagine a single Armenian for whom there are two sides to this question, the American press, for example, is much more ambiguous now than it was in 1915, when successive *New York Times* headlines ran: TALES

OF ARMENIAN HORRORS CONFIRMED (September 27); 800,000 ARMENIANS COUNTED DESTROYED (October 7); MILLION ARMENIANS KILLED OR IN EXILE (December 15). Other efforts at denial are more bald. The historian Susan Blair, doing research at the National Archives in Washington, found in 1982 that

> The volumes of records from the American Embassy in Constantinople from 1915 have been looted. The entire section devoted to social problems in the Ottoman Turkish Empire in 1915, which would cover the Armenian genocide, has been cut out of the bound volume, leaving only the stubs of pages. The rolls of microfilm covering the massacre of Armenians and Assyrians in northwestern Persia during the Turkish invasions of the area during World War I disappeared from the Archives' Microfilm Reading Room. I consulted the material one week, and the next week, when I wanted to check a reference the rolls were gone.

It happens—inevitably—in cyberspace, where on one private computer network this message was posted in 1994, turning matters upside down: "Your Armenian grandfathers are guilty of genocide."

Along with the denial of past horrors and therefore of the psychic relief of closure, of proper burial of one's dead, so to speak, there is the matter of systematic, ongoing cultural denial. Characteristically, concerning another ethnic group, the Kurds, Turkey employs the term *mountain Turks*. Lord Kinross observed in 1955 that "the Turks prefer to forget the Armenians." In Kars, the chief of police described to Kinross the eleventh-century Church of the Holy Apostles, of distinctive Armenian architecture, as originally a mosque, and "took the line that Armenia was largely a figure of American propaganda." And the marvelous deserted church of Aghtamar, standing solitary on a strange, beautiful island in Lake Van, legendary cradle of the Armenian nation, is, typically, described to Kinross by a Turk as a Greek church, "denying all things Armenian as a matter of course." The cathedral at Aintab is now a penitentiary, and a chapel at Erzerum a Muslim mausoleum;

other churches serve as latrines, hovels, and stables; some have simply been destroyed. This is the architecture whose apogee was reached in the seventh century, of which the great Russian poet Osip Mandelstam admiringly wrote: "The teeth of your vision crumble and break when you look for the first time at Armenian churches." And so it goes.

Who are these Armenians, anyway, who, according to Professor Leo Kuper, "were reduced in Turkey from about two million to less than 25,000 at the present time"? In his arresting prelude to *The Crossing Place*, the young English writer Philip Marsden tells of how, wandering in the hills of eastern Turkey and finding only the bones of long-dead Armenians there, he decides to go in search of live Armenians, from Venice through Lebanon, Syria, the Balkans, to the Crimea, and finally to the tiny besieged remnant, the former Soviet Republic of Armenia. This book is, then, a fascinating detective story, with a twist: the perpetrators have been discovered at the outset, along with the bodies; one is now in search of the spirit, which lives on. It is also, because of the author's self-effacing yet dynamically attentive personality, the tale of a knightly quest, moving in its gallantry, and requiring courage, tenacity, sensitivity.

The most impressive sign of Marsden's commitment is his decision to go first to the Patriarchate in the old Armenian Quarter of Jerusalem to learn the Armenian language, which, for Osip Mandelstam, "cannot be worn out—its boots are of stone." This could not help but endear Marsden to the Armenians, for whom the language has been for almost two millenia crucial to the survival of the *nation*. Unlike Lord Byron, who studied it for a season at the Mekhitarist monastery on the island of San Lazzaro in Venice as a penance for his sins but soon gave it up as an "obdurate" tongue, Marsden seems to have persevered. Later in the book, encountering hostility as the result of being mistaken for a Russian interloper, he is able to explain that he is not Russian but *an English*.

There have been other travelers among the Armenians, of course, with various motivations. Armenia has signified different things to different people. Each account reflects the historical moment or occasion, but also to a greater or lesser degree the temperament of the writer and, more broadly, his own culture. One of Marsden's merits is that while he has made a significant personal—indeed individualistic—investment, the result seems to me less of a projection, with Armenia as a backdrop, than in the case of some of the others. He has given himself up to the venture, and what he experiences impinges on him rather than the other way around. The American clergyman and writer George Hepworth, in his book *Through Armenia on Horseback*, explained back in 1898 that he had ventured forth because it was his "duty to take a bird's eye view of the Armenian region, where so many horrible massacres have taken place and to discover as far as possible the future prospects of this nearly exterminated race." He refers here to the order of Sultan Abdul Hamid, who in 1895 unleashed his Kurdish cavalry, or *hamidieh*, on the unarmed Armenians, causing the slaughter of between 100,000 and 200,000 of them. Hepworth's generalizations concerning Turks, Kurds, and Armenians betray only an occasional touch of *Orientalism*, though he does feel obliged at one point to state: "I don't think I am a bigot." On his return to Istanbul from the eastern provinces he asks of someone who is neither Turkish nor Armenian: "Are schoolbooks ever confiscated simply because the word Armenia occurs in them?"

"Without doubt," comes the answer.

"You are sure of that fact?"

"Perfectly so."

Hepworth presciently concludes: "Tranquility reigns at present? I do not think so. When the lapse of time brings inevitable forgetfulness of past horrors, when the Powers have too much business on hand to give attention to Turkish affairs, the sword will once again be unleashed."

Then there is the monumental *Armenia* published in 1900 in two hefty volumes by the Englishman H. F. B. Lynch, who states that the main "inducement was curiosity." Why write such a book, he asks rhetorically, and gives his own attractive answer: "It is very strange that such a fine country should have lain in shadows for so many centuries." Lynch especially concentrates, with an admirable thoroughness, on the topography of the region. He explains meticulously that he carried with him on his expedition "two aneroids, a boiling-point apparatus [he analyzed the chemical and mineral content of the waters of Lakes Van, Nazik, and Gop], a four-inch prismatic compass, used upon a tripod and carefully tested at Kew; lastly a rather troublesome but very satisfactory instrument called a telemeter, and made by Steward." He concludes his work by saying, "If I were asked what distinguishes the

Armenians from other Orientals, I should be disposed to lay most stress on a quality known in popular speech as *grit*. . . . They are not surpassed in this respect by any European nation."

As for Russian travelers, there is perhaps an exotic, even forbidden element to southern, mountainous Armenia. Mandelstam, in danger in Moscow, was dispatched to Armenia in 1930 by his highly placed protector Bukharin. His beguiling poetical *Journey to Armenia*, "a Sabbath land," is as much a projection of his own extraordinary imagination as it is a description of a real place in its own right, and was shortly followed by the cycle of poems entitled *Armenia*. According to the critic Henry Gifford, the Armenian interlude "ended five years of poetic silence." *Journey to Armenia* abounds in gorgeous metaphorical fancy: "You catch forms and colors—and it is all unleavened bread—such is Armenia." Another intrigued Russian, Andrei Bitov, in his interesting and original book *A Captive of the Caucasus*, published in the United States in 1992 but written much earlier, makes somewhat metaphorical use of Armenia, which seems to him, as an implicitly frustrated Soviet citizen, an attractively exotic, particularly liberating backdrop.

In 1975 Michael J. Arlen, of half-Armenian descent, published *Passage to Ararat*. In this little masterpiece Arlen explores his own inner topography concurrently with the outward exploration that he undertakes. Son of Michael Arlen (originally named Dikran Kouyoumjian), the fashionable Mayfair author of the wildly successful twenties' novel *The Green Hat*, Arlen wonders about the continuing psychic effect of a half-recognized genocide on the survivors and more particularly on their issue. His reflection, aptly cited by Marsden, bears repeating:

> I realized at that moment that to be an Armenian, to have lived as an Armenian was to have become something crazy. Not crazy in the colloquial sense of quirky or charmingly eccentric . . . or even of certifiably mad. But crazy: crazed, that deep thing —deep where the deep-sea souls of human beings twist and turn.

It should be noted here that along with the "colorful" Armenians Marsden engagingly portrays, he also depicts, with respect and tenderness, a gallery of "ordinary" people, in what is a far cry, say, from the admirable topographical investigations of his compatriot H. F. B. Lynch.

From the outset the history of Armenia has been relentlessly turbulent. On the one hand, it is hard to understand how the Armenians have survived three millenia as a distinct people, while on the other hand, the fact of having been perpetually under siege seems to have developed in them an implacable will against all odds to do just that. Traveling among them in the diaspora, Marsden finds that in exile "they are curiously resilient; only the Jews have resisted assimilation as fiercely."

Geography has played a major role in the turbulence. The location of historic Armenia, which has periodically varied in size from about 150,000 square miles to the 11,500 square miles of the present landlocked and blockaded republic, has always been a flashpoint, situated on the heavily traveled trade routes between east and west, control of which has been contested by the Medes, the Persians, Alexander's Greeks, the Romans, Byzantium, Georgians, Syrians, the Arabs, the Mongols, the Russians, and the Ottoman Turks.

The origins of this people are obscure. If you look in an encyclopedia under *Indo-European*, which has the most speakers of any language family, you will see Armenian listed way off by itself with only the vanished Thraco-Phrygian for company. Harvard scholar Sirarpie der Nersessian writes: "The Armenians had probably come into Asia Minor from the Balkans with the Phrygians, of whom, according to Herodotus, they were a colony. . . . Advancing eastward at the end of the eighth century B.C. they settled in the region of Mount Ararat."

Christianity was proclaimed the state religion by edict around the year 315; Rome followed in 335. The binding force of the religion has been very considerable. Christianity in turn directly engendered the creation of the written alphabet in 405, inaugurating a golden age of letters and a proliferation of monasteries dedicated to scholarship. Later, in the twelfth century, the patriarch Nerses the Gracious, was to write: "The monasteries have been the pillars of the country, the fortresses against the enemy, and shining stars." It is thus on the intertwined supports of religion and language that the Armenian identity stands. Armenians always resisted conversion, no matter what the cost. Although they were severely defeated by the Persians at the Battle of Avarayr in 451, who had sought to impose Zoroastrianism on them, the result was that the Persians did not subsequently find it worthwhile to insist. Similarly, within the pale of Christianity itself, the Armenians resisted the heavy hand of Byzantium (even though so many of its emperors and generals were Armenian themselves, notably Leo V, Basil I, and the charismatic John Tzimisces). Having subscribed to the Council of Nicea, along with the Catholics and the Greeks, the distinct Armenian church had gone its own way at Chalcedon in 451 on the issue of the nature of Christ. Religion and politics were not easily dissociated in that time: if there had then been agreement concerning theology, there might, for better or worse, be scarcely any Armenian identity today.

Constantinople fell to Sultan Muhammed II of the Ottoman Turks in 1453 and, according to the historian Vahan Kurkjian, he treated the Armenians with "kindness and tolerance." The *millet* system, which allowed minorities self-government within limits (but levied onerous discriminatory taxes as well) was one under which the Armenians thrived as artisans, merchants, administrators, and superlative architects. While the empire flourished, Armenians were considered an asset generally, but UCLA Professor Richard Hovanissian writes: "As the empire's administrative, financial, and military structure crumbled under the weight of internal corruption and external challenges in the eighteenth and nineteenth centuries, intolerance and exploitation increased," and "the decay of the Ottoman Empire was paralleled by cultural and political revival among many of the subject nationalities which were swept by the European winds of romanticism and revolt." Yet, although the Turks were later to try to justify their behavior by accusing the Armenians of disloyalty, they themselves had distinguished them from the other minorities by terming them "the loyal *millet*." At the height of the 1915 genocide, Talaat Pasha of the ruling Young Turk triumvirate tacitly confirmed that any grave disloyalty might be a consequence rather than a cause, when he rebuffed U.S. Ambassador Henry Morgenthau's pleas, saying:

> "It is no use for you to argue. We have already disposed of three quarters of the Armenians; there are none at all left in Bitlis, Van, and Erzeroum. The hatred between the Turks and the Armenians

is now so intense that we have got to finish with them. If we don't they will plan their revenge.''

The defeat of the Turks in the Russo-Turkish War of 1877–78, precipitated by the revolt of Bosnia and Herzogovina (with its subsequent, current repercussions), had ironically turned out to be disastrous for the Armenians, primarily because of British *raisons d'état*. While dismembering the empire to satisfy nationalistic aspirations of the Serbs, Montenegrins, Romanians, and Bulgarians, Europe gave the Armenians expressions of sympathy but left them altogether under Ottoman control. The sympathy may have made the Europeans feel good about themselves, but it largely served to annoy the Turks no end. Under Disraeli, at the Congress of Berlin, Britain had in effect acceded to a lip-service hands-off policy regarding the stateless Armenians in exchange for the right to administer the Ottoman possession of Cyprus, leaving them the focus of what was later to become a virulent xenophobia that flowered into Pan-Turanism, a movement obliquely foreshadowing Nazi ideology in Germany.

After the genocide of 1915 and the subsequent defeat of the Germans, along with their Turkish allies, the Treaty of Sèvres created an Armenian Republic, made up of both the Turkish and Russian parts. But neither the Azerbaijanis to the east nor the Turks to the west would permit any food supplies to enter Armenia; famine ensued. Vahan Kurkjian reports that from May 28 until December of 1919 more than 180,000 Armenians died of starvation and epidemic (one of whom was the mother of the artist Arshile Gorky). Within seven months Turkish armies under Mustafa Kemal crushed this infant state. The Armenians saved the remnant by accepting the protection of the Red Army; on the Turkish side recently repatriated Armenians were yet again forced into exile, this time permanently. Richard Hovanissian notes that in the subsequent Treaty of Lausanne, the absolute triumph of the presumably defeated Turks "was reflected in the fact that . . . neither the word *Armenia* nor the word *Armenian* was to be found. . . . Genocide had become the solution to the Armenian Question.''

The ensuing decades saw the smallest of the Soviet Socialist Republics faring relatively well, prospering largely because of a skilled labor force, even while chafing under the concomitant oppression. At least the traffic cops were, *mirabile dictu*, Armenian, as were the commissars; literacy was virtually universal, and there was more of a tacit acceptance of religion in this outlying region than elsewhere in the Soviet Union.

Early on, however, Stalin, as general party secretary, had slyly left the ancient Armenian area of mountainous Karabagh within the neighboring Azerbaijani Republic—not so perverse an act as it might seem, from the traditional Russian point of view, always sensitive where frontiers are concerned. A degree of inicipient instability was to be fostered, since this would always provide for a measure of influence in the Caucasus, as pretext for occasional intervention. Marsden shrewdly demonstrates the current manifestations of this quasi doctrine, though he perhaps underestimates tiny landlocked Armenia's need for a powerful if ambiguous and self-interested protector, with Azerbaijan to the east and Turkey to the west.

The accession of Gorbachev in 1985 and the advent of *perestroika* and *glasnost* were perceived to be an invitation to the Armenians of Karabagh to press their claims. Most Armenians felt they were misled by Gorbachev into a deleterious impasse. Azerbaijanis reacted violently; a pogrom in the town of Sumgait, where both peoples had lived peaceably, took scores of lives. Marsden points out that "the Armenians never forgave Gorbachev for not having sent in the troops earlier."

Nature then added to the travail. On December 7 of that year an earthquake struck Armenia, killing 55,000 people, and leaving 500,000 homeless, many of whom were the more than 150,000 newly arrived refugees from Azerbaijan. News footage shows Gorbachev on his visit looking shocked, even disgusted, when a man who had lost his mother in the earthquake profited from the occasion to ask him what he was going to do about Karabagh. When Gorbachev took him to task for his presumed inhumanity toward his own dead mother, the man shot back: "It's the same thing," with a look of contempt. Though Gorbachev apparently did not understand this man, Marsden would have. Having come to a hard-earned understanding, he writes that for the stubborn Armenians, with their long traumatic history of survival, "The loss of land was as deep a wound as the loss of life. That truth had haunted all the exiles I'd spoken to in the diaspora."

In the many months of his brave, solitary pilgrimage, crossing seventeen national frontiers, Marsden had traveled not to a state but to a nation. For Daniel Patrick Moynihan, as cited by University of Chicago's Gidon Gotlieb in his book, *Nation Against State*, "The challenge is to make the world safe for and from ethnicity, safe for just those differences which large assemblies, democratic or otherwise, will typically attempt to suppress. The idea deserves attention. As does the whole question of sovereignty."

Armenia is free and will doubtless survive, but possibly as the old American Indian reservations survived. Azerbaijan, so far unable to defeat the relatively small, fiercely determined enclave of Karabagh Armenians within its borders, has blockaded Armenia proper; the natural gas pipeline running through chaotic Georgia has been mysteriously, repeatedly, blown up. Winters claim the lives of infants. Once carefully tended boulevards are denuded of trees as they are cut down for firewood.

To the west, the Turks are guardedly hostile. As reported by Alan Cowell in the *New York Times* of April 18, 1993, Turkish president Turgut Ozal, two weeks before dying suddenly, remarked: "What harm would it do if a few bombs were dropped on the Armenian side by Turkish troops holding maneuvers on the border?" And in a dispatch from the capital of Armenia, *New York Times* correspondent Raymond Bonner writes just a year later of something so surrealistically strained that it must be true, concerning a parrot:

> The bird was one of two that had belonged to Mrs. Torosian's sister-in-law, who lives in Yerevan. The other one froze to death this winter. But as soon as the weather warms, the family will release this one. They cannot afford to keep it. It eats the food the family needs.

Bard College
November 1994

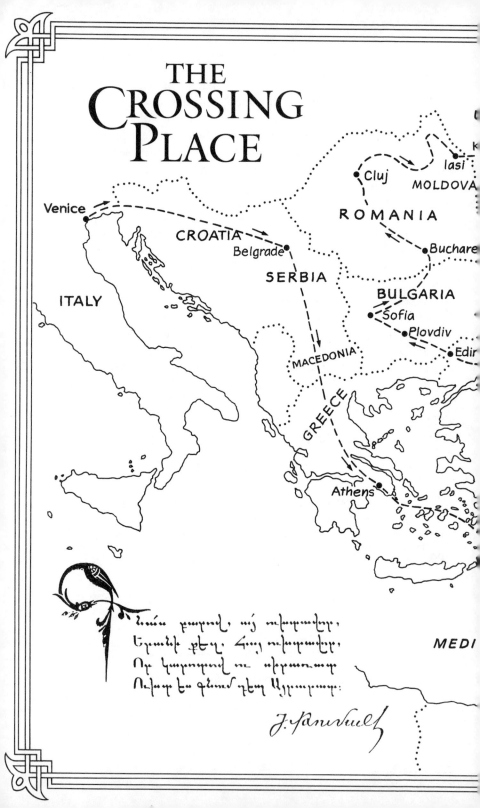

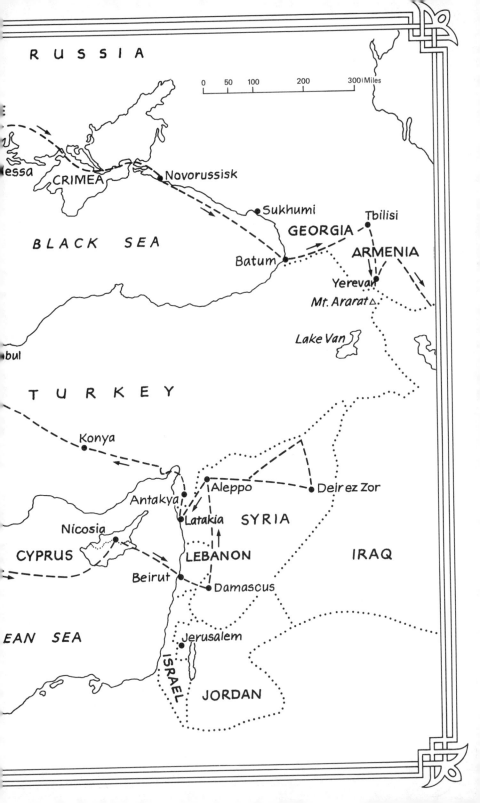

# PRELUDE

One summer, walking in the hills of eastern Turkey, I came
across a short piece of bone. It was lodged in the rubble of a land-
slip and had clearly been there for many years. I rubbed its
chalky surface and examined the worn bulbs of the joint; I took it
to be the limb of some domestic animal and dropped it into my
pocket.

Beyond the rubble, the land fell away to a dusty valley which
coursed down to the plain of Kharput. The plain was hazy and I
could just make out a truck bowling across it, kicking up a screen
of pale dust in its wake. I carried on down the valley. It was a strange,
still place and rounding a bluff, I stumbled on the ruins of a village.
A shepherd was squatting in the shade of a tumbled-down wall,
whistling. I showed him the piece of bone and gestured at the ruins
around him.

The shepherd nodded, wiping together his palms in an unambiguous gesture. He said simply, '*Ermeni.*' Then he took the bone and
threw it to his dog.

*Ermeni*: the Armenians. The guide books hardly mentioned the
Armenians. No one mentioned the Armenians, yet everywhere I
went over the coming weeks, every valley of that treeless Anatolian
plateau, was haunted by them. Arriving one morning on the shores
of Lake Van, I took a boat to the island of Aghtamar. The island had
once been the court of an Armenian king, the centre of a tiny realm
squeezed between Persia and Byzantium, but now it was unin-
habited.

Continuing north, around the lower slopes of Mount Ararat, I
came to the ruins of the Armenian city of Ani. Its extraordinary
thousand-year-old cathedral, in no man's land between the Turkish
and Soviet borders, was open to the sky, shelter for three ill-looking
sheep. A long way up a gorge near Digor, I found an Armenian

1

church so perfect in its design that at first I did not notice its collapsing roof, nor the gaps in its walls.

I left Anatolia with a clutch of half-answered questions. Who were these people, and what had happened? I knew about as much as most – that the Turks had done something terrible in the First World War, that Armenia was the first Christian nation, that it had hovered for centuries on the fringes of the classical world. But it was not an explanation. Everything that I learnt about the Armenians only served to deepen the mystery, to make them more surprising, more enigmatic.

The following year I was travelling through northern Syria and came across an archaeologist in Aleppo. He knew a good deal about the Armenians and one afternoon took me to meet Torkom, an elderly Armenian lawyer with a bony face and deep-set blue eyes. Torkom lived alone, at the top of a set of winding stairs. His room was dark and musty and filled with books. A few glass-fronted cases had been built into the wall for manuscripts and they glowed with a yellowy light; they looked like preserved organs in laboratory jars.

When he heard I was interested in the Armenians, Torkom peered at me suspiciously.

'Why?'

I said I'd been to eastern Anatolia.

'Yes?' I told him about the cathedral at Ani and the church at Digor. I told him about the bone and the ruined villages and he shrugged as if to say: 'What do you expect?'

But when I mentioned Lake Van, he said, 'My family was from Van. You see my eyes? I have Van eyes – deep blue.'

'Like the lake,' I said. He smiled and led me into a back room. A photograph of Mount Ararat hung on one wall. Beneath it was a large desk, covered in papers.

'Do you know anything about the marches?' he asked.

'Very little.'

He opened one of the drawers and handed me the xerox copy of a hand-drawn map. Years of interviews had gone into that map, he said. He had collaborated with an Armenian truck driver who knew every town and village of northern Syria, and they had spliced the oral information with the few written records to draw the map. It looked to me somewhat like a tidal chart: a mass of arrows curling and twisting down the page. But the arrows, when I looked closely, were overlaid on a map of the Near East and they all pointed in more or less the same direction, away from Anatolia, south towards the Syrian desert.

I spent the following day in Torkom's library.

On 24 April 1915 the Turkish authorities arrested Constantinople's six hundred leading Armenians. They rounded up another five thousand from the city's Armenian quarters. Few of these people were ever seen again.

In the interior Turkish forces began to deport the Armenians. Torkom showed me the published report of one of the only foreigners who had witnessed what these deportations really meant. Leslie Davis had been the American consul in Kharput. He had watched the Armenian groups come and go, and had listened to the rumours. Since it was wartime his movements were severely restricted and he had been unable to confirm what he heard. But one morning before dawn he managed to slip out of the town. He rode on to the plain of Kharput.

And wherever he rode he saw the Armenians. They were casually buried in the roadside ditches, their limbs half eaten by scavenging dogs; he saw the heaps of charred bones where the remains had been burned; he saw the swollen bodies of the newly dead and in places they lay so thickly in the dirt that his horse had difficulty avoiding them. As the day wore on, Davis rode further into the hills. He reached the shores of Lake Goeljuk. Here, in the valleys leading down to the lake, the scene was the same: corpses scattered amidst the thornscrub, bunched together in their hundreds – at the foot of cliffs, in gorges, in the hidden folds of land.

Those who weren't killed at once were gathered into convoys and driven south. These were the marches. Davis had managed to compile an account of just one of these dismal convoys; it had left Kharput on 1 July 1915:

| | |
|---|---|
| Day 1 | 3000 Armenians leave Kharput. Escort of seventy zaptieh under command of Faiki Bey. |
| Day 2 | Faiki Bey levies 400 lira from convoy for its safety. Faiki Bey disappears. |
| Day 3 | First women and girls taken by Kurds. Open violation by zaptieh. |

| | |
|---|---|
| Day 9 | All horses sent back to Kharput. |
| Day 13 | 200 lira levied by zaptieh. Zaptieh disappear. |
| Day 15 | Kurdish 'guard' take 150 men and butcher them, then rob convoy. Joined by another convoy from Sivas. Numbers swell to 18000. |
| Days 25–34 | Harassed by villagers. Many women taken. |
| Day 40 | Eastern Euphrates. Blood-stained clothes on river-bank; 200 bodies in water. Armenians forced to pay to avoid being thrown in river. |
| Day 52 | Kurds take everything, including clothes. |
| Day 52–9 | Naked, without food or water. Women bent double from shame. Hundreds die beneath hot sun. Forced to pay for water. Money hidden in hair, mouth, genitals. Many throw themselves into the wells. Arab villagers give them pieces of cloth out of pity. |
| Day 60 | 300 remain from 18000. |
| Day 64 | Men and the sick burned to death. |
| Day 70 | 150 arrive in Aleppo. |

When I rose after several hours of reading such accounts, I felt dazed and numb. I walked back into the centre of Aleppo, through the high, narrow streets with their 1950s cars and the clattering souks. But I could not erase the images of the massacres. I carried on walking until well after dark and by the time I returned to my hotel had decided to try and find out more. One place in particular had struck me – a certain cave at Shadaddie. I rearranged my plans: I took Torkom's map and a letter of introduction and left Aleppo for the desert.


South from the town of Hassakeh, the road ran straight ahead of the bus for mile upon mile. It dipped and rose and tapered towards a low horizon, but did not change direction. Beside it the telegraph poles echoed into the distance until the heat-haze dissolved everything into a shimmering mass. On Torkom's map, Shadaddie was no more than a dot in the desert. A thin arrow pointed down to it from Ras ul-Ain. Now it has become an oil-drilling station and in one of the pre-fab homes I found a technician who nodded when I gave him Torkom's letter: yes, he knew about the cave.

The technician drove me out of the town in a battered jeep. I sat half-hidden in the back and at the checkpoints crouched down behind the seat; we were now close to the Iraqi border and the oilfields were well guarded.

A dry wind swept through the flaps of the jeep. It sped out across the desert and into the jumble of hillocks ahead. It was a cool, unrelenting wind and in places it had scoured the sand from the bedrock and the quartzite gleamed beneath it as white as bone. Nothing grew here. The only things that moved were the lifeless profiles of the nodding-donkey pumps. We left the road and slowed on to a rutted track. All around it were the egg-like shapes of compacted dunes. We bumped along the track until the dunes gave way to a wide depression. The technician stopped the jeep and pulled on the hand-brake. Lighting a cigarette, he pointed into the hollow.

Flash-floods had cut a deep gulch which pushed down into the rock below. I followed its dry pipe-like channel to where it opened out suddenly into the mouth of a cave. Peering into the cave-mouth, I could see the chamber spread out as if from the lantern of a dome. I dropped down onto a damp, muddy floor. Three startled doves flew out through the skylight. At the foot of one wall, where the sun fell on it, was a green cushion of moss. Down to one side a passage led away into the darkness. The air was warm and heavy and I felt that here, if anywhere, was the Armenian story – hidden inside a muddy cupola, in an area sealed off by state secrecy, tucked away and buried in a hollow amongst a thousand other hollows, beneath the crust of a desert that stretched for hundreds and hundreds of miles in every direction. Here was where Armenia had ended.

I turned on a torch and went down the passage. There was no sign at all of what had happened, nothing to show that it had ever been anything but a vast storm-drain for the desert.

But for the zaptieh, it had provided a ready-made solution. As the mountains were emptied of Armenians so the Syrian desert filled up. The order came from Constantinople to clean up the area. All sorts of methods were adopted. Shooting was slow. Some were driven into the river. A great many simply perished from disease and hunger and thirst. Shadaddie provided its own natural apparatus. The passage was very long and very roomy.

The guards brought the Armenians here and pushed them in by the thousand; as more fell in so the first ones were forced down the passage. Then the guards dragged scrub to the entrance and set fire to it. That night they kept a watch over the cave, camping on the edge of the hollow. Then they returned to the town.

They might have got away with it (are there other Shadaddies that went unreported?), had a young boy not been able to get enough air from the depths of the tunnel to survive and, three days later, to crawl over the bodies and the ashes of the fire, back up to the desert.

The passage went on, curving and dipping in ways I could only imagine. I could see little in the yellow tube of light. The air became still and I could no longer feel the breeze from the entrance. I felt drawn on into the tunnel by a strange irresponsible urge. Each footfall seemed to take me further from the familiar. I felt a huge emptiness behind me – but a bigger one in front. I was trespassing, a grave-robber motivated by something darker than greed: I was driven by curiosity. I knew there was nothing I would find, but I carried on. I carried on without really thinking. I carried on because to turn back was to lose what there was left of Armenia.

My feet slid and splashed through unseen puddles. I steadied myself with a hand on the damp wall. I could feel the tunnel narrow and I began to stoop. Then one foot slipped on a mud bank and the torch spun out of my hand; it clanged against a rock and went out.

For several minutes I squatted there, quite still. I passed a hand in front of my face, and saw nothing. I turned my head one way and then the other, and soon did not know from which way I had come. I tried to imagine the smell of smoke seeping down the tunnel, and the noise – would there have been hysteria, or simply quiet resignation? Mothers murmuring for their children in the void, the few men too broken to care, the tangled bodies, the slow suffocation . . .

For an instant I felt the cave spin around me. Submerged by the horror it had witnessed, I was suddenly disoriented.

It passed almost at once. I crouched and ran my hands around my feet, probing for the torch, wrist-deep in the slimy clay, pushing through the cave's damp and formless floor. My fingers struck something hard. I clutched it and with the other hand found the torch, several yards away. I thought it must be another bone but when I switched on the torch it turned out to be a large crystal – five inches of transparent calcite in the shape of an arrowhead.

Outside again, the Armenian technician clapped a hand on my shoulder and smiled for the first time. He was worried I'd got lost. He lit another cigarette and started up the jeep. I wrapped the crystal in a scarf and buried it away in my bag. It seemed an appropriate relic from the cave: Armenia may have died here, but something survived. A year or so later, in Israel, I took it with my unanswered questions to Jerusalem.

The old city of Jerusalem, the holiest square mile on earth, is divided into four distinct quarters. Three of the quarters – the Jewish, Christian and Muslim quarters – represent the great monotheistic faiths that have sanctified and fought over the city for hundreds of years. The fourth quarter is the Armenian quarter.

That the Armenians have survived in this, the most intense of all cities, is proof of their extraordinary resilience. The Armenian quarter is in fact the longest established of them all – and it remains the most secretive. Much of it lies within its own high walls, where the laity live cheek-by-jowl with the monastic order of St James. It is closed to visitors and only for half an hour each day are non-Armenians allowed inside to visit the cathedral.

Peering into the side chapel of St James, which contains those of the saint's limbs which did not reach Compostela, I heard a voice behind me.

'Can I be of any help?'

A man with black-rimmed glasses introduced himself as George Hintlian, the community's historian. I told him I had seen Ani and Digor and that I had brought something from the cave at Shadaddie.

'I could tell you were not interested just in the cathedral.'

'How could you tell?'

'I could just tell.'

He took me up to his office and I laid the calcite crystal on his desk. He smiled and shook his head in disbelief. 'Let me show you around the quarter.'

For several hours we wandered through a labyrinth of crypts and alleys and sunny courtyards. He took me up over the roofs and in amongst the cloisters to meet the monks, and when I left he said, 'If ever you want to find out more about the Armenians, why not come and spend some time here with us?'

I left the crystal with George and within eighteen months I was back. My Armenian questions would not go away. I told George I wanted to get to Armenia and he said he could help. I stayed in Jerusalem for a few months, in a small, vaulted room on the border of the Jewish and Armenian quarters. The city was tense; Kuwait had just been invaded and all talk that autumn revolved around the likelihood of war. Jerusalem waited. The Israelis waited and the Palestinians waited; the Armenians waited between them. I waited – all the time planning a roundabout journey to Armenia, to seek out the Armenian communities that appeared to be scattered throughout the Middle East and Eastern Europe.

I took daily lessons in Armenian with a polyglot monk, took long walks with George, talked to everyone I could, and spent the rest of the time among the books of the Gulbenkian Library. I visited the Armenian community in Jaffa and a fifth-century Armenian monastery in the Judean desert; I spent a week with the Armenians of Cairo. And I realized more and more that the Armenian story was not so much one of massacre and persecution, as survival.

The first princes of Armenia had emerged in central and eastern Anatolia about six centuries before Christ. Five hundred years later, Armenia stretched fleetingly all the way from the Mediterranean to the Caspian Sea. At other times during these centuries the Armenian rulers paid tribute to the Persians, to Byzantium, to the Baghdad caliph, or some combination of the three. Even in these years Armenia's survival seemed improbable. Lying always on the fringes not only of opposing powers but opposing beliefs, the Armenians would adhere to no one's ideas but their own. In AD301 the Armenian King Trdat III became the first ruler to adopt Christianity – while in Rome the worst persecutions of Christians were yet to come.

When some years later Constantine chose the outlawed cult to be the cornerstone of Byzantine theocracy and the world's greatest empire, the Armenians still stuck to their own interpretation. In 451, at the Council of Chalcedon, the Byzantine bishops agreed some sort of Christian orthodoxy; the Armenians didn't even turn up – they were too busy fighting off the Sassanid Persians.

Even the earth itself seemed to conspire against them. Within a few hundred miles of Ani are the borders of half of the world's twelve major tectonic plates. In a single earthquake in the ninth century, seventy thousand were recorded as having been killed in one Armenian town alone.

Yet during this first Christian millennium, between the earthquakes and invasions, between the Mazdaeans, Manichaeans, Muslims, dyophysites and dualists, the Armenians emerged briefly to stage brilliant half centuries of their own, writing and building with passionate skill, before being stifled again by some rampant horde. In the ninth century Armenia emerged again as an independent state, centred on the city of Ani. I had caught a scent of that city's genius, sitting in its ruined cathedral a few years before. At one time Ani was bigger than most European cities. But in 1064 the Seljuk Turks swept up out of Asia and sacked it.

What should have happened then to this small people, occupying as it does the perennial buffer between empires, the most routed, trampled-over region on earth, was a gradual assimilation into its bigger and more powerful neighbours. Its scattered families should have struggled on for a couple of generations in exile, clinging proudly to traditions before intermarriage consigned them to history's roll of honour: a set of dusty ruins on the Anatolian plateau and some glass cases in the British Museum.

Instead the Armenian princes travelled five hundred miles to the south-west. There in the lee of the Taurus mountains, in Cilicia, they established a new Armenian kingdom. Many of those who didn't flee and who weren't killed by earthquakes nor slaughtered during the Seljuk invasion, but who remained on the land, were driven in 1604 by the Safavid Shah Abbas down into Persia. And those who survived both the Seljuks and Shah Abbas, and who didn't drift away beyond the Ottoman empire, who weren't killed in the pogroms of the 1890s, nor those of 1909, but who stayed in the villages, were rounded up in 1915, pushed down one of history's dark side-alleys and murdered.

More than a million Armenians died in the last years of the Ottoman empire, a half of Anatolia's total. The Turks had managed to do what numerous powers had tried before them: they managed to finish Armenia, though not the Armenians. In most of the world's cities you can find Armenians – Armenian newspapers in Armenian script, Armenian restaurants. In exile the Armenians are curiously resilient; only the Jews have resisted assimilation as fiercely. In the mountains of Colombia there is a small town actually named Armenia where they serve 'Antioch-style' beans. In Paris the first-ever café was opened in 1672 by an Armenian, as it had been earlier in Vienna, by the same Armenian spy who had helped break the Turkish siege. At the siege of Vienna the Polish King Jan's private doctor had been an Armenian, as was the doctor to the harem of Akbar the Great, the Mogul emperor whose adopted Armenian son was regarded by the Jesuits in India as the greatest poet of his time.

9

The 'Polish Byron', Słowacki, had an Armenian mother, as does the chess-master Garry Kasparov, as did Gurdjieff, as did the Abbasid Caliph al-Mustadi who ruled the entire Arab world during the twelfth century, except for Egypt where a few years earlier Armenian vizirs held power, and Jerusalem where the hereditary Crusader rulers had long had Armenian blood coursing through their royal veins. When Richard the Lionheart was married, in Cyprus, his best man was an Armenian; the last king of Armenian Cilicia, exiled in France, taught the French king to play chess. It has even been suggested that the Man in the Iron Mask was none other than the Armenian patriarch of Constantinople.

The first yoghurt in the United States was manufactured by the Armenian family Columbissian. The particular green ink of the US dollar bills was developed by an Armenian, as was the MiG jet, named after Mikoyan, whose brother was the longest-standing member of Stalin's Politburo, and the first to denounce him. Abel Aghanbekyan, an Armenian economist, produced the blueprint for perestroika.

They shouldn't really exist at all. They should have been destroyed, written out of history by its worst horrors. But they have survived. Instead of a footnote to the story of these border regions, the Armenians can be read like a kind of subtext.

With the Gulf War imminent, the Soviet Union crumbling and Eastern Europe in a state of dangerous uncertainty, it seemed the perfect time to set off around the Armenian diaspora, to try and reach Armenia itself. I prepared to leave Jerusalem.

In the library of the Armenian quarter, tacked to the wall, were the lines of the Armenian writer William Saroyan:

> I should like to see any power of the world destroy this race, this small tribe of unimportant people, whose wars have all been fought and lost, whose structures have all crumbled, literature is unread, music is unheard, and prayers are no more answered. Go ahead, destroy Armenia. See if you can do it. Send them into the desert without food or water. Burn their homes and churches. Then see if they will not laugh, sing and pray again. For when two of them meet anywhere in the world, see if they will not create a New Armenia.

Wondering what Saroyan meant by a 'New Armenia', and wondering what remained of the old, I said goodbye and left the monastary on a damp December evening. I headed for Venice, where there had been an Armenian community for more than eight hundred years.

# I

# THE NEAR EAST

They chose the Worst Thought, and then ran
to join Wrath.

From the Zoroastrian Gāthas, *yasna* 303, in which the
Deceiver tricks God into letting man acquire the wrong spirit.

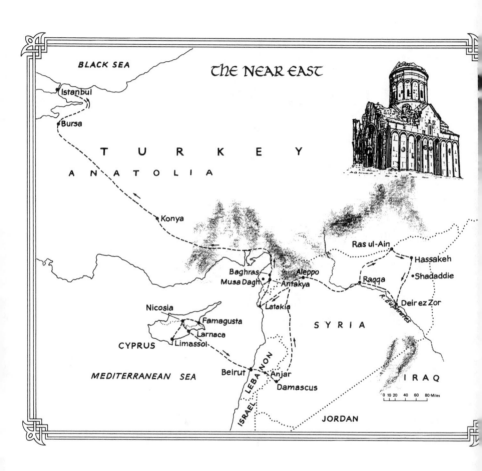

THE NEAR EAST

BLACK SEA

Istanbul

Bursa

T U R K E Y

A N A T O L I A

Konya

Ras ul-Ain

Hassakeh

Baghras

Musa Dagh

Aleppo

Antakya

Raqqa

Shadaddie

Latakia

Deir ez Zor

Nicosia

R. Euphrates

Famagusta

Larnaca

S Y R I A

Limassol

CYPRUS

MEDITERRANEAN SEA

Beirut

Anjar

Damascus

I R A Q

0 10 20 40 60 80 Miles

ISRAEL

LEBANON

JORDAN

# 1

I was looking a long while for Intentions,
For a clew to the history of the past for myself, and
    for these chants – and now I have found it,
It is not in these paged fables in the libraries (them
    I neither accept nor reject,)
It is no more in the legends than all else,
It is in the present – it is this earth today.

Walt Whitman

Venice was cold. Small ice floes littered the canals and drifted into
the lagoon like soggy notes. No one lingered long outside; the piazzas
were empty. But it wasn't just the cold. From the balustrade of a
palazzo on the Grand Canal, the students had draped a banner:
NO ALLA GUERRA! NO ALLA CATASTROPHE! The catastrophe for the
Venetians was that the Gulf war was scaring away the tourists. I had
the place almost to myself.

The Mourad-Raphaelian school was the only one for the children
of Venice's Armenian community. Its director looked more Italian
than Armenian; he wore scarlet socks and walked with short,
urgent strides. I met him hurrying away from the school. 'Please,'
he called back, 'wait inside! My car is in the middle of the road. It
is broken.'

'Your car?' In *Venice*? But he was already gone.

I pushed open the school's heavy oak door and entered a panelled
hall. Bright sun fell across the flagstones and through the windows
was a small courtyard. But there was no sign of life. Upstairs it
was the same – bare floors and echoing corridors. It seemed more
abandoned palace than school. Only the walls and ceiling, flourishes

of rococo plaster, gilded swags and voluptuous oils, seemed alive. Too alive, in fact. The overnight train to Venice had been a sleepless affair, and so much early-morning baroque made me a little nauseous. I found a window overlooking the canal and watched the sunlight flicker on its filmy surface.

The Armenians have long been in Venice. When it emerged as a power in the twelfth century they were already well established. Their talent for innovation, an exile's talent, litters the chronicles of the republic. Sinful Hagop set up a printing press in 1514 and produced the first Armenian printed book, while Anton Surian – 'Anton the Armenian' – built ships. Twice his own designs had helped save Venice: once with a frigate whose beam-mounted cannon swung the battle of Lepanto, and then again with a salvage ship that unclogged centuries of broken ships from the lagoon. But in recent years the community has been whittled away to almost nothing. Many of the old families have gone to Milan.

The director returned and showed me into a high-ceilinged office. The walls were refreshingly plain and hung with the familiar icons of Armenian exile: a view of Ararat, and large colour plates of half-ruined churches, standing alone in the mountain wastes of western Armenia, old Armenia, Turkish Armenia.

'Yes,' sighed the director. 'Not many are left here. You know, it's a full-time job being an Armenian.' He stretched his arms open wide, nodding at each of his hands. 'Here . . . and here. I struggle to keep up with my brother in Syria and Egypt, in America and Persia. If I relax for an instant, it is gone!' His arms flopped to his sides. 'You understand?' He picked up the telephone and tried to track down a mechanic.

Running a car in Venice also seemed a full-time job, so I thanked him and walked out again into the frosty streets.


I telephoned Father Levon Zekiyan and we arranged to meet in a small café near the Chiesa San Rocco. Father Levon held Venice's chair of Armenian studies. He was a tall man, with a distinct sartorial elegance. I'd been given his name in Jerusalem, but I'd seen it too at the head of various scholarly papers. He'd written a great number of papers, in several languages, and his footnotes were always a maze of different scripts. Enthusiasm for the minutiae of Armenian history set his conversation darting around the centuries, but did not make

him shy of the broad sweep. When I asked him the big question –
what keeps the Armenians Armenian – he paused for only a
moment.

'The whole thing,' he explained, 'comes down to a single idea.
And the key to it is the script. Mesrop Mashtots was our greatest
political thinker! In the fifth century he invented the alphabet and
realized Armenia as a power was finished. If the Armenians were to
survive without territory, they had to have a common idea, something that was theirs alone. The script embodies the idea.'

'And what is the idea?'

'Ah, you cannot describe it! You can give it a name but you cannot
describe it. If you are lucky, you will come to know it a little.' He
took a sip of wine and smiled. 'Our poet Sevak called it simply
Ararat.'

Ararat – of course. Ararat echoes around things Armenian like a
persistent refrain. It is the name of Armenian journals, Armenian
books, Armenian businesses and restaurants; in the United States
there is an Armenian credit card called Ararat, as is an Armenian
nursing home in California. The national football team is called
Ararat, and the mountain's dual-peaked profile had hung in every
Armenian home I'd seen so far. I knew it as a symbol of exile, staring
as it now does into Armenia from across the Turkish border. But
Father Levon's idea was much more than that. I began to see the
mountain as something more enigmatic: an article of faith, the survival of an animistic past.

Osip Mandelstam, after several months in Armenia, also became
aware of Ararat's peculiar presence:

> I have cultivated in myself a sixth sense, an 'Ararat'
> sense: the sense of attraction to a mountain.
>
> Now, no matter where fate carry me, this sense
> already has a speculative existence and will remain
> with me.

I had seen Ararat too – from Dogubeyazit in Turkey. But it had left
no particular mark on me. Perhaps I had to wait to see it from
Armenia.

I left Father Levon in the Piazza San Marco and took a boat across
the lagoon to the island of San Lazzaro. The afternoon was crisp and
beautifully clear. Only two other passengers were on the boat; one

17

of them was an Armenian monk. For more than two hundred and fifty years, San Lazzaro has been an Armenian monastery. It is now one of the great storehouses of Armenian culture, with its collection of thousands of manuscripts – pages and pages of Mesrob's script.

The monk from the boat passed me on to another monk who guided me around the monastery. Climbing the stairs to the museum, he asked me for news of the Armenian monastery in Jerusalem. I went in to some detail about the new patriarch and the bishops and the old retainers of the Holy Places, but I could see he had lost interest; they were members of the Brotherhood of Saint James, he was a Mekhitarist, a wholly different order.

San Lazzaro's museum, on the other hand, was a testament to the cohesion of the diaspora. Each exhibit, brought to the island by devoted pilgrims, was another dot on the Armenian map. It was like the collection of some well-travelled Victorian philanthropist. Under a Tiepolo ceiling, Persian ceramics stood with Iznik dishes and Kutahya ewers; there was an ivory Taj Mahal, some ivory filigree orbs (seven inside one another, like a Russian doll), a silver Ethiopian hand cross, St Petersburg miniatures, stamps, banknotes, a Crusader sword, a Canova cast of Napoleon's son, a Burmese boustrophedon manuscript explaining in Pali the initiation rites of a Buddhist priest, and a mummy. In 1925 Egypt's foreign minister, an Armenian, had brought the mummy, along with a Bubastis cat. The mummy was the monk's favourite exhibit.

He led me away from the main gallery to a room lined with the buckram spines of English classics. There, hanging over the door, was a portrait of Lord Byron. All through the winter of 1816, several times a week, Byron crossed the lagoon to visit the monks of San Lazzaro. He developed a fascination with Armenia, discovering among other things that it was the supposed site of Earthly Paradise.

'Their country,' he wrote, 'must ever be one of the most interesting on the globe.'

In this room Byron took on the Armenian language. His letters tell of his endeavours: 'In the mornings I go over in my gondola to hobble Armenian with the friars . . . my mind wanted something craggy to break upon . . . this was the most difficult thing I could discover . . . a Waterloo of an alphabet . . .' In Venice itself, his pursuits were easier: '. . . the lady has, luckily for me, been less obdurate than the language . . .' After some months his visits to San Lazzaro dried up.

The next day, before leaving Venice, I called ahead to Cyprus. I told Garo Keheyan, an Armenian I'd met in Jerusalem, that I planned to be in Nicosia in a few days. Crossing the Rialto that evening I saw the Grand Canal just beginning to ice over. In Trieste there was a night train to Yugoslavia. It snowed heavily in the night and at Belgrade a guard stumbled along the track to thaw the points with a flaming torch. The train ploughed on, south through Serbia, through dead valleys and silent forests, beneath swollen clouds. The day slid past in a series of frozen images: a man with a gun on an icy pond, the breath of a horse at a level-crossing, a yellow pig leaping in the snow.

The following afternoon at Piraeus was warmer. A ship from Odessa was in port and the Ukrainians lined the docks' perimeter fence. By their feet lay piles of china plates, plastic dolls, knives, forks, and tins of caviar. I bought a bottle of Armenian brandy from a stern Russian woman and carried on past the ones with smiles and powder-blue eyes and no goods at their feet, prepared to go to any lengths for hard currency.

The ship to Cyprus was practically empty. Half a dozen people gathered in its burgundy lounge as if for a bad joke: a Jew, a priest, a London cabbie, and a Greek cabaret artiste. The Orthodox priest settled down to watch a TV game show while the cabbie vilified Saddam Hussein for the 'artiste'. I took the brandy and sat with the Jew, an antiques dealer with shoulder-length hair and dark, smiling eyes. He was on his way to marry a girl he'd never met. A friend in Lithuania had sent him her picture and now they were to meet at a certain hotel in Cyprus, go through the civil ceremony, and start anew in Haifa.

'Call me a fool,' he said. 'But I feel good about it.'

I drank to his bride and he asked me what I was doing in Cyprus.

'I'm on my way to Armenia.'

'Armenia? What are you going to find there?'

'I have no idea.'

'So we are both on a mystery tour!'

It was well after dark when the ship hauled in her warps and eased away from the dock. The antiques dealer suddenly thought of something: 'I remember there were some Armenians in Cairo. Extraordinary people. They had an expression – perhaps you've heard it. They used to say that the Armenians were "caught between the hammer and the anvil".'

'And they say that if the hammer falls often enough you end up with a diamond.'

After a day and a half we berthed in Limassol and I took a bus up to Nicosia. There I went to find Garo Keheyan whom, I hoped, would be able to advise me. I was trying to get back to the Armenian communities of Syria. There were two options: to go straight there, by boat to Latakia, or to go via Beirut. A lot of Armenians lived in Beirut; it had at one time been the most important city of the diaspora. But while the Gulf war continued, I was not keen on going in. Nor did I have a Lebanese visa. But then I had no Syrian visa either; in fact I had no visas for any of the countries I wanted to visit before Armenia – nor for Armenia itself.

In part this was due to the confusion of the Gulf war and the mess of the Soviet Union. But I saw it also as a test. The Armenians have travelled these regions more consistently, more zealously than any other people. They have always lived by travelling – as merchants, adventurers or pilgrims – with all the cunning and enterprise that it requires. That the Armenians remained so mobile, and yet survived as a distinct people, was a miracle that I still had not understood. When borders were sealed by warring empires – Mameluke and Seljuk, Seljuk and Abbasid, Ottoman and Safavid, Safavid and Mogul – the Armenians' network of exiled communities spanned them all. Often they were the only link between rival courts and carried messages in their own script like a code. Because of the eternal instability of Armenia itself, the rigours of a peripatetic life were part of being Armenian; frontiers and wars just an everyday obstacle. My own journey would have to be an experiment in this.

Garo shrugged when I asked him if I should go, and in truth I'd already decided. He knew the Lebanese consul and telephoned her to vouch for me. All I needed, she said, was a letter from the British High Commission to free them of any responsibility. I secured the visa and arranged – through Garo's own travel agency – a passage to Beirut. I had two days before the boat left; the Armenian network was already proving its worth.

Garo was not just a travel agent. He was also Cyprus's Brazilian consul, director of a bank, a property developer, a would-be publisher and a power-broker of the Armenian republic's burgeoning foreign affairs. But his real enthusiasm was reserved for esoteric thought. He had a library full of ancient wisdom and a Great Dane named Plato.

Nicosia, he explained, had its own mystic – the Magus of Strovolos; not his favourite, by any means, but worth a hearing. That week he was giving a series of lectures. We drove through Nicosia to Strovolus, known to be the city's dullest suburb. The day's lecture was in a large shed in a leafy garden. A group of Germans filled the room and hung through the open window to catch the Magus's words. He started by talking about psychotherapy. Literally the word meant 'healing the soul'. A misnomer, explained the Magus, for the soul is the one part of us that is never sick. It is the other things, the worldly things like doubt and desire heaped around the soul that make us sick.

The 'Magus' took his title from the priestly caste of Zoroastrians and displayed in his teaching some of the dualism that they had taught. Dualism was outlawed by the early Church, like so much else that was good, but it survived in Armenia. It found its way eventually into Western Europe to become the basis for the great medieval heresies, the Albigensians and Cathars. It was Armenian exiles – ever the carriers of Oriental ideas – who are believed to have introduced it.

The Magus sat on his stool in a grey, button-up cardigan, spreading his appealing heresies in mellifluous tones, speaking of the powers of auto-therapy, of modern evils, of peace. And it was all grist to the mill for the gentle Germans who sat with eyes closed, palms upturned. His American supporters, wary of the war, were not so loyal. They had stayed at home and sent as proxy a set of small tape recorders which whirred and clicked at the Magus's feet.

For fifteen hundred years Armenians had been fleeing to Cyprus – heretics, subversives, exiled princes and kings, poets, monks, pogrom

21

survivors and orphans. Once there, things have become little easier.

They watched the island shift from one power to the next – from Abbasid to Byzantine, Byzantine to Knights Templar, to French Crusader, to Venetian, to Ottoman, to British, and from British into civil war. Looking at the island on the map, it appears somehow anvil-shaped, and there's never been a shortage of people to wield the hammer.

The Nalchadjians had been particularly unlucky. On a hot June afternoon in 1963 the Nalchadjians were married at Nicosia's Armenian church. It was a glamorous occasion. The Nalchadjian factories in Famagusta and Kyrenia were large and prosperous, and the couple stepped from the church into a cheering bay of Armenian well-wishers, who had gathered beneath the cypresses.

Mrs Nalchadjian had kept something of her dark, Armenian beauty, but the factories had all gone. I went to see her in a small, third-floor flat in Greek Nicosia, which had the advantage of being close to the new Armenian church.

'Yes, it was a wonderful service,' she sighed, turning the page of her photograph album. 'The shooting didn't start until the reception.'

When he heard the shots the vartabed left the party and hurried through the deserted streets to lock up the church. It was never used again.

Mrs Nalchadjian turned the album's last page, which was empty. 'For our daughter's wedding. She's engaged to an Armenian doctor, a lovely man. But he lives in Beirut and things are still a bit difficult there.'

'The church,' I said. 'What has happened to the old church?'

'I don't know. Some say it's a café, others that it's destroyed. No one's been back.'

At the Greek checkpoint, I signed some papers and they let me through. I walked on past the UN checkpoint, through no man's land, to the Turkish checkpoint. There, I signed more papers and pledged I'd be back before the border closed at dusk.

While Greek Cyprus has grown fat since the occupation, and its roads purr now with German cars, the Turkish side has become something of a backwater. It is like a sleepy Anatolian town, with peasant families living in the wrecks of old Ottoman villas, grazing sheep and moustachioed cloth merchants with rolls of suiting tucked under their arms. All that still lives of a non-Turkish past are the rusting hulls of Morrises and Hillmans.

The church was hard to find. Victoria street had looked easy on the map, but it was a Greek map and all the names had been changed. Asking for an Armenian church was even less tactful here than in Anatolia. So I idled past the fruit stalls and abandoned *hans*, the foundries and workshops, followed the zig-zag of the Green Line until, not far in from the western wall, I spied the telling pinnacle of a church tower.

The high gate was padlocked. Its wrought-iron whorls were trussed with barbed wire. A board had been crudely tied to the gate: a victory targe with a soldier bursting from the red and crescent moon of the Turkish flag. Behind it the courtyard appeared untouched from the day of the Nalchadjian wedding. The cypresses were gone and the flagstones bordered with weeds, but it had about it the air of neglect rather than destruction.

Nor was the church a café. That too was abandoned and tufts of grass billowed from its walls. Another Armenian church in ruins. I tried to get in but on the other side was a military assault course, all raked dirt and poles and rope-nets and pits. When I went a little later to Famagusta to see what had become of the fourteenth-century church there, I found it also adjacent to an assault course. There were the poles and rope-nets and pits. I began to wonder whether Armenian churches might form some essential part of Turkish military training.

The following day I left Nicosia to catch the boat to Beirut. In Larnaca a warm wind blew off the sea. The gulls spun in idle circles above the empty hotels. Pinned to the menu-board of one, coyly avoiding any mention of the Gulf War, was a letter from the Cyprus Tourism Organization: 'We regret the decision of certain tour operators to repatriate their clients from Cyprus. It is as calm and safe as it used to be, and as beautiful for holidays.'

That evening on the docks, waiting for the French to load their military supplies, a Lebanese came up to me. He had a three-inch scar on his jaw.

'You going to Lebanon?'

'Yes.'

'Why do you go to Lebanon? Lebanon is not a good country.'

'I've heard it's a beautiful country.'

'You have friends in Beirut?'

'Yes,' I lied.

'Good, but don't go to West Beirut. If you go to West Beirut, you know what will happen.'

I could guess.

'They will take you away.'

# 2

The exile understands death and solitude in a sense
to which an Englishman is deaf.

Storm Jameson

The sun rose behind a bank of dark clouds, spreading shafts of light
into the pale sky above. It gave the impression of some vast Georgian
fanlight and I stood at the ship's rail, watching its reflection in the
still water, watching the bow-wave as it flopped over and shattered
the water. It was just before seven.

The clouds grew larger and turned out not to be clouds at all, but
the mountains of Lebanon. They ran up and down the coast, sheer
and very dark. Ten miles to the south they fell to a strip of flat land
which stuck out to sea like a tongue. From it rose the square blocks
of Beirut. Looking at the distant, sun-lit profile I felt as though I was
seeing for the first time some notorious celebrity, a mass-killer, a
rampant dictator, there in the flesh. Since the Syrians had mopped
up the last of General Aoun's forces a few months before, there had
been peace, but it was an uneasy peace. Much of the city remained
in the hands of the militias, and almost all of the land outside. Beirut
at that time was still the most lawless city on earth.

But for me, it was indispensable. Beirut had long been Armenia's
unofficial capital-in-exile. In the good years the Armenians had operated like a semi-autonomous republic; more than a quarter of a

million of them had lived here, with powerful links all over the world. They controlled a great deal of Beirut's trade and much of its industry. Although half of them had emigrated, the community had survived. The Armenians were the largest of the Lebanese minorities to have remained neutral throughout the war.

I had exactly a week here before the deadline for the land offensive expired in the Gulf. I did not want to be in Beirut for that. I wanted to be well clear of the Lebanon, to have reached Syria. It had been a long, sleepless night. The bars and decks of the ship echoed with the chatter of returning Lebanese. They were all young, all Christian, and all draped in a kind of transparent, satin-jacketed machismo. Among them tottered the relief guard for Beirut's French embassy, making the most of their last few hours of leave. I talked for a while with a group of officers while they gesticulated over half-bottles of claret; others played roulette with fat, gold-chained Beirutis, while the ranks with their tanned Legionnaire faces burnished with sweat, bellowed at each other around the bar, then dozed head-down on the saloon tables. And over the whole scene, ignored by all, the Saudi desert flickered from two televisions.

In the morning, the French looked groggy and depressed. I waved goodbye on the quay at Jounie and headed up the short ramp and on to the street. I watched the open-backed trucks take them away and the bleary faces staring back as if from a guillotine tumbrel.

I placed my bag on the sea-wall, contemplating my next move. I looked up the road, and looked down the road. I leaned against the wall. Beside me were a couple of crates of red mullet and a fresh ray which flapped about in the dust. A fisherman sat on the rocks mending his nets. The sun had cleared the mountains and shone on the wheelhouse of a scuttled coaster; the torn fringes of a shell-hole curled out of its top-sides. It was a lovely Mediterranean morning, but I felt ill-placed to enjoy it. Who could I trust? Which areas of the city were safe?

I found a taxi; the St Christopher dangling from the driving-mirror was reassuring. We drove in towards Beirut along a coast road littered with the signs of war, between the shoreline and the stern rampart of the mountains, beneath a thirty-foot, Rio-style Christ and the church of Notre Dame de la Délivrance crying 'Protégez-nous!' from its concrete pediment. And everywhere hung the faces of half-ruined buildings, shrapnel-scarred and lifeless.

Ten miles was about half-a-dozen checkpoints. We were waved

through them all. A convoy of war-weary tanks rattled past. I watched the phalanx of Beirut's tower blocks grow larger in the windscreen and thought how normal they looked. But their approach made me nervous. When in Antelias I saw a church and its drum and the distinctive crenellated cone, I felt a sudden relief; I recognized it as an old friend.

'Here!' I leaned forward. 'Drop me here.'

The taxi swung off the main road. Weaving to avoid the shell-holes, it pulled up to a pair of black, wrought-iron gates. On them were fixed the twin crosier and mitre of the Armenian Catholicosate of Cilicia.

From Cyprus I had tried to telex the monastery in Antelias, the main centre for Beirut's Armenians. But my message had failed somewhere. At the gate they had no idea who I was. I presented a to-whom-it-may-concern letter, in Armenian, from the patriarch in Jerusalem and the young priest nodded. He led me to the residence of the Catholicos and left me with a secretary who in turn took me into a large, teak-panelled office. At the far end, behind the broad raft of his desk, sat an elderly cleric.

His Holiness, Karekin II, Catholicos of Cilicia, spiritual leader of perhaps a third of the world's Armenians, was a man of some presence. He was a small, thick-set man with canny blue eyes that missed nothing. He had had a difficult war; that much was clear from the weariness in his face. He would tense occasionally with some sudden irritation and, half in jest, blame the war every time he reached for one of his cigars, their silk bands personalized by a loyal Armenian from Kuwait: HH KAREKIN II. In Beirut, even spiritual leaders had to behave like warlords.

We had lunch alone in his private dining room. There was a long table and two windows. One of them looked out on to the coast road and over the Catholicos's shoulder I could watch the traffic limp up on to a battered fly-over. Beyond the fly-over was the sea.

'Artichoke,' he said. 'I hope you like artichoke.'

'Artichoke's fine.'

'My doctor says it's good for the nerves.'

For a while we tugged at the leaves in silence. The Catholicos's cook stood attentively at the kitchen door, an elderly Armenian with his shirt done up to the neck. He took away the plates and the Catholicos began to talk.

'Can I make a point to begin with? That you look at the Armenian Church not, as so many others have, as a thing of archaeological interest, but as a living church.'

I told him that was exactly what I was looking for in the Armenians as a whole. 'But perhaps some Armenians are guilty of that too.'

'What makes you say that?'

'Well, Armenian history – it's quite a burden to bear'.

I told him of an image of the poet Gevork Emin's that had particularly struck me: he had compared the Armenians and their past to a peacock and his fan – all that was most impressive was behind them.

He nodded. 'Of course the Church must combine tradition and hope. In the East we integrate things much more. You in the West, you think religion and politics must be separate. It is absurd to divide things like that!'

And there I thought I heard the echo of his critics, the dilemma of his own position: a religious leader caught between the complexities of Armenian politics and the Lebanese civil war. For years he had struggled to keep the Armenians free of the local feuds and alliances. It had just about worked. Now, he said, the country's leaders were coming to him privately and admitting that perhaps the Armenians had been right all along. 'Positive Neutrality' the Catholicos called it, but it made me think of the hammer and the anvil. Muslims suspected the Armenians because they were Christian, and Christians chastised them for not being true to their colours. But the real Armenian battle was always elsewhere – with the Turks and the lost lands of Anatolia. On the boat from Cyprus, a Lebanese had said that the Armenians were feared – 'tough like old boots', ruthless in the defence of their neutrality. If one Armenian died, he said, the next day there'd be two or three bodies lying in the streets of the perpetrators.

The Catholicos finished eating and unwrapped another cigar.

'It was the shelling that got to you,' he said.

The last year had been the worst. Auon had been up there in the hills, the government forces down below. The monastery was in between.

The monks took shelter in the underground printing press. The young ones would run across the compound to the store for food.

For two months they spent the nights down there, sketching each other by the light of hurricane lamps, playing Risk, while the Catholicos would sit apart from them all, grimacing at each blast, chewing on a cigar and writing a long meditation on the war entitled: *Cross Made from the Cedars of Lebanon.*

The Catholicos gave me a room in the monastery. There was a patch of new plaster where a shell had fallen through the ceiling. I spent the evening there reading *Cross Made from the Cedars of Lebanon,* struck by the sense of constriction of an urban war.

In the morning an engineer drove me into Bourdj-Hamoud. The deadline in Kuwait was ticking away; the engineer said Saddam would pull out, but I wasn't so sure. More than seventy years earlier, in the wake of another war, the Armenians had arrived on the edge of Beirut. They were in rags and, for the most part, without shoes or possessions. They were the dazed survivors of the Turkish massacres and scavenged and combed the beaches for anything of value. In time a crude shanty grew up and this they called Camp Marash, after the region they had left. They knew that soon the order would be given to return. But it didn't come. The Armenians were still there. The shanty had survived in pockets but in the main Bourdj-Hamoud was a modern town. And it was the only place I saw in Beirut that seemed busy. With the city centre off limits, it had come into its own. The place bustled and thrived with commerce, attracting Beirutis of all factions to do what Beirutis like doing best – shopping.

'You know what the Armenian hobby is?' The engineer was striding down Bourdj-Hamoud's main street.

'What's that?'

'Building. When a Lebanese gets some money, he'll buy clothes or a car. But an Armenian, well, he'll get some bricks and put them one on top of another.'

It was true – Bourdj-Hamoud was scattered with mini-cranes and cement-mixers. And there was something else. I had been nowhere yet where Armenians were in the majority, where shop signs were first in Armenian, then in Arabic, where Armenian was spoken in public, where Armenians were treated by Armenian doctors, had their teeth pulled by Armenian dentists, meat cut by Armenian butchers, and cloth cut by Armenian tailors, where the bookshops had whole sections on Charents, Totovents and William Saroyan. There was an Armenian football team and everywhere, splayed out beneath shrapnel-dented cars were the bodies of Armenian mechanics. The streets bore the names of the lost towns – Aintab, Marash, Adana – and there seemed to be in them an assurance, a swagger, I had not seen before. It was almost as if the Armenians belonged here.

I left the engineer at one of his building-sites and went off to track down a painter who they'd told me about at the monastery. Yervant lived on the second floor of a rocket-scarred block. It was his parents' flat, but they were seeing out the war in Cairo. He was in his mid-thirties and had swarthy Armenian looks, with thick, wedge eyebrows and a heavy flop of dark hair. His stance was sprung with a peculiar, rigid intensity, as though in constant anticipation of something. He would often run his hand across the bristly nape of his neck.

His flat was a dark place. Though he'd been there for years, it still had an empty, itinerant feeling to it. There was a blood-red carpet on the tiled floor and blood-red seat covers.

Over the sofa, like an antimacassar, was a Manchester United scarf. 'I have a Manchester United t-shirt, Manchester United socks and Manchester United pillow. You know why Manchester?'

'Because of the Armenian community there?' Manchester was where the first Armenians settled in Britain.

He shook his head, and flashed a smile. 'When I heard the name, I thought – it is Armenian: *manch-es-ter*. "You are a baby!"'

Off the main room was a studio where stacks of canvasses leaned against the walls. Yervant was an expressive painter, with a pallet of subdued, earthy colours – grey-blue, brown, and a dull mustard-yellow which cropped up in all of them. Some were figurative – portraits with wide eyes and no mouth; others little more than swirls of colour slapped on like butter. The best ones were a series of dark, misty shapes which seemed partly dead rock and partly alive: mountains, he explained, Armenian mountains, which he'd never seen.

'Eight months work. All of this.' There were dozens. 'Two hundred – when I began I could not stop. I had no control. Then last year two tanks were down there shooting. All night they fired. First one, then the next. I took my brushes and after that, when there was shooting and everyone went to take shelter, I came to my studio and painted. I could not stop!'

Through Yervant the war began to come into focus. It seemed to have forced out of those who did not flee a kind of raw volatility, which became so ingrained that no one noticed it any more. If they did, it was as a matter of pride. *Liberté totale* was something Yervant mentioned often. To him it was the principle for which the war was fought, but to me it seemed no more than a description of its worst excesses.

We walked later by the sea. Yervant loved the sea. He did not notice the years of dirt and broken things that swilled about in its swells. He breathed in deeply and squinted along the shore.

'I like the peace here, don't you?'

The traffic bumped and growled along the freeway behind us. A couple of fishermen argued on the rocks. I nodded.

Yervant carried on answering my questions about the war. He ran through a catalogue of chaos, bombings, kidnappings, snipers, checkpoints when they killed at random, days when they fired ten shells a minute, all day.

One morning last year he had been shaving when there was a massive explosion. He thought it was an earthquake; on the radio they said it was an earthquake. But in fact it was a gas storage-tank hit by a shell. One piece of the tank had landed outside an Armenian school in Bourdj-Hamoud, nearly two miles away. The piece, said Yervant, was big enough to park two cars underneath.

On another occasion a running street-battle had spilled over into Yervant's building. There was shooting on the stairs and a militia man burst into the flat. Yervant was waiting there with a revolver. He killed the man before he even knew anyone was there.

Yervant gripped my arm. He pointed to a flock of herring-gulls gathered to squabble over some waste. 'You like birds?'

'Yes, I do.'

'Me too. In the war I would come down and shoot them with my gun. My friend in Canada says there you cannot do it. You must have a licence. A licence – imagine that!'


One afternoon, through a series of introductions, I traced another side of Beirut's Armenians in another darkened room in Bourdj-Hamoud. Here the atmosphere was quite different. Half a dozen men in track-suits sat around a television, cracking pistachio nuts. There was none of Yervant's eccentric tension, but instead a kind of palpable toughness.

The youngest of them was Manouk. He was little more than

twenty and was small and wiry and wore a neatly clipped moustache. It didn't take long before we were talking about Karabagh. The Turks and Soviets, he said, were helping to flush the Armenians from their villages. Every day they were being killed. Driven from their villages and killed – just like 1915. Now. Today! And what was the West doing? Nothing. As always. Just carrying on their love affair with the Russian reformers.

I told him that Armenia would have to fight its own battles from now on and he agreed. And in fact I knew that they were, these ones in this room. I had heard of the arms that filtered through from Beirut to Karabagh. There was a sharper spirit here. It was in Manouk and the others, in their crunching of pistachios, in the pages of the Armenian magazine *GAYDZ!* (meaning 'flash of fire'), with its images of oppression, of heads under boots, nooses and cages, and the technical diagrams of a Chinese grenade-launcher, an M-16 and a Kalashnikov. It had been there also, in the late 1970s, when the Armenians too learned the effectiveness of small paramilitary units.

Both were based in Beirut: ASALA (Armenian Secret Army for the Liberation of Armenia) and JCAG (Justice Commandos of the Armenian Genocide). Of the two the JCAG were much the more secretive and sinister, and operated with surgical efficiency. One FBI officer was quoted as saying, 'The Justice Commandos were known as a singularly effective group of assassins. When they went to work somebody usually died.' There was something very Armenian about the JCAG. Their operation in sixteen different countries, their attention to detail and meticulous planning, their expertise with firearms and explosives, the way they traced the movements of their victims (invariably Turkish diplomats), getting so close to the cars when shooting that powder burns were often found on the skin.

And it occurred to me, listening to Manouk recounting their methods, that I'd heard precisely the same language used to explain the pre-eminence of Armenian goldsmiths.

This is how it would happen. You'd be in a taxi. You'd be watching a wrecked building pan across the window or the sun play on a sheet of high glass. You'd be thinking about something else entirely. In Kuwait there would be some atrocity and you wouldn't yet know and the taxi would pull up in a strange courtyard and there they'd be waiting for you, five of them in black t-shirts tugging at your door. And then? Would the Armenians be any help? Part of me wanted to find out. But another part, and much the larger, feared kidnap more than death.

I was thinking about that after my meeting with Manouk. It was a bright afternoon and I was in a taxi with three Arabs. I was looking at the sun play on the sea and thinking that I now had only two days before the land offensive was due to begin when the music on the radio was interrupted and I could make out the names – America, Saddam Hussein, Kuwait, Britain. The Arabs started talking with the driver – about what? About the Bastard Americans, about the Bastard British! About the Great Satan and the Little Satan! About me. I cursed my foolishness. We plunged into the back-streets, heading west. I leaned forward and said where are you going, I wanted Bourdj-Hamoud. But the driver just shook his head. Damn it, what's happening? The car slowed and turned into a courtyard and the Arabs got out and one of them leaned back in and said: 'My friend, you better be careful.' And the driver pulled away again and the buildings in the streets seemed suddenly sharper as I searched desperately for something I recognised.

Armenian script. When I saw it appear above the shops, I felt for the second time the relief of sanctuary and realized how much, in a Middle East where I felt an unwelcome alien, I depended on the Armenians. So much so that later that day I gave in. I'd promised myself I would not go into West Beirut: West Beirut was under Muslim control, kidnap country. But there was an Armenian there going to Yerevan and I needed to speak to her. The Armenians said they'd get me in, by ambulance, and we were waved through all the checkpoints.

As I waited to meet my contact, the door of the office suddenly burst open. A man stumbled over the threshold, sweating and short of breath. 'You have a British here?'

'Yes,' I said.

'You must leave at once. You have been seen.'

I left. I climbed into the back of the ambulance and we headed out of West Beirut towards the Ring and the burnt-out strip of the Green Line. An Armenian nurse sat with me. 'Don't worry, we'll soon be through the checkpoint.'

'I'll be glad to get back to Bourdj-Hamoud.'

'They took two yesterday. A French and a Belgian.'

'Where?'

'Just near here, but they were drug dealers. They shouldn't have gone in. We have an expression in Armenian that a broken jar breaks again on the way to the rubbish tip.'

The evenings in Antelias, with the monastery gates locked after sundown, were long and dark and empty. On my last night a thunderstorm tumbled down from the mountains. The lights failed, came on again, then disappeared altogether.

I stood up from the desk in my room and went to the window. The rain was falling with a tropical ferocity. It sluiced off the flat roofs and filled the headlight beams of the traffic – bobbing Buicks, battered Mercedes, empty trucks swishing into the night. A pack of wild dogs splashed through the puddles. Two Lebanese soldiers crouched beneath their rain-capes on the turret of a tank. Then for an instant Beirut was lit up by lightning and the thunder again took a whip to the hills.

There was a knock on my door. A young priest holding a candle said His Holiness would like to see me. I followed him through the darkened passages to a room with a great arched window that rose from the floor and surveyed the courtyard below. Often I had looked up at that window and watched the bishops pace behind it like caged birds. Now the rain spotted its surface and ran down it in wide rivulets. The Catholicos sat alone watching it in the dark, preying on a large cigar.

'Please, sit down,' he said.

We sat in silence for a moment, looking out at the rain.

'You will not see me again,' he announced.

'Oh?'

'Lent is coming and I am tired. I shall go to Oxford to rest.'

'A retreat?'

'A retreat.' He looked away and again we were silent while the rain hissed outside. The Catholicos looked down on the flooded courtyard like a brooding general. Then he asked, 'And you?'

'Damascus,' I said. 'I will leave tomorrow for Syria.'

'You will have trouble in Syria.'

'I was hoping perhaps you could help me cross the border.'

'I will leave a letter for you, but I would not go to Syria. The police will make trouble.'

I could not tell him that in fact I would be relieved to be out of the Lebanon, that at least in Syria there *were* police. So I thanked him for his advice and for all his help, and wandered back through the unlit cloisters to my room.

Early the next day an Armenian photographer took me into Bourdj-Hamoud to find a lift to the Syrian border. It was a bright morning. The night's storm had left its mark in shining pond-sized puddles and the traffic was heavy. Cars queued three deep at the checkpoints, impatient to get into the city to trade and shop and busy themselves in the Beiruti way. No one, except me, seemed at all bothered that in about twelve hours' time the deadline for the land offensive in Kuwait was due to expire.

Coming through the checkpoints in the other direction were dozens of vehicles with skis strapped to the roof. That year on Mount Lebanon the snow had been frightfully disappointing.

'Terrible,' the photographer lamented. 'All thin and slushy.'

'I'm sorry to hear it,' I said.

'But this year they are all going skiing. If there's one thing the Beirutis are good at, it's forgetting,' he chuckled. 'I mean, does this seem to you like a city that's been sixteen years at war?'

'Yes,' I said. 'It does.'

# 3

History will search in vain for the word 'Armenia'.

Winston S. Churchill

After all, who now remembers the Armenians?

Adolf Hitler, discussing use of his death-squads

The main road from Beirut to Damascus had only been open a few weeks. Lebanese government forces controlled it to the pass below Mount Lebanon, Syrians beyond that. Shared taxis had begun to ply the route between the two cities, braving the checkpoints for the sake of a good fare.

Looking back down towards Beirut, it could have been any Mediterranean town with its bushy-pine slopes and the dust and the terraces and the olive groves. From a distance it looked like Nice or Genoa. But the road was scarred with tank tracks and by the time we reached the abandoned hill resorts of Aley, Sofar and Bhamdoun all the villas – once the summer courts of the Gulf sheikhs – were utterly destroyed. At the pass of Dahr-al-Baidar, where the Syrians took over, fog brushed the mountain slopes and piles of snow lay beside the road. At the checkpoint, an old Volvo burst into flames. The Syrian soldiers dashed about in a panic, piling snow on the bonnet to smother the fire, barking orders, letting the traffic through without question. The Armenian taxi-driver accelerated past them with relief and we started the long, sweeping descent towards the Bekaa valley.

For me, the Bekaa embodied all the most dangerous aspects of the Middle East. From years of news reports and hearsay, I imagined a place something akin to the Valley of the Shadow of Death or one of the inner circles of Hell. I saw a dark shadowy declivity into which crawled extremists too extreme for Beirut; I pictured Western hostages tied to the bottom of cars and, from above, Israeli planes bombing and strafing its southern reaches. Out of the valley came trained terrorists and hashish (for both of which it was the world's leading supplier), and each year the Syrians earned more than a billion dollars from the opium. Even its name sounded dark and threatening: Bekaa – like a rifle shot or a cry of *jihad*.

So it was a surprise to find that the valley was very beautiful, that the Hizbollah and their hostages woke to mornings of a brilliant, feverish light; that the militias – Palestinian, Shiite, Kurdish – could run their combat training against a backdrop of sensuous, flesh-smooth slopes. But I was pleased to get across it, through the narrow corridor of Syrian control, up to the Lebanese frontier on the far side. At the Syrian border beyond, I waited seven hours for a visa. President Assad scrutinized me from three walls with his benign bank-manager's stare.

Just before four o'clock, an official summoned me to the desk. 'Border closing.'

'My visa?'

'*Bukra*. Tomorrow.'

'Tomorrow Damascus will say yes?'

'Maybe yes, maybe no.'

Damn you. I was now caught in no man's land – unable to get into Syria, and unable to re-enter Lebanon; I'd used up my 'une seule visite' visa.

Only a few carefully placed US dollars eased me back across the Lebanese border, back into the Bekaa. In a few hours' time the allied forces would launch their offensive in Kuwait and the Bekaa Valley was the last place I wanted to be.

Once again the Armenians were able to offer me protection. Just up from the border post I found the village of Anjar, where a series of bubbling springs leave a smudge of green on the dry slopes. The village was made up entirely of Armenians and they welcomed me in. Just outside, the Syrian secret police had set up camp. I didn't think I had much to thank them for, but the sight of all their military hardware between me and the Hizbollah was something of a relief.

There was a doctor named Caspar who ran an occasional clinic in Anjar. I'd met him in Beirut but today he was here. I found him in his surgery with a queue of patients; he said he'd be half an hour and advised me not to leave the building. So I waited beneath the anatomical diagrams and listening to the stern advice to young mothers, reflecting that in fact I was glad to be in Anjar, to have the opportunity to trace one of 1915's few episodes of successful defiance.

The story of Anjar is a story of exile and return, and exile again. A conglomerate of six old Armenian villages, Anjar's people came originally from an area around the mountain of Musa Dagh, at the far northern end of the Levantine coast. The town is divided into six segments, which retain the names of the villages that they left. When in July 1915 the deportation order reached Musa Dagh, Armenian opinion was divided. Some said they should resist. Others saw there was no point; the Turkish forces were far too strong and the order, after all, was only for deportation. About sixty families complied with it. They were never seen again.

The rest took to the mountain. On its seaward edge they stretched two large shrouds between the pines. One had a cross on it, the other, in English: 'CHRISTIANS IN DISTRESS: RESCUE'. The opposite slope they defended against repeated Turkish attacks. There was little ammunition and still less food. After more than seven weeks, supplies were virtually exhausted. But then one morning, the wind blew away a sea-mist and just off the coast lay the French ship *Guichen*. Four thousand villagers scrambled down the cliff and were ferried aboard. They were taken south, to Port Said.

For four years they sheltered in tents on the edge of the Sinai Desert. After the war Musa Dagh came under French rule, so it was safe to go back. The Armenians returned to their beloved villages and found their clapboard homesteads half-hidden by mulberry trees, and the apple orchards a tangle of weeds. They set about clearing the orchards and restocked the mulberries with silk worms.

But in the 1930s, new pressures came to bear on the region. Eager to keep the Turks at bay, the French conceded to them the sanjak of Alexandretta – which included Musa Dagh. Once again the Armenians were forced to flee. This time the French gave them land in the Bekaa Valley. Many died in the harsh winters but others held on, convinced, like those of Bourdj-Hamoud, that it was only a matter of time before they'd be allowed back. It soon became clear after the Second World War that Musa Dagh would remain in Turkey. The Armenians resigned themselves to permanent settlement in the Bekaa, not at the camp, but at Anjar where the spring-fed soil and distant peaks reminded them of home.

Below the springs they cut irrigation ditches and planted poplars along their banks. They'd grown apples before, so they grew apples here; before long Anjar's orchards were the best in the country. They built neat houses, neat and diligent in the old way, and laid them out in a grid with a church at its head. They prospered in Anjar; there was something about the site. One man, ploughing nearby, unearthed some old stone which turned out to be the remains of an Ummayyad palace, now one of the Lebanon's most prized ancient sites.

During the most recent fighting Anjar had swelled with refugees from Beirut. Caspar explained to me that it wasn't just the shelter, it was the land itself. The springs and the poplars and the abiding sense of a distant mountain; there, he said, people felt more at ease, closer to Armenia. In times of trouble they gravitated to Anjar.

Mount Sannin was undoubtedly a powerful presence. It rose steeply from the far side of the Bekaa, screening Beirut. Its snow-topped peak shone in the sun. And perhaps for the Armenians it made a good substitute not only for Musa Dagh but for that other mountain, the first mountain, the one they had fled centuries before. For local lore has it that from Anjar's spring the first rainbow rose and, using it to navigate, Noah had steered the Ark to shore on Sannin's rocky summit.

Caspar helped me track down Tomas Habeshian, one of Anjar's grand old men. We met him on the church steps, a tall, straight-backed man in an astrakhan hat. He stretched out his left hand to greet us; his right was crippled with arthritis.

Driving down through the town (the Armenians forbade me to walk: 'Not safe,' they said) we spent much of the rest of the afternoon in Anjar's tea-room, while Syrian jeeps bounced bask and forth outside the window, and the proprietor laid his best cakes before us. 'On the house!' he said in honour of Tomas.

He had been little more than ten when he fled with his family up the slopes of Musa Dagh. The whole thing, explained Tomas, had really been a big adventure. No, he didn't recall being frightened. He remembered climbing the trees and larking around the rocks, but fear, he didn't think that was a part of it. What he did remember was Kavanes and his quixotic antics. An Armenian of the old school, Kavanes had lived all his life on the land and was full of a peasant pride that Tomas, as a boy, found comic. He was nearly sixty when they went up Musa Dagh armed only with hunting rifles and flint-locks, and a few sticks of dynamite. Early on, Kavanes stepped forward to volunteer for an attack.

'He took the dynamite and put a pistol in his belt. Down the hill he went.' Tomas leaned forward and hushed his voice. 'Slowly, slowly, from tree to tree. He came out of the woods and crept up to the slope above the Turks. He lit the fuse and lobbed the dynamite down. One, two, three . . . Nothing! So he lit another. This time – PAF!

'You know, I think Kavanes was more surprised than the Turks! We watched him turn and run back up the hill in fright. He felt sure the Turks were following him. They were running at him, they grabbed his coat, but still he tried to run away, pulling and pulling. He took the pistol and fired it over his shoulder, and the noise terrified him so much he thought it was him who had been shot and fell to the ground.

'He touched his forehead: no blood! He got up and started to walk towards us. I can walk! And he looked behind him and all along, it had been a branch that had caught his coat. There weren't any Turks. All of us in the trees were laughing so much, but he was trying to look like a returning hero!' Tomas took off his glasses and wiped his eyes. 'Oh, that Kavanes!'

Tomas was one of the few still alive who had survived the whole saga. He gazed now through the window, quiet and sad after his picaresque, and the sun brought out the creases on his face. I felt a strange awe at the alien experience of this man's life and how its suffering had not left him bitter like so many, but poised and full of humour.

I asked him, 'Do you have a family?'

'Yes. In America mainly. Los Angeles.'

I couldn't picture this proud old man in California. 'Have you been there?'

'Oh yes.'

'And you liked it?'

'I liked it.' He looked away. 'But I could never live there. America is no place for an Oriental man.'

\*

Caspar passed me on to some friends who said they could put me up for the night. Four generations sat on divans around a hot barrel-stove. A two-year-old girl sat on the knee of her great-grandfather, tugging at his whiskers. Her mother, Anahid, carried in a tray of rattling glasses. It was a warm, homely room and, for a moment, I forgot all about deadlines and the hostility of the Bekaa.

A man with a feathery moustache leaned over and poured me a glass of arak. 'What are you doing here?'

'Trying to get to Damascus.'

'Well, I'm trying to get back to Kuwait.'

I said that perhaps now he would not have to wait long.

'I have waited long enough!'

'Why the hurry?'

'Three kilos,' he winked at me. 'I have three kilos of gold in a Kuwaiti bank.'

I pictured the gold sitting now in a Baghdad vault, but did not mention it. I turned instead to Anahid who had retrieved her daughter from the old man's hair. 'You know, it's not a bad place, Anjar. Better than America – I'd never bring up children there!'

'Why not?'

'It's so dangerous.'

'And the Bekaa is safe?'

She sighed. 'Well, it's home. I went to Los Angeles and I felt afraid even to step outside. All those drugs and murders. I was glad to get back.'

I'd never thought I would hear that from a Lebanese Christian, here in the Bekaa. Anahid's brother, Levon, had come down from Aleppo for a couple of days. He was more Levantine than Armenian, with eyes full of dark, undirected resentment. He heaved down another shot of arak, leaned towards me and jabbed at the window. 'He's just a few kilometres up there.'

'Who?'

He grinned at me and sank back in his chair, but did not answer.

'Who?' I said, annoyed.

'Your Terry Waite!'

'Levon!' snapped his sister. 'Quiet!'

I told her not to worry, but the cosiness of the room had gone. There was silence and no one could look at me. Levon proposed a toast to the Western hostages but it was timid and forced, and fell flat. Later they all left and I was shown into a small bedroom. I pushed open the window and looked out across the valley. It was a clear night and very cold; the moon glowed deep blue on the snow of Sannin.

In Kuwait the deadline was about to pass but here in the Bekaa, with its strange medley of militants and the dispossessed, its gaolers and hostages, all was quiet.

# 4

In exile one lives by genius alone.

Vladimir Nabokov

Behind the wheel of his crimson, 1960s Plymouth Fury, its interior flushed with bordello-red velvet upholstery, Stepan looked very small. But he was the wiliest man I met in the Middle East, where wiliness counts for everything. He could only have been Armenian.

I met Stepan in Anjar. He had quick, dark eyes and his energy palpitated from his wiry frame. He was going to Damascus and on a sunny morning we drove back to the border. Today the Lebanese would not let me out of the country unless they were sure the Syrians would let me in. And I couldn't confirm that without getting across the two miles of no man's land. It posed no problem for Stepan. To him and his Red Beast, the route between Anjar and Damascus was routine. He took my passport and swung the Beast round in a wide arc up towards the frontier. He didn't even slow down to go through it, but simply hung an arm out of the window and waved to the border guards. They waved back.

In less than an hour the crimson roof topped the hill and was back.

'It's good?'

He nodded. We accelerated up over the hill, through no man's land and down to the Syrian border. There I left it all to him. We passed from one office to the next, waited while a South American diplomat checked two feather-boaed dancing-girls into the country; collected stamps and filled in forms; I fielded strange questions about my family and my contacts in Beirut, and assured them I'd never even thought of going to Israel (I'd hidden all my letters of introduction from the Jerusalem patriarch). At some stage Stepan paraded the palms of the border guards before me: 'Ten US dollars here . . . five there . . . nothing for him . . . one hundred Syrian pounds.'

And then with a nod we were through the frontier, with a Syrian major propped between us on the bench seat, being waved through customs and the remaining checkpoints, bouncing and rolling down a runway of a road into Syria, towards the desert, beneath a winter sun that picked out every crease and knuckle of the dry cliffs.

Stepan slid a tape into his cassette machine. 'Frank Sinatra – "Fly Me to the Moon". My favourite one!'

'Stepan, you did well,' I said. 'Thank you.'

He laughed and said, in Armenian, 'This man here is secret policeman. I know them all and this one is bad. He told me they sent four telexes yesterday about you to intelligence in Damascus. You are lucky!'

Not luck, I told him, but another triumph for the Armenian network. It had been the toughest border to date. After several weeks on the road it seemed a great achievement and bolstered my faith in the Armenians. The dozens of other hurdles between here and Armenia looked smaller and strangely, unexpectedly, I found I was delighted to be back in Syria. I really didn't think I'd get in.

Between us, the secret policeman leaned forward and pointed down a bank. The wreck of a car lay upside down thirty feet below. 'Yesterday,' he said, 'I was in that car. Three times it turned over.'

'Weren't you hurt?' asked Stepan.

'My driver, he is in hospital. But I was all right. God makes sure the good men survive.'


Stepan banked the Red Beast down through the outskirts of Damascus. The modern city was little more than a series of wide, straight boulevards and elaborate fountains, the sure mark of a grim dictatorship. We left the major on the steps of a ministry building and headed towards the Old City. Stepan pulled up at one of the gates.

'Follow the Street Called Straight until you reach the Gate of the Sun.'

I nodded.

'There on the right you will see the Armenian church of Saint Sarkis.'

'Right.'

'Ring the bell many times. The doorman is often drunk.'

But it was Sunday and the door was open. The liturgy had just finished and half a dozen Armenians sat drinking coffee with the priest.

I handed him my letter from the Catholicos in Beirut. He received it with enthusiasm and he showed me a room at the top of the Armenian school. The place was only half built and building-dust lay like a patina on the mattress. For a long time the door wouldn't open, then it wouldn't shut.

'I hope it's all right,' he said.

'It's fine. I'm very grateful.'

I meant it. In Beirut I'd been warned about Damascus hotels: full of dangerous extremists. I wasn't sure I believed it, but was pleased – at this time especially – not to have to find out.

Off the Street Called Straight, in amongst a warren of cobbled alleys, I found a sun-lit courtyard which corresponded to my directions. Cloistered by horseshoe colonnades, the tiled floor was awash with soapy water. A woman bent over it, scrubbing vigorously.

'Hagop?' I called.

She gestured to a staircase in the far corner and eyed me as I tip-toed across her morning's work. She was not pleased and a hail of Koranic curses followed me up the stairs.

Hagop was a friend of Yervant, the gull-shooting painter in Beirut.

'See him,' urged Yervant. 'See if he is OK. He has had some problems . . .'

Hagop had the Armenian penchant for dark rooms. All I could see to begin with were narrow strips of light slanting through the shutters. The window was open and I could smell the baker's ovens below and hear the hum and clatter of the souk. Hagop sat on a divan and the smoke from his cigarette rose and curled in and out of the strips of light. He had a thick, modulated voice and his English was good.

'How is Yervant? I think the war was bad for him. I don't know why he didn't leave.'

'He's glad it's over.'

I could see Hagop more clearly now. He was a compact figure in t-shirt and jeans and no shoes. His legs stretched along the divan, crossed at the ankles. All his movements were slow and measured and his thin lips twitched slightly as he spoke.

He re-lit his cigarette. 'I have been planning for some time to return to Beirut. When this Gulf situation is sorted out, I will go back. For now I have taken this room. I feel happy in this room.' He pulled his palm slowly across his forehead. He did not look happy. 'I have been reading some things by our Gregory of Narek, from his Book of Lamentations. You like his work?'

'Yes – very much.'

'For me Gregory is a master. I hear his voice between the lines. You know how he writes and it seems so hopeless? About how he feels like the foal of an ass, or a broken lock in a door, and that he could not tell all his sins even with a sea of ink and a grove of reeds? Yet I feel such joy reading him.'

Hagop smiled to himself. He and Gregory had little in common. Both of their families had come from the mountains around Lake Van, both shared the Armenian passion for jeremiads. But Gregory, born in the tenth century, had been an intensely pious man, a mystic, devoting his life to prayer and rarely moving from the monastery. Hagop on the other hand could hardly keep still. His story as he told it, of a water-boatman life skimming across the surface of the Middle East, made me realize how precarious the diaspora now was. He had spent fifteen years in a worldly frenzy of travel; there were few towns in the Middle East he had not been to, few things he had not traded. Borders of every kind had tumbled in his path and now there was nothing new.

But he had resisted going to Turkey. Someday he would, but for the moment, well, Armenians are not welcome. I tried to describe for him Lake Van and its high, blue light and the mountains around it. He sighed and shook his head; it was a world away from here.

Hagop's grandfather had been seven when he'd seen Lake Van for the last time. The Turkish zaptieh came to the village and drove them all out. Those who weren't shot at once were marched down from the mountains towards the desert. Twenty-five of his family left; only he and a cousin survived. The old man never spoke of these things. But shortly before he died he sat young Hagop at his feet and calmly told him everything.

The village was not big. There'd been a fountain in the square where the horses drank and sometimes water from the trough would slop over into the square. The people gathered at the fountain before the march. He remembered then how silent the older marchers were and the shouts of the zaptieh. He remembered them taking his sister, and the woman who wandered off into the desert with the guards running after her and shouting, 'Come back! Where are you going?' and she saying simply, 'I am going to the funeral of God.' He recalled the thirst of those dry regions of southern Anatolia; the marches followed the old road beside the river but they could not drink. His brother cried and begged for water and his mother scooped a cupful from the imprint of a donkey's hoof. A day later the boy died; his mother was dead within a week.

Hagop's grandfather and his surviving cousin had somehow reached one of Aleppo's orphanages. From there they moved to Beirut. They both married at about the same time orphaned girls from the same region around Van. But for his cousin the weight of what they had been through overwhelmed him. With his wife expecting their first child, and the next generation ensured, he hanged himself.

Hagop's father meanwhile built up a business in Beirut retailing European clothes and again had one child, a son. Hagop himself grew up to an easy life. He was bright, indulged by his father and exposed to all the temptations of Beirut in the late 1960s. Studying at the American University he became involved in the lucrative fringes of Beiruti commerce. Within a few years he was running a dubious venture trading antiquities. The war stifled that operation, but soon all sorts of other things were passing through the crumbling capital: raw opium, guns, hashish from the Bekaa valley.

Hagop was drawn in by it. His business spun higher; the possibilities seemed limitless. But he began to make mistakes and for six months fretted in an Egyptian jail convicted of currency smuggling. Then he began to dip into his own bags.

One night in northern Iraq, in the town of Mosul, he stepped on to the flat roof of an apartment block. It was a hot night and he was twitchy and wide-eyed from months of cocaine use. He stood on the parapet and saw the edges of the night flashing with orange. Part of him knew these were the well-head fires of the desert oil stations, but as he watched them, they grew, ringing his own horizons so that he could no longer move. He thought he was in Hell. All that his grandfather had told him came back. He saw the Turkish zaptieh riding beside the convoy. He felt his throat parched and saw the damp imprint of the donkey's hoof. He felt his tongue fur up and stick in his mouth. His face flushed with heat. When he looked down and saw his own skin peeling, he tore off his shirt and ran inside. Drinking from a bottle of water, he had hallucinations of a quite different kind: the village near Van with his young grandfather squatting in the shade of a walnut tree, splashing in the fountain's overspill.

'That was worse than the flames,' said Hagop. 'I realized then what it was to be Armenian. That village I saw is now always with me.'

Thereafter Hagop was a different man; he became a committed Armenian. He started to study music seriously and combined it with his other resolution – to live in Armenia, Soviet Armenia. He gained a place at the Conservatoire in Yerevan. That was two years ago.

He lit another cigarette and looked at me darkly. 'Let me tell you about Armenia. Great Armenia! When I first arrived in Yerevan, I couldn't believe it. Armenians in an Armenian city, in the shadow of Ararat. I got involved in everything – political meetings, the arts. I spoke to the composers and the poets and read many books of Armenian history. I even started to write an opera based on the court of the Bagratids at Ani. I became a "Good Armenian". But after a while something changed.'

Hagop was there when they started to kick against Moscow. Yerevan became charged with the idea of change; intellectuals saw the hold of the Kremlin weakening. At last they could speak out. But the new climate had its darker side: liberalism belied anarchy, nationalism became a by-word for banditry. Guns fell into the wrong hands and decades of bitterness and frustration spilled over in peculiar ways.

Late one October night Hagop was walking home through Yerevan. A car pulled up and the rear door opened. Two Armenians climbed out and bundled him into the car. They pressed the muzzle of a Kalashnikov to his cheek and drove him up to the mountains. There they forced him to kneel and to clear the rocks from a small patch of ground.

'Now, dig a grave!'

For three hours they toyed with him, threatening to shoot him, abandoning him for a while, then returning. Just before dawn they took him down to Yerevan and dumped him outside the railway station.

'I still don't know what they wanted. They knew I was from abroad. I offered them dollars – but it wasn't money. I stayed in Yerevan a few months longer, but after that night, things were not the same. If you reach Armenia, be careful.'

'And are you still a "Good Armenian"?'

He smiled for the first time. 'I've no idea. But I am certainly more Armenian.'

When I left Hagop it was almost dark. For some time I wandered, half lost, through the narrow streets around the souk. Not for the first time I felt numb and baffled by Armenia. I was haunted by the image of a flame and the Armenians spinning round it like moths; like Hagop I now felt by turns drawn in and repelled by it. At the end of the evening I returned to the gate of the Armenian compound. I rang the bell but there was no response. I called and threw pebbles at the guard's window. Nothing. I was tired and distracted and abandoned myself to going into the city centre, and the hotels I had been warned against.

Two of them turned me away when they saw my passport. In a third they grunted and gave me a room. I lay on the bed and idly watched the cockroaches pad across the wall. In my fatigue they became allied tanks in the Iraqi desert . . .

I woke from a sweaty dream in which Palestinian guerrillas were kicking down the door. I took off my shirt and saw with some alarm the Hebrew letters of its label. I'd bought the shirt in a department store in West Jerusalem. All the anxiety of the past few days spilled over. Convinced I'd be taken for a Mossad agent, I pulled out the label and cut at it until the patterns of the letters were no more than formless shreds of cotton on the floor.

The following morning I took a bus to Aleppo and saw again the wide-open face of Syria. Between the bunched-up chaos of Damascus and Aleppo the horizons fell to a flat, featureless desert. The gates had closed on the hubbub of the souk, the everyday mayhem of Arab towns, and the world was suddenly still and quiet. I thought of the silence two years ago at Shadaddie and the dark silence of the cave, and before that the silence of the hills around the plain of Kharput. Silence was the seal on the Armenian massacres: Turkish silence, Armenian silence, desert silence. I still had the sketch map I'd been given then in Aleppo. It was now annotated with dozens of notes and I planned to go back with it to the desert north of the Euphrates. But first I needed a few days in Aleppo, a few days of planning, a few days with those who'd survived. Since the exodus of Armenians from Beirut during the civil war, Aleppo's community has swelled dramatically. Now there are close to one hundred thousand Armenians living in the city.

If Aleppo can be considered something of an Armenian centre, then its own centre must surely be the Baron Hotel. At the foot of the Baron's sweeping double staircase dozed a portly golden retriever. From time to time a chamber-maid or guest would step over her but she did not move. Crossing the parquet floor I propped my bag against the reception-booth and asked for Baron Mazloumian. ('Baron' is the Armenian 'Mister' dating from the Crusades when the Armenians noticed that all the best French names were preceded with 'Baron'. Mazloumian was the hotel's proprietor.)

'At a quarter past ten every evening he comes in to do the telexes.'

So I wrote him a note, arranged a room and, in the late afternoon, stepped out into the fading yellow of the town. Aleppo was fleshier than Damascus: more Arab, less Ba'athist. Along the outside of the pavements, loose calico swung against the hips of the desert drovers; on the inside hawk-eyed merchants squatted beside cheap watches, lighters and rainbow racks of useless plastic things. In the shadowy hinterland were the cinemas. Posters made banal promises of semi-nudity, gun-laden banditry and rough justice. In one were rag-doll bodies swinging from garrets, in another beckoned the pink chiffon charm of Schehrazade, through another galloped the Mongol hordes. I plumped for *A Town called Bastard* and paid fifteen Syrian pounds for a broken seat.

Ten minutes was all I could stand – and all it took for the carnage on-screen to spill into the aisles. Several boys wrestled on the floor. Others yelled support or argued nonchalantly in groups while bursts of automatic gunfire rattled unnoticed from the speakers. It all seemed too familiar.

Behind the cinema were the open-fronted workshops of the Armenian mechanics. A bare-footed boy was chasing and coaxing a tractor tyre along the cobbles. The monochrome interiors echoed with metallic sounds and it seemed that nothing in that street was not dedicated to restoring – as swiftly as possible – life to broken cars. The row of workshops looked like beds in a busy field hospital. I thought of the adage about Armenians in Syria, that without them the government would collapse: Assad depends on his secret police, and the secret police depend on their cars – and no one can fix cars like the Armenians.

Near the place of the mechanics was a subterranean arcade full of photographers' studios, many of them also Armenian. I needed a new stock of passport photographs for my on-going quest for visas and pushed open the door of Kevork's Yerevan Foto Studio. Photography, like fixing cars, is also a talent of Armenian exiles. Karsh of Ottowa, who gave us the grizzly-sad picture of Hemingway, who snatched Churchill's cigar from his mouth in order to make him angry enough for that famous bullish portrait, was born of Armenian parents in Mardin, southern Turkey. In Beirut I'd been to the studio of Varoujan Sethian who flicked through his portfolio of official portraits: the leaders of Qatar, Abu Dhabi, Bahrain (not Jordan, as King Hussein has his own Armenian photographer). He had had four Lebanese presidents in his studio in recent years (two had subsequently been assassinated). And his pictures of President Assad had now been reproduced and posted in offices, in car windows and on almost every street corner in Syria.

Kevork's Foto Studio was more commercial. He cupped my chin in his hand, then bent down behind an old plate camera.

'Yes, sir. Very good. Hold it like that. You married? . . . You have pretty girl? Very . . . nice!' His flash bowl bathed everything in a sudden white light and it was done.

Kevork had started as a darkroom assistant when he was fifteen. His parents had both been from the orphanages, too young to remember anything about how they got there from Armenia. They had had one child and no money. When he was sixteen Kevork borrowed thirty dollars from an American to buy a camera. The American clearly did not expect, or want, the debt repaid. But Kevork turned up five months later at the Baron Hotel and gave the American his cash.

'I used to work sometimes all night in the darkroom, but the chemicals made me ill.' Now Kevork had his own family to help him out. 'Let me introduce you!'

He assembled them in the studio. 'Now. This son, he do video US

51

system. Other son do video European system. My wife, she do Muslim weddings.'

'Why don't you do the weddings?'

'Christian gentleman no go to Muslim wedding.'

'Why not?'

'They may kill him.'

'So what sort of photography do you do?'

'Propaganda photo.'

'Propaganda? For whom?'

'All people – government people, family people. I do work for blind.'

'Blind people?'

'Yes. They like holy place propaganda. I do moskies and shrines.'

'But they cannot see your pictures?'

'Of course not – they are blind.'


I was back at the Baron by ten fifteen and Krikor Mazloumian was there in his office, checking the ledger against the day's telexes. As the hotel's tourist trade had slackened so its telex machine rattled into service for Aleppo's Armenians. Soviet Armenia was opening up and the Levantine diaspora was again learning to combine its two driving passions: business and the homeland.

It was a high-ceilinged room, with the telex in one corner and Armenia's modern iconography pinned to the flaking walls. The snowy summit of Ararat hovered above Krikor's head; on the opposite wall Yerevan's Martyrs' Monument stretched its brutal limbs over the Eternal Flame and, above a battered grey filing cabinet, a map showed the borders of old Armenia stretching across the east of Turkey.

Krikor reached into the filing cabinet and fumbled around. He came out with a bottle of Armenian brandy. 'You don't speak German, by any chance?' he asked, filling two plastic beakers.

'No.'

'Pity. Chief of Police gave my son this letter he'd been sent. Asked him to work out what it says. I know a little German, but this baffles me. Something about love or something . . .'

He shook his head and muttered while he looked for a place to put the letter. He had an old-world charm but his speech, like all his movements, was slow and listless. He was blind in one eye and pretty blind in the other. Light annoyed him and round his forehead he wore a visor made from an old box of washing powder: 'Omo for the brightest wash – Omo for the cleanest whites'.

After some minutes he closed the ledger, pulled down his visor, took the beaker of brandy and began to talk. The story of the Baron Hotel, like most Armenian stories, starts in Anatolia in the last decade of the nineteenth century. It was then that Krikor's grandmother left Kharput for her pilgrimage to Jerusalem. In Aleppo she stayed in a *han*, with the desert merchants and their animals. There was no hotel. So she bought a small premises near the souk. 'Being a good Armenian, she named it the Ararat Hotel.'

Her son later rebuilt it, with an Armenian architect from Paris. And since then it has remained more or less unchanged. The parquet floor is still the same, the dark stained panels and the dark double staircase; the prints on the landing are still of the London–Baghdad Simplon Express (seven days: safety / rapidity / economy), and all the place lacks as a perfect period piece is a few aspidistras, spreading their languid fronds across the foyer.

During the First War the hotel was taken over by the Turks. 'What champagne will you be serving at your Easter?' asked Abdulahad Nouri Bey, a notoriously cruel member of the Deportations Committee.

'Easter', replied Armenak Mazloumian, 'begins on the day of your departure.'

When they got news of their own deportation, the family managed to escape to the Bekaa valley, with the old matriarch, Krikor's grandmother, claiming that the eighty children she brought with her were all her own kin. But the hotel came into its own after the war, with Syria under French control. The 1920s and 30s were heady days at the Baron. Aleppo stood at the exotic end of the Grand Tour and the Baron was the only place to stay. Krikor had a bi-plane and would take favoured guests flying over the desert to the ruins of St Symeon Stylites. Amy Johnson stayed at the Baron, so did Diana Cooper. Agatha Christie sat in one of its rooms, writing *Murder on the Orient Express*; the Household Cavalry stayed and ran a mock hunt up and down the stairs. A framed copy of T.E. Lawrence's unpaid bill stands in the reading room. But now few people came to Syria, still fewer to the Baron.

The fat old labrador squeezed through the door. 'Oh. Pasha,' muttered the Baron fondly.

'Pasha?' I said. 'Like the Turkish governors?'

But he laughed. 'No, not *Pasha*. *Portia* – Shakespeare. *Merchant of Venice.*'

The Baron asked me to lunch the next day. 'Just something simple' was five courses and didn't end until it was almost dark. Our table of seven was the only one laid in the hotel's large panelled dining room; the Kurdish waiter was attentive to a fault, serving everyone with great scoops of green dal and running round in a frenzy of high spirits. He had just heard from Radio Monte Carlo that the Kurds had shot down three of Saddam's combat helicopters.

At the head of the table Krikor sat flanked by three fat Armenian women on a week's holiday from Yerevan. They looked very Soviet in their long black leather coats and dyed hair, and said nothing throughout lunch. I felt a little low to think that Armenia, the object of my journey might in fact be more Soviet than Armenian. But Mrs Mazloumian, English by birth, had a different view of Soviet Armenia. 'Sometimes I think I like it more than my husband does.'

'Really?'

'Yes, they're so gay. I had thought it would be grey and drab, you know, *Russian*. But when I got there, it was livelier than Aleppo.'

'You surprise me.'

'And Edjmiatsin's so beautiful. I defy anyone to go there and not come out a better Christian.'

Opposite me sat an American journalist.

'We don't like journalists very much,' challenged Mrs Mazloumian. 'They've come here before and written some frightful nonsense.'

The American muttered some apology, but he was a little nonplussed. He was Jewish and Jews in Syria – beyond the walls of the Baron – are not very welcome.

'Where are you based?' I asked.

'Bonn.'

At the end of the table Krikor's eyes lit up from amidst his silent menagerie. 'Bonn! So you speak German. The letter! Where's that letter?'

The Kurdish waiter went off, a little too eagerly, to get it from the telex room.

'Well, it's a strange German,' said the journalist. 'From Slovenia, I think. A girl . . . she's fallen in love with a Syrian policeman. "I need that man!" She cannot live another moment unless she finds that policeman.'

'Poor girl!' said Sally Mazloumian, who had also lost her heart in Aleppo. She had come out in 1947 as a nurse from England. Krikor was enchanted by her; they used to meet beneath an almond tree on the hotel balcony and within a short time were married. She had lived at the hotel ever since.

Yet her introduction to Aleppo and its Armenians had come much earlier. When she was a girl in England between the wars, Sally used to watch with particular dread the approach of a grey, willowy woman up her family's Yorkshire drive. This woman would come selling strange things from abroad. They used to call her Pilgrim-Frances but Sally saw her as somehow ghostly and cold. Even the woven, rainbow-coloured runners that Pilgrim-Frances brought with her seemed pallid when Sally thought of who had brought them. Pilgrim-Frances had a sister – known universally as Miss Roberts. They had both come from a small village in mid-Wales. They were devout, serious girls and, when they received a ten thousand pound legacy, decided to dedicate their lives to the Armenian orphans of Syria.

Pilgrim-Frances stayed in Britain, knocking on the doors of country houses, while Miss Roberts went to Aleppo to receive the money that her sister raised. She lived with the orphans, sleeping on a damp mattress and, even on the coldest days of winter, wearing only cotton dresses. One day Miss Roberts heard from Pilgrim-Frances that in England King George V and Queen Mary were to celebrate their jubilee. At once Miss Roberts set her orphans to work on embroidering a special tablecloth. She designed it herself, with a set of matching napkins.

When the work was finished they packed it all up and Miss Roberts took it to Mr Parr, the British consul in Aleppo. She told the orphans that soon the King and Queen of England would be eating off their tablecloth and brushing their royal lips with the napkins! But Mr Parr received a terse note from the Foreign Office: the Palace could accept no gifts unless delivered personally. Couldn't an exception be made? These Armenian children lived in miserable conditions and had suffered so much at the hands of the Turk. No exceptions, said the Foreign Office. Krikor remembered a distraught Mr Parr at the bar of the Baron. They agreed that there was only one thing he could do. Mr Parr sent an official letter from the consulate. He thanked Miss Roberts and the Armenian children for their delightful tablecloth and napkins. He signed it on behalf of His Majesty King George V.

And out of his own pocket, Mr Parr enclosed a cheque for twenty-five pounds.

Shortly afterwards old Mrs Mazloumian – Krikor's mother – gave Miss Roberts an overcoat for the winter. She couldn't tolerate seeing this poor Englishwoman in rag-dresses any longer. Miss Roberts was very appreciative. But the next day the coat was wrapped around some young Armenian. Shortly before the Second World War there was a particularly cold winter. The orphans were no longer that young but Miss Roberts continued her work, still in her cotton dresses. After one too many of the cold desert winds, she caught pneumonia and died.

Back in England Pilgrim-Frances received the news. She felt suddenly alone. She took her sister's letters to a family who had been kind to her in the past. But they were out, all except the young daughter. Sally reluctantly opened the door and let Pilgrim-Frances in. She sat and listened to her reading the letters and, seeing the woman close to tears, found her old aversions going. She heard about the desert and the dusty town of Aleppo, about the bustling bazaar, the world's largest covered market and the Armenian orphans, and about the coming and goings of the Baron Hotel, not realizing for a moment that this distant place would eventually become her home.

The next day was a Ba'athist holiday. It was the day that, a quarter of a century earlier, the Syrian Ba'athists had split away from the Iraqi Ba'athists.

'I just wish they'd thought a little more about how it sounds in English,' said Mrs Mazloumian at lunch. 'Rectification Day sounds, well, so *uncomfortable*.'

One and a half courses was all I had time for; I was leaving for the desert and had to catch the train to Raqqa.

The Kurdish waiter showed me out. 'Well?' I said as he opened the door. 'When will the Kurds take Mosul?'

He leaned towards me and grinned broadly. 'Two, maybe three days. Then Saddam finished!'

# 5

I rode over land everywhere sown with grain;
villages were visible all around, but they were
empty.

Alexander Pushkin, *Journey to Erzurum*

From the railway, sweeping round Aleppo's southern flank, I
watched the city centre thin to suburbs the colour of milky tea. The
sun dropped down between low, mud-wrapped buildings; tousle-
haired children chased whatever they could through the alleys –
dogs, hens, footballs, each other; seeing the train, they chased that
as well. Beyond Aleppo were strange villages with houses shaped
like Hittite helmets, then the stagnant swamps and far-off roads, and
then just the desert, rocky and lifeless behind the swells of trackside
cables.

I was glad to have Aleppo behind me, even after only a few days
there. It felt good to be away from the Levantine cities, the threatening closeness of Beirut and Damascus, away from the need to be
chaperoned and to chase up contacts, and free too of the Armenian
communities.

After a long evening in an Armenian club or in one of the neat
private houses, I often stepped back into the town with a sense of
relief. I wanted to strip off the weight that they hung on me, the
cuff-clinging bitterness, the weight of Turkish injustice; I longed to
be rid of the massacres and the exile, the whole weary burden of

57

the Armenians. But if it wasn't that that drew me, then what was it? What a cosy lie I was living, to suppose that the Armenians were anything more than a savagely persecuted people! To search for this other thing, this older thing, was nonsense. There was only the tyranny of the massacres. But what of the centuries before when it should have collapsed, and what of the spirit of Ani and Digor, and why the tenacity of the diaspora?

I took out the sketch map of the marches. From the west and central areas of Anatolia, and from the old Armenian kingdom of Cilicia, the arrows weaved down towards Aleppo, converging at Raqqa. I had first heard about Raqqa from an old man in Cyprus; he had escaped the killings by crossing the Euphrates on an in-flated goat skin. Raqqa was the western-most of the concentration centres.

It was mid-evening when the train reached the concrete shell of Raqqa station. The darkness pressed in upon the town's fringes and it was very cold. Pools of orange light lay beneath the street-lamps, but they were few and far between and I walked somewhat blindly into town and found a room in the town's only hotel.

In the Al-Waha restaurant, I pulled my chair closer to the paraffin stove to warm my hands. I looked idly at the menu and its kitsch cartoon logo of an orange ball of a sun and emerald green date-palms and an absurd long-lashed camel by an oasis. I felt a little warmer for that. Beneath it the name Al-Waha was written in three scripts – Arabic, Roman and Armenian. *Armenian*. I had no idea there were still Armenians in Raqqa. Nor had the wall-eyed waiter, who received my enquiries about them with blank ill-temper. Soup or shashlik, he tapped the menu with his pencil. You have soup or you have shashlik.

The next morning I went to find the Ojayli brothers. 'Ask anyone where they live,' they'd told me in Aleppo. 'Their family used to own most of Raqqa.' Dr Ojayli was one of Syria's leading writers, but he had left for Damascus. I found his architect brother climbing into an old, beaten-up Pontiac.

'Armenians?' He shook his head. 'My grandmother used to have Armenian orphans in her house. But I don't think there are any in Raqqa now.'

I told him about the menu in Armenian and he shrugged. 'Probably it came from a restaurant in Aleppo.'

He was going to the excavations of an Abbasid villa and asked me to join him. We drove through the town's main street while traders from the villages thronged around the car. Once the Euphrates had run here, beside the old walls, but in the last thousand years it had migrated several miles to the south, away across the valley. In its place a stream of red keffiyehs and yashmaks bobbed along the road. Overhead, President Assad was cloned on a hundred lines of plastic bunting; the crude stencil made him look like a matinée idol.

In 1915 Ojayli's grandfather had been mayor of Raqqa. Another cousin was the telegraph operator and would tell him in advance of the arrival of the Armenian convoys. He would then send people into the desert to meet them and do what he could to help. Hearing of his leniency, the Turkish authorities removed him. Ojayli said that when he had been a student in America, sometimes there would be a knock on his door and it would be an Armenian. 'One of them came across two states to see me when he'd heard my name. "Your grandfather", he said, "rescued my grandfather."'

After the Abbasid villa, we drove back along the main street and Ojayli carried on various conversations through his window as we nudged through the crowds.

At one point, he turned to me and said: 'I'm wrong. This man says he knows an Armenian cobbler.'

'Where?'

'He has a shop towards the Gate of Baghdad.'

We found the cobbler in the back of a dark, mud-walled shop. He had a slow smile and gave us coffee but said little. My questions brought only grudging, evasive answers. He did not like to talk about Armenian things. But as we left, he told us: 'My father will speak. You should see my father.'

His parents lived in a new building on the edge of the town; concrete dust still lay on the communal stairs. Their flat was very neat and smelt of new paint. In one corner of the sitting room, wrapped in a dressing-gown, was the cobbler's father. His fingers were long and arthritic, and bent sideways like the bristles of an old brush. But he shone with an elegance that belied his age; he leaned towards me like an exiled prince, reliving the strained reminiscences of home. In his wheezing laughter and sudden quiet anger, there was survival, not the weight that bowed so many of the other Armenians. This man was close to death – at times he could hardly breathe – but he was alive.

His family had always lived around Urfa, from far, far back – near the beginning, he said, and flicked his crippled fingers in a gesture of eternity. Raqqa was no more than eighty miles south of Urfa. But what did that matter? He shrugged. It might as well be eight thousand; he could never go back.

The cobbler's family had come from one of the outlying villages. They had escaped the massacres by hiding with some Kurds. He himself had been five in 1915 and only remembered returning to the farm a few years later, when the war was over. The first thing he did was to run to the small patch of garden his father had given him. The tomatoes he'd planted had gone. Disappeared! But he cleared the ground again and replanted it. He was soon growing, with some pride, most of the family's vegetables. When he was twelve he went out to pull up some carrots and a voice cried: 'Put them back! They are not yours!' A Turkish soldier stepped out from under a fig tree; their farm, he said, now belonged to the government. This time they knew they would not come back. They left on two carts and ended up in Raqqa. The cobbler had married an Armenian girl a decade younger than him.

Now, more than fifty years later, she crossed the room to give him his bottle of medicine and spoon out the last of their time together.

In Jerusalem there had been an old woman whom I visited a number of times. She was small and timid, and sometimes as she talked would sob so discretely that when it first happened I thought she was just coughing. They'd found her with countless other children in the orphanages of Aleppo. She would ask me about the places I had been to in eastern Turkey and would listen intently. When I came to Bitlis, she interrupted; yes, it may have been Bitlis, she said, what are the mountains like there? No, perhaps it was Van, or Moush. In truth she did not know; this woman had no idea where she'd been born.

In the east, in the vilayets of Van and Bitlis, the 1915 massacres had been perpetrated in part by a mobile force which grew to about ten thousand strong. They were commanded by Djevdet Bey, brother-in-law of Enver Pasha, known by some as the 'horse-shoer' for his practice of having horseshoes fitted to his victims. He named his troops *kasab taburi*, or 'butcher battalions'. Ousted as governor of Van by local Armenians in the middle of May 1915, Djevdet Bey took his troops and vengeance west to the town of Sairt. There he hanged the Armenian bishop before killing the greater part of the remaining Christians. On arrival in Bitlis, he rounded up the twenty or so Armenian leaders and hanged them. With the *kasab taburi* surrounding the town, he ordered the collection of all able-bodied men. They were taken to a patch of open ground beyond the town. There they were forced to dig trenches before being shot and buried in them. The women and girls were handed out among the local Turks and the Kurds; most of the rest were taken to the Tigris and drowned. Some fifteen thousand Armenians were killed in Bitlis and many more had died by the time the *kasab taburi* had toured the local villages.

In one sense the massacres appear appallingly orchestrated: the systematic removal of an ethnic group who were perceived as a threat, whose loyalties were doubted, who undermined the eastern borders. Armenians were first disarmed, then rounded up, the men killed, and the rest either killed with them or driven south towards the desert. But how much the Armenian massacres were planned in advance remains unclear, as does so much surrounding the events of 1915. Few papers survive and, in a way that perpetuates their crimes, the Turks have continually denied what happened. Often too the Armenians have done little to help their cause. The aftermath of the massacres produced odd reactions in Turks and Armenians alike and, at different times, both parties have done their best to eradicate the memory.

For years after 1915, the Armenians were silent; they sought to forge new lives in the Middle East, in Europe and America. Survivors would not talk about it; some changed their names and tried to bury their Armenian past. They suffered the same shame of many of the Jewish survivors of the Holocaust, the shame of surviving while so many died. Without such perverse logic, many went mad. But in the 1960s, around the time of the fiftieth anniversary, a new generation of Armenians started to bay for justice. Unprotected by their parents' sense of shame, they started to quiz them about what happened and interest groups gathered to lobby for recognition of the 'Armenian Genocide'.

In a California hotel, at the beginning of 1973 an elderly survivor of the massacres invited two Turkish diplomats to his room. He shot them dead and set off a spate of Armenian terrorism. But the violent fringe was always a minority; in a hundred other ways Armenians pressed for recognition of what happened in 1915.

The Turkish reaction was to counter the claims: the so-called massacres are just an Armenian stunt, the propaganda of embittered extremists. As the Armenian voice became louder, so the Turks were pulled further into their denial. Yes, Armenians died at that time, but so did Turks. It was simply a war between the Ottoman army and Armenian separatists, and in war there are victims. With so little photographic or documentary evidence, such denials challenge the evidence of the survivors. It all happened a long time ago and far away in the distant Eurasian provinces of the Ottoman Empire. Who can really be sure now what went on?

The Turks, it would seem, are not trying to reconcile their own individual guilt – by the 1970s almost all those directly involved were dead. There are those who simply believe it did not happen. Given the blurry evidence, a cold denial is very effective – not in disproving it but in helping it to be forgotten. A counter-claim undermines the notion of the Armenian genocide as a historical fact. It chastens those who might mention it in passing. It is the censorship of doubt. Editors and writers feel their pens falter over the page at 'Armenian genocide', obliged to qualify the words, to tone them down, or simply to delete them.

The campaign has been many-pronged. In 1934, MGM were persuaded to abandon a film of Franz Werfel's *Forty Days of Musa Dagh*; the Turkish government had threatened to ban the distribution of all US films in Turkey. More recently scholars have been commissioned to publish work disproving the Armenian claims. PR companies have lobbied governments, newspapers, academic institutions. Armenian churches in Anatolia have been bulldozed and dynamited. Any Armenian monuments that survive tend to be reattributed 'Byzantine' or 'Anatolian'. 'Armenian' has become a non-word in Turkish historiography.

I heard the story of an art conference in Ankara, in which a British scholar, giving a paper on *kilims*, suggested that one of his exhibits showed 'Armenian' influence. The Turkish convener of the conference stormed to the front and demanded an apology; the scholar returned home.

At the School of Oriental and African Studies in London, there is a small section in the library which deals with the Armenian massacres. A number of the titles have been defaced. A book, for example, entitled *The First Genocide of the Twentieth Century* by the Armenian, Mark D. Bedrossyan, has had scratched on its cover the simple, unambiguous legend: FUCK OFF.

The Armenians are by no means innocent in this battle of words, just as they were not all innocent victims in 1915. They have published some dubiously sourced evidence of their own, muddying the already muddy waters of evidence. They have resorted to terrorism. But behind the violence, the claims and counter-claims, the 'client-history', it is clear that something very terrible happened to the Armenians: they were driven from their land, they were killed in vast numbers and they have been continually denied recognition of either of these things. Already I was aware of the intensity and confusion of exile, and the strange doubts that the Turkish counter-genocide campaign evokes in Armenians. Other peoples' land now lies beneath their feet. They pine in exile for something most have never seen. Perhaps Armenia only exists in their imagination.

I spent only a day in Raqqa and then took a bus across the desert to Ras ul-Ain. On the sketch map, the arrows of the deportations entered Syria at two main points. While those from Cilicia and central Anatolia converged on Aleppo and Raqqa, from the eastern plateau − from Van and Moush and Bitlis − the Armenians were marched to the terminus of the railway at Ras ul-Ain. Some were then taken by rail from there to Aleppo. But most never went west. Along a line running through the desert between Ras ul-Ain and Deir ez Zor were witnessed some of the worst scenes of 1915−16.

The desert's baked surface was dotted with stones. Nothing broke the crust except for the long, drawn-out scar of the road. To the south was a row of hills, spread like crumpled linen beneath a grey horizon. On the bus the Kurds and Arabs sat in a contemplative silence, their sun-furrowed jowls bouncing with each bump of the road. We arrived in Ras ul-Ain with the sun long gone and the wind blowing straight out of the heart of Turkey. The desert stars shone coldly overhead.

I asked about a hotel but there was none. Trusting to luck, I entered a dingy café and there met a teacher who said he could put me up for a few dollars. I spent the evening with him and his veiled wife and five children, propped on cushions on the floor, trying not to think that this man's grandfather probably had Armenian blood on his hands.

But when I showed him my letter, in Arabic, explaining what I was doing, he said: 'I speak Armenian.'

'You do?'

'My father was Armenian.'

It never failed to surprise me; even though I was looking for it, it surprised me. Scrape away at the surface of any of these Middle Eastern towns and a little of the Armenian motif came up, like some code in a medieval palimpsest.

Later in the evening, a stream of people came to visit. They left their shoes in the porch and came into the room to talk and finger their wooden beads. They were all related.

'This my cousin,' said the teacher.

'*Ahlein.*' I shook hands.

'This my wife brother.'

I nodded.

'This his wife, my cousin . . . her brother, my wife sister . . . her husband, wife cousin . . . his brother . . .'

And so it went on, until the evening was over and they'd all gone and the teacher said to me: 'Sleep here, by the stove. Tomorrow we go and see police.'

'What?'

'Secret police.'

Damn it. He was Mukhabarat. Everyone was Mukhabarat. I should have known. 'I don't think it will be necessary.' I said.

'No, no. Don't worry. Your own safety. Secret police my best friend.'

That was what did worry me.


The morning was crisp and beautifully clear. Walking with the teacher to the police station, I glimpsed the green of the springs as we passed, the 'Ain' of the town's name. It was here that the Armenian convoys had converged. The teacher hurried me past. That was all I'd be able to see. Couched as he was in Levantine courtesy, this man had placed me under arrest. The authorities would pack me off away from the desert and the border regions, back to the old castles and bazaars of Aleppo that the foreigners so admire. What was there, after all, to see in Ras ul-Ain?

The police chief sat in a darkened room; through the open door were almond trees and a drained swimming-pool. His desk was flanked by six telephones and a short-wave radio. He had that special talent for looking tough and ordinary at the same time; you could pass him twice on the street without noticing. But there was no doubt about his authority; his slow, fluent movements were full of it. The teacher looked nervous in his presence.

The chief read my letter, tapped a pencil three times on his desk and smiled.

'Everything', he said quietly, 'is all right.'

'So,' I said to the teacher, outside the gate. 'Everything is all right.'

'Yes. That is good. Now we go and see secret police.'

'Well, who was that then?'

'He was secret police. Now we see military secret police.'

The military secret police had more guns. They searched me at the gate. The chief's office was closed but a group of agents stood outside waiting for the key to be brought. I wondered which one was in charge, which one I should fawn to. Was it the fat one in the middle, or the one with a cruel smile? Was it the young one with a pistol in his belt or the quiet one with the prayer-beads?

When we all entered the office, the pecking-order became clear. The fat one sat nervously on the bed and cracked a joke (number three), the cruel one leant against a filing cabinet near the desk (number two), the one with the pistol made the tea (number four). Number one took his place behind the desk, working the beads through his stubby fingers, telling me my letter was not necessary and that if there was anything at all he could do to make my stay in Ras ul-Ain more comfortable . . .

Doubly relieved, I walked out into the sun. 'Now, we can go to the springs.'

'Yes, of course.'

We passed the fruit market and the butcher's stalls and the teacher stopped at a gate. He looked at me sheepishly. 'Here, we must see police.'

'More police? Is everyone in Ras ul-Ain a policeman?'

'Not every man. But many.'

This one had none of the civility of the others. He was older and hid behind a harsh, angular face and a tiny moustache. Around his office three Arab farmers fidgeted expectantly. I dreaded to think how much of their lives depended on the whim of this man. Cocking his head, he looked me straight in the eye. I stared back. I began to feel an extreme distaste for him. He continued to stare. Outside a motor-bike backfired and an ass neighed in shock. Then he looked down and wrote something on a pad.

'You will report in the next town to the police and in all towns.'
He smiled unconvincingly. 'Let us be glad that the sun now shines
between our two countries.'

'Yes,' I said. 'Let's be glad.'

So I did reach those springs below the town. I had another battle
there with the teacher. Appointed to keep an eye on me, he couldn't
understand why I should want to slip his clutches and be on my
own. In the end I wasn't sure either. There was nothing much to see:
a man scrubbing his brightly coloured bus in the shallows, another
skinning a six-pound carp, women beating the dirt from blank
squares of calico. I walked on beside the stream where it bubbled
and murmured over the pebbles, and watched the low swelling of
water at the spring-head. Tiny trout fingerlings hovered in the pools
and water-boatmen scuttled across the surface. I sat on the bank and
at my feet slow eddies tugged at the willow-fronds.

How many died here? Fifty, sixty thousand? And what is that
anyway – a good football crowd, a large town? It made even less
sense here, sitting beside the water, than when I'd first read about
it. In Jerusalem, I had spent much of my time among the books of
the Gulbenkian library, following the loose threads of Armenian
history. But the massacres, I put off until the end. What I'd been
reluctant to start absorbed me at once; it was that that I had been
afraid of. Everything else seemed meaningless when set against the
reports of 1915.

Leaving the library after those sessions, I struggled for understanding. I wanted the courtyard outside to look different. I felt dazed
and curiously grubby – as though simply by reading about it, I had
participated in the obscenity. In 1915–16, the spectacle of Ras ul-Ain,
one of the worst of the concentration centres, produced similar feel-
ings of vicarious shame. Everywhere lay groups of Armenians, near
the springs, by the roadside in goat-skin shelters or unprotected
beneath the sun. More kept arriving. Thousands were killed here or
taken on into the desert. The authorities struggled to keep the
numbers down and for many typhus and dysentery brought a swift
dehydrated death. The desert wells were choked with corpses and
the naked decomposing bodies of women lay on the roadside for all
to see. Turkish foot-soldiers used to avert their eyes when they
passed through Ras ul-Ain. There was a saying among them: 'No
man can ever think of a woman's body except as a matter of horror,
instead of attraction, after Ras ul-Ain.'

Men in patterned sweaters had come with their families down to the springs for lunch; there was a small café beside the stream. Someone had put a speaker on the grass. The children threw sticks in the water and Julio Iglesias and Charles Aznavour (a French Armenian) wailed among the willows. Through the thin foliage the sun fell and dappled the grass and the faces of the children, but it was too early in the year to be warm. Repelled by the scene, I walked along the bank and found the teacher talking to a friend.

'This is Serop,' he said. 'He has restaurant. Very good – Serop Restaurant.'

'Serop is an Armenian name,' I said.

'Yes, I am Armenian.'

Him too. I asked him the obvious questions but he did not respond. They seemed suddenly trite and irrelevant. I was beginning to see the springs as everyone else did, simply a pleasant place to be when it was hot.

With his brother, Garabed, Serop had also secured the lease to the government restaurant of Ras ul-Ain. It was just above the springs, an ugly concrete structure. Inside, seated pointedly at opposite ends of the room, were two groups of the secret policemen. I nodded politely to each group.

Garabed was more forthcoming about the massacres than his brother. 'Yes. Many were killed by local people. Just up behind here.' He said, no, he had no qualms about being here and explained quite matter-of-factly how Circassians would line the Armenians up against one another and compete to see how many they could fell with a single shot. He said that in their gardens, people were still digging up skulls. He was about to tell me more when one of the Mukhabarat called for more meat. I waited for him to come back and carry on, but he avoided my gaze and busied himself around his guests. Clearly talking to me was not a good thing to do.

So I left the restaurant, thanked the teacher for his help and walked up above the springs. A desolate piece of land stretched over a low hill, too high to receive any benefit from the springs. The spiky limbs of leafless trees clawed at the sky and between them old buildings and graves lay neglected and half-ruined. Here, if I wanted it, was the landscape I'd expected, a dead landscape. But it seemed overdone, as though a film crew had prepared it for a scene of mass killing. Its ruins had little to do with the atrocities. I did find the grave of one Armenian: but it was recent, 1946–1976, a car accident.

I felt a little baffled by my reaction to Ras ul-Ain: the springs were too idyllic, too pretty, to help me understand what happened here. Yet when I found somewhere suitably ugly I was equally unconvinced.

I carried on down the river, past the clutch of willows by the oasis, past the mosaic of plots it fed, and on into the desert where the river's gully cut a tentative line south towards Hassakeh. Tufts of small trees rose from it, but beneath my feet the ground became dry and the soil turned to dusty clods.

Every day for a month, in April 1916, the Turkish authorities would select three or four hundred Armenians from the camps at Ras ul-Ain and bring them down here to be slaughtered; their bodies were then thrown into the river. For several miles I walked a broad corridor between the river and the road. Ras ul-Ain became no more than a swathe of green behind me and the desert flattened itself in front. This was the route to the cave at Shadaddie and all the other anonymous desert places which now cover the remains of Armenia.


Out of the muddle of stories that I had thought about at the springs, one in particular now preoccupied me: that of Talaat Pasha and Soghomon Tehlirian. None of the other Young Turks who emerged from the Turkish revolution of 1908 proved quite so ruthless as Talaat Pasha. He did not have quite the zeal of Enver Pasha, nor his intelligence, but in his shameless efficiency he was by far the most dangerous. By the time Turkey entered the war in 1914, Talaat had murdered his way to the top. More from political expediency than any form of vision, he upheld the ideology that had risen from the ruins of the Ottoman empire: a secular pan-Turkism, in which a new Trans-Asian state would rise to unite Turkic peoples from the Balkans to the Himalayas.

There can now be little doubt that Talaat was the Turkish leader most closely involved in the Armenian massacres. Frequently he was called upon to receive Henry Morgenthau, the American ambassador in Constantinople. Morgenthau would remonstrate with Talaat while Talaat would brag of his success in 'dealing' with the Armenian question. On one occasion he said: 'The massacres! What of them!' On another he asked Morgenthau to procure the money held in the US by Armenians who had been killed. Morgenthau stormed from the room.

Meanwhile in the interior Soghomon Tehlirian felt the blade of Talaat's policy. The son of wealthy merchants in Erzindjan, Tehlirian was eighteen when the order came. It was early June, 1915. The Armenians of Erzindjan were to gather their valuables and prepare to leave the city. They were to be deported for their own safety. There would be a full military escort to take them to the south. But on the very first day of the march, just beyond the edge of town, the guards turned on the convoy. They began systematically to rob the Armenians. At the same time the Erzindjan populace joined in and for a while there was total mayhem.

Tehlirian saw his sister taken by one of the guards. His mother cried, 'May I go blind,' and was felled by a gunshot. His brother was attacked with an axe; his head was split open and he died before Tehlirian's eyes. All around was shooting and screaming, and the bodies of the dead lay thickly in the dirt. Tehlirian himself was struck with something – an axe or a rifle-butt – and remembered no more. He came round after two days, surrounded by bodies.

With the help of the mountain Kurds he escaped to Persia. After the Russian advance he managed to get back to Erzindjan and recovered four thousand eight hundred gold pieces his family had hidden in the house. For several years he wandered rootlessly through the Caucasus, the Balkans and western Europe, learning a little of the languages, keeping to himself, then moving on. By the end of 1920 he was in Berlin. There he took a room and began German lessons. Sometimes the weight of his experiences would overwhelm him and he would draw the curtains in his room and play the mandolin and sing Armenian songs. 'They do have such sad songs,' his landlady recalled.

One day he saw a group of three men walking near the zoo. He followed them to a cinema and watched them say goodbye. One of them, whose hand the others kissed, was addressed as 'Pasha'. Tehlirian recognized his face from newspaper pictures. It was Talaat. After the final defeat of the Turks, Talaat had fled Constantinople. He was court-martialled *in absentia* and sentenced to death. He was rumoured to be in Berlin, living off a ten-million-mark bank account, but no one had confirmed it.

A few days after sighting him, Tehlirian had a dream. He saw the corpses of the convoy and his mother rising from them, saying, 'You know Talaat is here and yet you do not seem to be concerned. You are no longer my son.' Tehlirian woke from the dream and vowed to kill him. He tracked down Talaat's apartment and took a room opposite. One morning he watched the old Turkish leader step out of the building and walk towards Berlin's zoo. Tehlirian left his own room, caught up with Talaat and shot him dead. He made no attempt to escape and simply addressed the crowd: 'He was a Turk. I am an Armenian. It is no loss to Germany.' The German court acquitted Tehlirian, who denied premeditation. (In fact he had probably been working as a Dashnak agent, but this did not come out at the trial.) He died in California, an Armenian hero, at the age of sixty-three.

Within two years the remaining two members of the Turkish triumvirate were also dead. Enver Pasha was killed leading a revolt, near Bukhara, pursuing the Pan-Turkist cause. It was an Armenian, allegedly, who fired the shot. Jemal Pasha was shot by an Armenian in Tiflis.

In 1943, Hitler released Talaat's body for re-burial in Turkey. It now lies, in a state mausoleum, in Istanbul.

It was getting dark. Grey rags of cloud pulled across the horizon. The desert stretched towards them, flatter now in the dusk, less delineated, harsher. The road had looped far away to the east. I cut across towards it and climbed its stony embankment. A pair of headlights loomed out of the night and two very stern-looking government officials gave me a lift towards Hassakeh.

The next evening I reached Deir ez Zor. It was after midnight and I was suddenly very tired. I walked through the ill-lit streets, on a familiar trail of flea-ridden hotels which were all full. I conceded in the end to the Waha Tourism Hotel, just outside the town. The hotel had been converted from the temporary huts of an Italian team who had come to build a paper mill for the Syrians. The huts were neat and well-built in the Italian way, but the factory had not been a success. No one thought, it seems, that getting wood pulp would pose a problem in the desert.

In the morning, at breakfast, two Texan oil consultants came up to my table.

'You mind if we join you?'

'No, go ahead.'

'My name's Jim, and this here's Paul.'

I nodded to each of them. Paul wore a red keffiyeh round his neck. He smiled easily and had wide Texan eyes. He had on a bright red sweater and wore sun-glasses over the top of his head. Jim was enormous.

'Well, Saddem's sure kicking the ass out of those Kurds,' explained Jim as he lowered himself into a chair. 'Just heard the radio report. Bet those boys as wishing they'd just kept quiet.'

Paul put his hand beside his mouth and yelled across the room. 'Hey, Hassen! Get your ass down here. We're all kinda hungry.' Then he turned to me and winked. 'We bin living here for months. Everyone's pals now!'

Hassan brought a salver of meat.

'Now looky-here, Hassen, you be a bit quicker next time.' He peered at the salver. 'Watch you cooked up for us today? Looks like a lil ole chickun. You want some chickun, Phillup?'

'I've already eaten.'

'Aw well. Jim?'

Jim had started on the war again and as he placed half the chicken on his plate explained how 'Saddem sure got his ass licked' and how 'them Rackees were no match, it was kinda sad . . .' as if it had been a baseball game.

In the reception hut I found another itinerant worker – a Yorkshireman. He knew the area well. I spread my map out before him and asked him how to get into the desert.

'What's to see oup there?' His wide Yorkshire vowels fell incongruously in the room.

'I'm interested in the Armenians. Many died here during the First World War . . .'

'Aye,' he said.

'You know about it?'

'Aye.'

'How come?'

'Ahm Armeniun.'

'What!' I checked myself, and smiled. 'I'm sorry. Your English . . .'

He'd learnt English from a Barnsley widower in southern Spain. He'd also taught himself Italian, French and Spanish; I wondered in what sort of accent he spoke them. For ten years he had sold Spanish leather to the tourists in Seville, before returning to Syria to became the manager here, at Deir ez Zor's Waha Tourism hotel. Like Serop in Ras ul-Ain he had ended up precisely where his own people had perished, rising from their ashes like some phoenix of hotel management.

Deir ez Zor had been the largest of the concentration centres; it was the last place, the last destination for the Armenians. All the arrows on my sketch map pointed towards Deir ez Zor, though not all, by any means, reached it. Its name has become synonymous with 1915 and has about it a curious resonance of finality. The desert around Deir ez Zor is the very antithesis of the world that was destroyed, the old pastoral life of the Anatolian villages, the two and a half thousand years of civilization.

By 1916, the numbers at Deir ez Zor had reached a critical level. In April, the Turkish authorities removed the governor, who was considered too lenient, and replaced him with a man named Zeki Bey. In the main Zeki Bey let the desert do his killing for him. He had many thrown in the Euphrates, but the desert was easier. On one occasion he put five hundred in a stockade where long before they died they'd been driven mad by the sun. He also had gangs of Circassians. He would select groups of Armenians from the camps and walk them north into the desert. There the Circassians would shoot them, trampling the bodies with their horses to make sure. Zeki Bey would watch the whole thing through a telescope.

Many estimates put the death toll at Deir ez Zor in six figures, although in fact – and this somehow makes it worse – no one really has any idea. Even during his brief few months of office, Zeki Bey probably accounted for about twenty thousand. At his trial at the end of the war, a figure of ten thousand was mentioned, to which he replied, 'You are impugning my honour. I disdain the ten thousand figure. Come on, raise it!'

I asked the Armenian manager what he knew about these things and he led me to the open door and pointed towards a straight track that led down to the river. The camps, he said, were all around here. I walked along beside a ribbon of flat, cultivated land. It was criss-crossed with stands of willow and blotched where the swamps wallowed beneath bamboo groves. Towards the Euphrates a few fat cattle lumbered through the grass and the egrets stooped and padded among them like fastidious detectives. But that was all. Since I'd left Aleppo I had not seen anything to suggest what happened in these regions. I hadn't expected to find anything new – I had enough images of my own. But I had thought that seeing the places might make it easier to understand. It hadn't; it had made it harder. I had been to a quiet oasis, and was now walking a pleasant strip of land beside the sacred Euphrates. Who was to say that that was not all these places were? And I sensed for the first time the madness of having to prove it happened. How shrill the cries become when there's so little evidence, no corpse to grieve! What was it to mourn amidst that uncertainty, in exile, with nothing to touch, no preserved Auschwitz, nothing but an ancient language and a broken generation now almost extinct – and for a monument the blank wastes of the desert?

It was a crisp morning and the Euphrates was in spate, swollen with snow-melt from the Anatolian plateau. The flow was fast and even, and I watched the bulbous eddies twist and spin as they sped past the banks. Some miles further on, the belt of fields narrowed beside the river and I could see beyond them to the railway embankment. I crossed the track and slid down the clinker on the other side, on to the desert floor.

For half the day I walked north. The wind blew without pause, lurching over the low mounds to chase the dust and ruffle the sprigs of wild marjoram; the sun fell through hazy furrows of high cloud. And I came to a place where there was just the tan pebbly surface and the sky, where the railway was far behind, and there were no well-head fires and no Bedouin flocks. The heat-haze hovered like water on the horizon and across it appeared suddenly a man on a bicycle. I waved to him and he pedalled out of the distance and came over. He stood for a moment with me and the wind hummed in the tubes of his bicycle, but he said nothing.

Then he swung his bicycle away and I called after him a speculative 'Goodbye!' in Armenian and he looked around and stopped. Then he headed back towards the horizon and for a long time afterwards I wondered if he had not been some sort of ghost.

# 6

My God, in what a century you've caused me to live.

St Polycarp, second-century Christian martyr

The journey back to Aleppo was a trial. The train left Deir ez Zor the same day, but late, after midnight. All I wanted to do was sleep. There were no seats. I squatted against a wall in the corridor of the third-class carriage amidst a group of rapacious-looking villagers. At some point in the previous four or five days two hundred US dollars had gone missing from my supply, my only funds to get me to Armenia, and I was in no mood for bonhomie.

The man next to me tugged my arm: 'Sir, sir. Why you here? Why you travel donkey-class?'

'Because I have no money.'

'You are Europe man? Europe men all rich!'

'Not me.'

He frowned. 'Then you must be donkey.'

'Yes, yes. I am a donkey.'

I turned away and tried to get back to my disturbed sleep. The train thundered through the desert and the loose fittings of the donkey-class carriages rattled like a milk tray.

It was breakfast time when I pushed open the doors of the Baron Hotel. There was some solace in its familiarity. Portia lay asleep at the foot of the stairs. A family of Soviet Armenians stood in the hall, surrounded by a low rampart of shopping, and the whole place echoed with its reassuring 1930s charm. Sally Mazloumian said that she had given me until today; then it was the authorities and a search party. Only the Kurdish waiters had changed. They sat in silence in the dining room, staring at the floor, their enthusiasm muted by Saddam's reprisals.

Krikor was in the telex room. 'Glad you got back safely. Where to now?'

'Turkey.'

'Look out for those bloody Turks, won't you. Don't breathe a word about what you're doing!'

'I'll keep quiet.'

I too had heard the stories of police harassment, expulsions and imprisonments. Anyone poking around Turkey after the Armenians is running a risk. I'd secured letters to say that I was a student of Seljuk and Byzantine architecture, but the biggest fear was losing my notes. With the help of Toros Toranian, one of the Aleppo community's most ebullient members, I photocopied them and sent the copies home.

Toranian was a distinguished-looking, silver-haired man. He was a great talker. Driving through the city to the Armenian district, he hardly drew breath. Every building elicited an anecdote. He pointed out the Armenian clubs and told me how for forty days after the Spitak earthquake the Armenians had hung the schools and churches with a black shroud. (In Jerusalem they had a similar story: everyone had spontaneously appeared the day after the earthquake wearing black. It made me think of the idea of morphic resonance, the shared impulse of migrating birds or the movement of shoals of fish. And I wondered again whether the Armenian genius now gave its best to the expression of grief.)

Toranian's flat was compact and neat, as he was. Every inch of wall was covered with the work of Armenian artists. He had written a book about the Aleppo-born Armenian Carzou, and the painter's brightly coloured prints dotted his collection like harlequins. On the piano (every Armenian diaspora home has a piano) was a photograph of Toranian's mother. Once seen, her monochrome presence dominated the room. She stared in harsh judgment on everything in it, just as if she herself still sat there. That one photograph overshadowed all the paintings.

'Fifty-five at the time of the photograph. I think it was the head that gave her that look.'

'The head?'

Toranian's grandmother had taken her five-year-old daughter to the Anatolian town of Roomkeh, not far from their own village. She left the girl with a Kurdish family and set off south, on foot, knowing that the order for deportation was imminent. For two years, Toranian's mother lived with the Kurds. There were other Armenian children in the town but they were forbidden to meet. Even so, some of them would occasionally rendezvous in secret by the river. Once, not many months after they arrived, they were walking together along its leafy banks. Suddenly in the water, Toranian's mother saw a familiar face.

'Look!' she exclaimed. 'It is brother Hagop. He is swimming!' And she ran up the river to greet him. She was delighted to see someone she knew, an adult, after so many strangers.

'Hagop!'

She parted the reeds. 'Hagop! Hagop!' She had watched him swimming before; he was always swimming!

Just then the current caught him and for an instant he disappeared. When he surfaced again, she saw that it was not Hagop, but only his severed head.

'After she told me that story,' explained Toranian, 'I could never look at her without seeing that head in the river. Only when she died, and her eyes were closed for the last time, only then did the head disappear.'

'How did she get to Aleppo?'

'My grandfather had been fighting for the Turks on the Caucasian front. He fled the army, reached Roomkeh and rescued her. He walked to Aleppo with my mother on his shoulders. She was married at the age of fourteen, but by eighteen she was a widow.'

I bent to look more closely at the picture. Behind her stern, matriarchal mask, behind the granite expression, there was something else, a flickering look of the old Armenians. I'd seen it in some of the survivors, but more clearly in the family daguerreotypes of the nineteenth century. It was not the look of suffering or persecution, but a kind of peasant confidence, a fullness in the cheeks and around the eyes, a look of the land.

*

At the end of the first week in March I left the Baron Hotel and the Mazloumians, and set off for Turkey. Before the border, they'd said, you'll find a small group of Armenian villages. To the west of Aleppo the Latakia train eased out of the desert and into land that was almost green. The baked-mud walls of the beehive huts looked out of place, now sheltered as they were beneath high gum trees. I felt a surge of high spirits at the sight of life, green life, rows of bean-plants and damp soil. Losing the land, I had come to realize, is as much the legacy of 1915 as the massacres; it had marked the end of belonging. When Armenians told me of the atrocities it was always with a curious detachment. But when it came to the land, to talking of the lost land, there came into their voices a strange note of convic-tion, a sense of real grievance. Perhaps, I thought, it really is a more pervasive loss; either that, or it is the only aspect that can be given any shape at all.

Through the train window, the land continued its slow regener-ation. The valleys, now lush and cut into verdant squares of pasture, cast a bright mid-morning spell upon me and I sat contemplating the fields and—

'My friend!'

—their compelling beauty and the bushy rims of the high contours and—

'Monsieur!'

—the cloudless sky above. 'What is it?'

The man in the next door seat was tugging at my sleeve.

'Yes?'

'Look my watch! You know who is on watch, my friend?'

He thrust his wrist at me. He had a Mickey Mouse watch. But instead of a grinning cartoon stencilled on the face there was a pic-ture of Assad. He looked ridiculous.

'Yes.' I turned back to my meditations and a small village and the dusty yards full of sheep—

'Listen, my friend.'

'What!'

'Oh, my friend. Don't be serious.'

'What do you want?'

'I am Alawi man.'

That made sense. Assad himself is an Alawi and they enjoy a certain clan status. Many are Mukhabarat. He asked where I was from.

'Britain.'

'Ha! Britain no good. Once you had half the world. Now you are satellite of America . . .'

I could do without that. I stood and walked down the aisle. At the end of the carriage a dark, demure-looking girl sat hunched over a text, mouthing it silently. I glanced at it as I passed; it was an Armenian prayer book. I greeted her in Armenian.

'You're Armenian?' she asked.

The Alawi had followed me and pushed through. 'No, no – he is British! No good British man!' He laughed and held the girl with his lingering stare.

I squatted down to talk to her. 'Look, maybe you can help. I'm trying to get to the Armenian villages at Kessab.'

'I am going there!' she said. 'My family lives in Kessab. I will show you.'

The carriages shuddered to a stop at the Latakia terminus. We climbed down on to the platform. The Alawi would not leave us alone. He whispered to me, 'Why you feel sorry for the Armenians? My friend – why not Palestinians? Every day they die . . .'

I said goodbye.

'Oh, my friend!' he called to our backs as we left the station. 'Come my house! I have very good girls. We don't do bad things, we do maybe some thing. They very nice girls. Christian girls. My friend . . .'

Packed to its aisles, the bus up the coast to Kessab was a little pocket of Armenia. Armenian replaced the Arabic of the bus station. We shared Armenian news, of the Aleppo community and Beirut, before turning to Karabagh where Soviet forces had just emptied an Armenian village and stirred up all the anguish of that old wound.

Nudging the southern-most border of Turkey, the villages of Kessab are all that survive of the old Armenian settlements that were scattered around the see of Antioch. They pre-date even the medieval Armenian kingdom of Cilicia. They are true Armenian villages, some of the very few that are left.

Now the main village, falling between terraced plots, looks like any other Mediterranean village. Ruddy-faced men work the vineyards, ferrying their plump, headscarved women around on tractors; half-wild dogs scavenge in the dust and the boys ride whining two-stroke mopeds up and down the square. And like any other Mediterranean village, Kessab is peppered with building sites; it has become the summer playground for the Aleppo community. I arranged a room with the Armenian Protestant priest and went with him to call on Bedros Demyrdjian, Kessab's oldest citizen.

Bedros was ambling slowly through his nineties; he was uncertain quite where he'd got to. He sat on the edge of his straw mattress, smiling, and the late sun fell across his shoulders and on his old, leathery cheeks and highlighted the remaining white hairs of his head. He had about him a kind of weathered assurance; he had lived all his years here, in the same house, with its thick walls and rafters and wooden stairs. All his years, that is, except one.

They'd come with six hundred soldiers (another survivor remembered a hundred and fifty). He watched them stop in the square, then fan out to collect the villagers. That afternoon the whole village was trooped down the hill past the terraces and vines, past their ripening fruit. Several days later they arrived at a camp near Aleppo. There Bedros got wind that they were headed for Meskeneh, near Deir ez Zor. During the night, he slipped past the guards and escaped. He travelled to Latakia and for seven months lived in hiding. Arriving back in Kessab he found the houses looted and the fruit ruined. Over the years he managed to piece together the fate of his family. Out of thirty-two, only eleven survived. Four of them were burned in caves. Others, he was told, died in the sun or threw themselves in the Euphrates or were taken out in boats and drowned. The closer I got to Turkey, to old Armenia, the more matter-of-fact the telling of these tales became. But Bedros had not suffered the double blow: the killings and the exile. He still lived where he'd been born.

He was looking out of the window, at the hill above the village. His face was age-scored and leathery, and oddly placid.

I asked him, 'Couldn't you have gone up the hill like those at Musa Dagh?'

'Musa Dagh is a good mountain and ours is not.'

'What do you mean?'

'Water – there is no water here.'

Water, of course – the currency of these regions.

Now Bedros lived alone. All his family had gone to Los Angeles.

'And you?' I asked. 'Weren't you tempted by America?'

'No. There I would have to work for someone.' He took a bony hand to his chin. 'Here I have ten thousand square metres under apples.'

The next day I had planned to cross the border but I awoke ill. My stomach became a battlefield of sudden, sniper-like pains and manoeuvring aches. I stayed in my room with the World Service, Doctor Zhivago and a paraffin stove which kept going out. I ran out of matches and ten bombs went off in Turkey; Zhivago, meanwhile, spent two years as doctor with the partisans. Pasternak's portrait of a muddy, crumbling Russia seemed a pertinent one. This is the natural state of affairs, he was saying, chaos and savagery. Dictatorship, more than communism, had placed a seventy-year lid on that, but now we were back to the post-revolutionary mess.

During the years of civil war in Russia, Armenia achieved, for the first time in nearly a thousand years, a fragile independence. Turkey had its own internal difficulties and, for once, the Transcaucasian states – Georgia, Azerbaijan, Armenia – were left to their own devices. It was not, though, a happy period. Armenia fought a war with Georgia, suffered pogroms in Baku and had one in five of its population die in a particularly savage winter. When Turkey had regrouped in 1920 it cut swiftly into the new Armenia, which was in turn forced back into the arms of the Bolsheviks. Looked at that way, from the high ground of history, it seemed hard to avoid the parallels. Now Russia was too weak to help, Armenia would be swamped again by whichever power emerged in the region . . . I blamed this dangerous thinking on my stomach and, turning over, went to sleep.

It was late afternoon when the Armenian pastor put his head round the door and asked if I was up to going with him to see one of his favourite families.

The Boymoushdians lived in a neat bungalow at the top of the village. The Turkish border ran along the ridge above them. Their porch had the sweet smell of stored apples. Inside, old Agnes Boymoushdian sat fingering the folds of her housecoat. She stared up, unblinking, at a point somewhere above the window and gripped my hand tightly as I sat down beside her. She was quite blind.

Yes, she remembered the Army coming. She remembered the rich ones bribing the soldiers and being taken away separately. She remembered the young couple who hid in the bushes and the baby that had to be strangled to stop them all being found. She remembered the months in strange camps and the slow marching by day, and then people gradually drifting back to the village, some who'd escaped, some who'd been in different camps. But she didn't remember seeing the rich ones; no one ever saw the rich ones again. They went to Deir ez Zor, she said.

The following morning was misty and very wet. I packed up and prepared to cross into Turkey. In Norayr's general stores I stood and waited for the rain to clear. A man sauntered in, a red-faced country Armenian, with mud splashed all over his boots and hands, and a great scab of it on his neck.

'Don't hurry!' he said, lighting a cigarette. 'Don't worry!'

He stood with me at the window and we watched the rain fall in slim glassy columns from the awning. It was Sunday and up the hill the bells of the Armenian Apostolic church rang out in crisp unison. The Catholic church was silent. But from the Evangelical church opposite came the sound of a piano and eager hymns. A woman, late for the service, dashed up the steps and shook her umbrella before going in.

'Don't hurry! Don't worry!' The country Armenian grinned.

When the rain had stopped I said goodbye to him and to Norayr and found a lift down the hill. I walked to the frontier. It was a minor crossing, cut through thick pine forest and there was no one there but the border guards.

The Turks were petulant. 'Where is your visa? What you do in our country? You have no visa.'

I told him I didn't need a visa.

'Hm.'

He stamped my passport and I walked on through. A filmy mist hovered around the treetops and clung to the ridges and peaks above. Ten minutes up the road, I slipped in among the trees.

It had been several years now since that first trip to Turkey. Though I tried, it seemed impossible to rise above the view of the Turks I had acquired in the meantime. It had crept in unawares, into the breach left when reason failed to explain their treatment of the Armenians. It had hardened when I learnt of the continuing campaign of denial. Yes, I had become partisan. I couldn't help seeing this country as somehow usurped. But for the moment it looked innocent enough. The forest floor was soft and mossy; honeysuckle snaked around the foot of the pines, and the blackthorn was already in blossom. I crossed a series of damp fields, passed some steamy-flanked horses and, soon after midday, walked up the main street of Yaylandagi.

# 7

'Proud? No! Think what we might have done if we
had been able to stay in Armenia.'

Nairi, architect at the Armenian-built gates to the old city of Cairo.

It took several days to travel up through the sparse middle of Turkey.
They were isolated days. I had no Armenians to root out; outside
Istanbul only a handful has survived: plenty of Armenian sites, but
no Armenians.

A local bus spilled me out on to the streets of Antioch, which
for more than seven hundred years had had a largely Armenian
population. I found a small journeyman's hotel in the Zenginler
Mahalesi, the old rich quarter (now the poorest). A few chairs were
arranged around the lobby window and there I spent a large part of
the afternoon waiting for the hotel's only stove to be lit. I still felt
ill and it was very cold. A policeman came in, rubbing his hands.
But the duty porter, a rotund man, took nearly an hour of shuffling
around to empty the ash, gather fuel, tear up newspaper, read
the colourful story of a local brothel raid and finally to pull out
some matches. I stretched out my hands to the heat. The duty porter
eased himself into a chair next to the policeman, and the policeman said that it's a pity Antakya doesn't have more brothels to
raid.

Once alight, the barrel-stove lulled all three of us to sleep. Only the policeman's snoring disturbed it, and the sudden clatter of his automatic rifle falling to the floor.


'Musa Dagh? Where is Musa Dagh?' I asked the following morning in the fruit market at Samandagi. No one knew.

I pointed to a mountain looming over the town: 'Musa Dagh?'

'Jebel Musa.'

Of course! Musa Dagh is what Armenians call it. So much for my discretion.

The name 'Musa Dagh' is actually Turkish, meaning the 'Mountain of Moses'. But since 1915 it has become known as the place that the Armenians held out, the place they defied the deportations. Franz Werfel's best-selling account of their defence, *The Forty Days of Musa Dagh*, has further soured the name for the Turks. Reluctantly they have been forced to adopt the Arabic version 'Jebel Musa'.

The Armenians of Musa Dagh had ended up in Anjar in the Bekaa valley, where I'd seen them a few weeks earlier. Remembering the stories of Tomas Habeshian, I skirted round the mountain's lower slopes and came to the seaside town of Cevlik. It was as grey and damp as any off-season resort. Hotel signs squeaked in the wind; up-turned dinghies lined the esplanade and half a dozen boats lay stern-on in the quay, like horses sheltering behind a fence.

I'd climbed perhaps a third of the mountain before the rain came down in earnest. It swept down the slope with long diagonal strokes and the down-draught sent a ruffled skirt of water out into the Mediterranean. I took cover in a small cave and found there three fat cattle and an old cowherd. He scratched in the dust with his stick, and muttered and grinned, but we had no common language. Had he been alive, I wondered, in 1915? He looked little younger than Tomas Habeshian. I examined his boots and his muddy trousers and the familiar contours of his face. Put him in the Armenian villages of Anjar or in Kessab, and he would not be out of place. Peasant Armenia and peasant Turkey were indistinguishable; perhaps, paradoxically, that was what made the massacres so savage.


The next day was grey but there was no rain. I took a bus north out of Antioch to a small village on the edge of the plain. Above it, propped on a crag, was the castle of Baghras, one of the most embattled fortresses of the Near East. The first stone was laid here in 969, by Nicephorus II Phocas, the Byzantine Emperor. He was of the Macedonian dynasty, in fact more Armenian than Macedonian. It is possible too that he employed Armenians to build it; at the time they were acknowledged to be the most competent military architects in the Levant.

Baghras's position above the Antioch plains made it a prize acquisition. It changed hands with almost comic regularity. From Byzantium it soon fell to the Arabs, then to the Armenians, then to the Seljuk Turks, to the Crusaders, back to Byzantium, back to the Turks, then to a combined Crusader force, back again to Byzantium, then the Armenians again before becoming the headquarters of the Knights Templar. And all in the space of two hundred years.

No one takes much notice of it now. Winding up the rocky track above the village, I met only a single drover. He *yo!*-ed his beasts to stop and pointed with his stick to a narrow gap in the cliff. I hauled myself up the rock and out on to the walls of the crumbling bailey. Spread below were apple orchards and bare poplars and a bare minaret, and in the distance the puffy clouds rolling like white-crested waves down the plain. At my feet was a familiar pile of rubble. This was how it had begun, with broken rock in the abandoned villages of Anatolia, with a broken bone, with the broken ashlar of Ani. This was what had launched my Armenian journey: a few traces of vanished life, the fossil remains of Armenia.

For at least six years, from the age of six, all my spare hours were spent with a geological hammer, in old quarries, on sea-cliffs and in gorges. I had boxes and boxes of rocks, but none of them quite like the lump of Portland stone that I found beneath a laurel bush shortly before my eighth birthday. One blow of the hammer and the stone fell open along a hairline. Curving out of the stone was the outer shell of a giant ammonite. It took more than a month to chip away the matrix and when it emerged, fully unwrapped, it was nearly two feet across. I put it on a shelf in my bedroom. But as time passed, so the spell faded. To my eyes, the ammonite became strangely still and dead. Had something really once lived inside it? I diverted myself instead with books that reconstructed its habitat – those swampy Jurassic shallows and the giant ferns and scaly reptiles. And then the books too paled and the ammonite was lost and only two decades later, faced with the cathedral at Ani, did I recall the surprise of first discovering it, that same sense of order in a random landscape.

The first art historian to examine the ruins of Ani, at the turn of the century, was an Austrian by the name of Strzygowski. He was so taken aback by the ancient Armenian capital that he became convinced he'd stumbled on one of the great links in the evolution of Western architecture. He concluded that 'Greek genius at St Sophia and Italian genius at St Peter's only realized more fully what the Armenians had originated.' His ideas have since been largely pooh-poohed by the scholars. Too speculative, they sneer: no proof. But I have always felt rather sorry for Strzygowski, bowled over as he was by Ani, seeking to overturn the Classical hegemony, to advocate a more Oriental provenance for Western architecture, and being lured by the sight of Ani beyond the narrow bounds of 'acceptable' scholarship.

I too have still seen nothing in these regions that comes close to Ani. It is a place of haunting genius. Perched on a bluff above the Araxes gorge, now in no man's land between Turkey and Armenia, its half dozen crumbling structures were the work of masons and architects at the very height of their craft.

The masterpiece is the cathedral. It is not big, no bigger in fact than any large English parish church. Yet it achieves an extraordinary sense of space; it seems twice the size inside as out. Every detail, all the blind arcades and the niches of the outer walls and the looping arches and the grand central apse is perfect, perfectly designed, perfectly executed. And they all combine seamlessly in a whole that is neither pious nor overbearing. The cathedral at Ani seems to me no more and no less than a celebration of form. Like Strzygowski, I felt unwilling to accept that this building, and the Armenians who built it, were some sort of cultural cul-de-sac.

In north-western Europe, Gothic architecture appeared virtually fully formed in the early twelfth century. Within the space of a few decades many of the great cathedrals had been completed. The introduction of rib-vaulting and the pointed arch enabled its sudden growth. But there was nothing Gothic or Teutonic about these devices at all; the term was coined in the Renaissance whose pioneers saw something pagan, almost demonic, in the pointed arch. They blamed it erroneously on the Goths, forest-dwellers to a man, who were so savage that the only shelter they could construct was by pulling together the whip-like trunks of small trees: two trees made an arch, four the wooden ancestor of the rib-vault. In fact these structures were extraordinarily efficient. The sense of space and height in Gothic cathedrals is due more than anything to the load-bearing qualities of the pointed arch.

If not from the forest, where did it come from? In Christian architecture it appears first in Syria in the eighth century. From there it trickled into the Mediterranean and up into Italy. But its use by the Normans was undoubtedly inspired by their crusading adventures in the Levant and Anatolia. At this time – the turn of the twelfth century – the Seljuk Turks were also new arrivals in the region. They were building zealously. They fused central Asian traditions with those they discovered in eastern Anatolia. They began to build in stone rather than brick, and for this they employed the region's most proficient masons: the Armenians.

In the cathedral at Ani, built at the end of the tenth century, the Armenians had already used pointed arches and clustered piers and it was this more than anything that tempted Strzygowski to feel, sitting in its semi-ruined interior, that he was in a prototype of the great European cathedrals.

The Seljuks sacked Ani in 1064 and its cathedral became a mosque. Using Armenian masons, they went on to develop what in Ani had been merely transitional. Seljuk mosques in Diyarbekir, at Sairt and Gaziantep, but most of all the Great Mosque at Bitlis, show a use of pointed arches and rib-vaults very similar to that of Gothic. And the Great Mosque at Bitlis was, according to Burney and Lang's study, 'a product very largely of Armenian architectural genius'. Armenians built both for Seljuks and the Crusaders. Who is to say that they did not act as the bridge between them?

But it is hardly proof. At best it hints at something. All sorts of builders and labourers came to early medieval Europe from the Near East, and some from Moorish Spain. Undoubtedly Gothic architecture, as Romanesque before it, gained something from all these groups. It is tempting to think that it was the Armenians, brilliant masons that they were, passionate builders of churches, ever industrious and innovative, who were among the most influential. How many of the great surviving monuments of this era include demonstrably the work of Armenians: the restored dome at Istanbul's St Sophia, many of the Seljuk mosques, the castles of the Crusaders, the ribbed dome of the Great Mosque in Cordova, all three of the remaining Fatimid gates in Cairo. Anatolia, the Levant, Spain – what other people had the Armenians' mobility and their skill in masonry?

I climbed down from the castle and on the edge of the village came across a young shepherd on a rock – a reluctant-looking shepherd, dressed in jeans and orange satin jacket.

I told him he had fine sheep.

'No good sheep! I want car. You have car?'

'No.'

'What you do here? Castle?'

'Yes.'

'It is no good, broken castle.'

On the main road I hailed a *dolmus* and headed up over the ridge to the coast and the port of Iskenderun. There, waiting for a bus to Konya, I ambled along the seafront, beneath the date palms, among the lunchtime crowds, the office workers and the baggy-trousered peasants, the balloon merchants, the nut-sellers and shoe-shiners, the hawkers of plastic toys. Just offshore a scattering of yawls and coasters lay motionless on the midday sea.

I was jolted out of my sunny trance by the sight of Ataturk. He appeared to be surfing. Raised on a marble plinth, he rode a large black wave into the town. With him came the popular pantheon of dictators – the engineer, the soldier, the broad-hipped woman, the peasant, the manual worker. All posed beneath the Turkish flag and an olive branch. Thus the Turks had landed in the province of Hatay. In 1938 Ataturk won it from the French by agreeing to stay out of the coming war. But by the time it was annexed, he was dead and it is doubtful anyway whether he ever had any intention of joining the war.

At some point in the small hours of the following morning, the bus left me on the shadowy outskirts of Konya. I walked into town and found a hotel where I slept late and woke to a bright morning; the air had a crispness to it that was partly the altitude and partly early spring. I was, they told me, the first tourist, like the first cuckoo, and beyond the town's grey roofs, beyond the plain, the snouts of extinct volcanoes were still white with snow. I spent the morning ambling round Konya, fighting off rug merchants, drinking bitumen-like coffee and lying on a hot navel-stone in the town's old *hamam*. When I emerged from that, with rubbery limbs and glowing skin, it seemed that spring had been brought about two weeks closer. The Seljuks adopted Konya as their capital in 1097, the same year the knights of the First Crusade took Nicaea. It was the greatest of the Seljuk capitals. In it their building flourished with all the geometric exuberance of the Classic period of Islamic architecture. But in Konya it was an Armenian, Keluk Abdullah, who was among the greatest architects; according to some, he was as much of an influence on Seljuk building as later Sinan the Great was to be on Ottoman. In the courtyard of the Alaettin mosque, I'd heard there were mausolea of Armenian origin. The mosque sat on top of a small knoll in the centre of the town. It is one of the oldest occupied sites known to man, where the first settlement, according to Phrygian myth, appeared after the Flood. But it was closed for renovation. I had a brief argument through a crack in the fence and the foreman reluctantly let me in.

In a cement-scarred courtyard I found the two *gumbats*, the Seljuk tomb towers. They were short, decagonal structures, like stubby obelisks with conical roofs. The Seljuks had left a trail of these *gumbats* all through central Asia. Their invasion route – from Oxiana to Konya – can be traced by them. They are exclusively Seljuk structures, but in Anatolia they underwent two changes. The star-shaped column was abandoned for a polygonal or rounded form, and the brick of Persia was replaced with stone. Both these developments point to the use of Armenians.

Walking around these *gumbats*, I was struck as at Ani by their austere symmetry, as though building them was some sort of ritual indulgence, a worship of form. There is a sense in which this architecture and all the rhythmic, patterned architecture of the Near East is an expression of the deep reverence for the laws of God – not His stern, moral laws, but the perennial cosmic laws that govern all things. In these gumbats can be traced the Babylonian forefathers of Copernicus and Newton. Geometry is the mother of the sciences and architecture in its purest form is a geometric exercise, a microcosm. All those pioneering civilizations who explored geometry produced buildings that reflected it. The Egyptian pyramids and Babylonian *ziggurats* are oriented and proportioned on geometric principles, and the 'golden section' proportions of Greek temples give them a beauty that depends on the subliminal recognition of some universal order. The cathedral at Ani makes full use of golden sections and so-called sacred proportions.

The Armenians, in the first millennium, were great scientists, great geometers. They had access to all the ancient traditions of knowledge and were active in Baghdad when many of the early scientific studies were made. The seventh-century Armenian scientist, Ananiah Shiragatsi, born at Ani, angered the priests by suggesting that the world did not in fact rest on the backs of three elephants, but that it was round. He even suggested that when it was night on one side, it was day on the other, and that the moon shone from the reflection of the sun and the Milky Way was a concentration of stars (all of this was eight hundred years before Galileo.) He devised too an immensely intricate calendar, based on a 532-year cycle.

The Armenians had their own numeral system. Recognizing the limitations of Greek, Roman and Persian numerals, they adapted their own alphabet for mathematics. The thirty-six letters fitted neatly into four sections of nine: units, tens, hundreds, thousands (the zero came later). Large numbers could be written, and manipulated, with ease. It was remarkably sophisticated. While most early systems used an additive principle, the Armenian numerals were based, as ours now are, on multiplicative and additive rules. The Roman system, for example, is fine for buying cloth or counting cohorts, but try multiplying XLIV by LII. Clearly the Armenians were using their numbers for more than just trade.

Ananiah Shiragatsi's manuscript calculations show such a variety of advanced uses that one American mathematical historian, Allen Shaw, has concluded:

> The Armenian alphabetic system is more perfect than any of the other ancient alphabetic systems. The only missing symbol in the system is zero, which was discovered and used later in the eighth century. The present writer holds that the origin of our common numeral system is *Armenian* or *Graeco-Armenian*, worked out at the court of the Baghdad Califs, possibly under the patronage of Harun al-Rashid.

No other people has been quite so haunted by the demons of disorder as the Armenians, with their centuries of invasions, exile, massacres, earthquakes. They have tried constantly to tie down their ever-shifting world with numbers, to palliate themselves with pattern. All their endeavours – art, science, even commerce – have been attempts to tame these demons. Their response to the chaos around them has been to dig, dig deeper, deeper into business, deeper into the mysteries, deeper into knowledge, in the hope that somewhere there is solid rock. So all the ruined churches of Anatolia, these *gumbats* at Konya, all Armenian architecture with its geometric temples, are not what they first appear. They are not so much a reflection of order as a defiance of chaos; not so much assured as hopeful; not so much a statement, as a prayer.

An endless snake of scarved Turkish women winds past the tomb of Mevlana, founder of the Sufi order of whirling dervishes. The women give off strange muted chants and raise their hands in prayer before the tomb, which is draped in a leather cover, mounted with black satin and embroidered with gold-threaded Kufic. One man, muttering Koranic invocations, traces the concentric pattern of a Persian carpet, another prostrates himself. A gold-braided colonel bends down to whisper to his daughter. There is a sense of rapture and reverence.

Kemal Ataturk's dream of a modern, secular state appears to have failed – though not through want of trying. Within a couple of years of the declaration of the republic in 1923, all religious orders were banned, *medreses* closed, and women discouraged from wearing the veil. But the greatest betrayal to Turkish tradition and to Islam – in which the very script of the Koran is the manifestation of God – was to extract the Turkish language from Arabic letters and squeeze it into Latin. Anyone who has seen a Turkish newspaper will understand that it was not an easy job. The story goes that Ataturk saw an Armenian in Aleppo writing Turkish phonetically in Latin script. 'So it can be done,' he said and commissioned the Armenian to work on the current phonetic system. The polyglot is remembered as 'Hagop Dilacar', or 'Hagop who opens the language'.

That same evening I nearly missed the train to Bursa. The road to the station was suddenly blocked by vehicles stopped for evening prayers; yet another thing to set Ataturk turning in his grave.

Around 1400, the Ottoman Turks succeeded the Seljuks of Konya as Anatolia's dominant Turkish clan. In Bursa, just south of the Sea of Marmara, they waited to pounce on Constantinople and bury, finally, a thousand years of Byzantine power. With none of Konya's pious conservatism, Bursa is now a bustling, modern town, with fashion boutiques and fast food, and its own peculiar shade of yellow smog.

Stalling for a day before my own final assault on Istanbul, I went to visit Yesil Camii, one of the earliest of the Ottoman mosques. From the sultan's gallery I looked down on the interior. A muted galaxy of tiles faced the walls and stalactite masonry hung from the recesses but the building lacked the exuberance, the intricacy of the Seljuk mosques. It was stolid, almost monolithic. The Ottomans seemed to be saving their energy for the empire-building to come; the Seljuks, on the other hand, having reached Konya, had dissipated themselves in beauty and Sufi mysticism. Behind the mosque's sobriety, its gloomy *iwans*, its high tutelary *mimbar*, was the pastiche of a people new to building. Seljuk, Byzantine, Persian and Mameluke details had been balanced and fused into something that just about passed as a distinctive style. According to an inscription near the door, this pastiche was the work of one Yegyazer Kalfa. In old Turkish, Kalfa means simply 'master builder', but Yegyazer was in fact an Armenian.

Eager to escape Bursa, its yellow smog and green mosques, and keen suddenly to leave behind all those buildings and dead rock of the past few days, I took a cable car up to the mountain of Uludag. The afternoon was bright and warm, and the sky cloudless. Snow still lay thickly over the forest, but had been cleared from the cobbled road which weaved its way down through the trees. For some time I sat on a high granite boulder which rose above the tree-tops. There was the occasional distant whine of a small aircraft and every now and then one of the boughs would shake off its snow and swish free. To the east, for as far as I could see, the mountains dipped and rose beneath the forest. Serrated ridges cut the horizon. Beyond them, out of sight, was the Anatolian plateau, stretching unbroken to Lake Van and the Caucasus, to Persia and the Syrian desert. It is one of the most fertile regions on earth. Once Byzantium's larder, it has yielded also signs of the first cultivation, the first pottery, the first towns. It has spawned some of the greatest of the early civilizations, Hittites, Urartians, Phrygians; and its rivers had nurtured others, the Sumerians, the Assyrians, the Babylonians.

A few Assyrians survive, but otherwise it is the Armenians who, as a distinct people, lived longest on that land. Where exactly they came from no one is quite certain. Perhaps, as Herodotus suggests, they were neighbours of the Phrygians, or perhaps they spread east from the Balkans. They may simply have risen from the pool of nameless clans who roamed around the high plains. All that is known for sure is that around the sixth century BC, a people calling themselves 'Hai' appeared among the beaten Urartians. They paid tribute to the Persians and called their satrapy 'Hayastan', the name still used today by Armenians for their own land. The Armenians see themselves as an indigenous Anatolian people and it is that more than anything that makes exile so hard to bear. Losing your land is one thing, but losing *this* land, this fertile plateau, that's quite another.

I approached Istanbul with a strange sense of ennui. It was a grey, foggy morning. The train wound through an interminable shambles of half-built suburbs and chemical works. It came to rest in a terminus dressed up as a German palace. The Teutonic, schloss-like front glared back across the Bosphorus, back from Asia into Europe. But that morning there was nothing to see but fog.

The Galata ferry, across the Bosphorus, was loaded with office workers. My rucksack sat clumsily against their briefcases. Beyond the gunwale and the colourless slick of the sea, tall slender ghosts loomed out of the mist. The booms of cargo ships? More industrial chimneys? No, the minarets of Sancta Sophia and the Blue Mosque; then the walls of the Topkapi Palace and the mass of roofs and domes that squabble over the back of the city.

I crossed the Golden Horn from Galata on a bridge that wobbled and whose parapet was a thicket of fishing rods. I climbed up the hill into Istanbul proper. I passed through strangely silent souks, beneath grime-blackened buildings, past swarms of students and Kurds, troops of riot police, a cripple with a yo-yo, a woman with a monkey, a gypsy with a dancing bear, and the Ukrainians again, down from Odessa, lining the walls by the main bazaar, touting for hard currency with their sad piles of worthless goods.

# 8

Say Istanbul and Sinan the Great Architect comes
   to mind
His ten fingers soaring like mighty plane trees
On the skyline

Bedri Rahmi Eyugoblu, *The Saga of Istanbul* (Trans. from Turkish
by Talat S. Halman.)

In amongst the fish and fruit of Galata's covered market was a doorway and in the doorway a screen. Behind the screen was an
Armenian church and beside that a small alley which led to a wooden
door. The door was locked. Peeling back a net curtain a woman
peered at me suspiciously until I greeted her in Armenian. Then she
opened the door and I stepped again into that half-hidden world of
the Armenian diaspora.

The building was the office of *Marmara*, Istanbul's Armenian newspaper. Sitting with the editor, in his sharp Italian suit and red socks,
was the director of Venice's Collegio Armeno. It had been a good
two months since I'd seen him, on that first icy morning beside the
canal. He seemed surprised to meet me here; for him it had been
twenty years since he'd been in Istanbul. But it wasn't so much the
coincidence, as the fact that I'd made it here at all. I asked him if
he'd managed to fix his car yet and he laughed, telling me how, just
after I'd left Venice, they'd had to send the ice breakers along the
Grand Canal.

I spent the rest of the morning in a spare corner of the office,
reading. I found a story about a bomb in Beirut. Looking closely at

the picture I recognized the room I'd had there, reduced to rubble. There was also a new book about the Balian family, Istanbul's most accomplished nineteenth-century architects.

The more the Ottoman empire declined, the more opulent their buildings became. And no one contributed more to the decadent nineteenth-century style than two generations of the Armenian Balians. Page after page illustrated the scale of their work – the vast white Selimiye barracks, the Nusretiye Camii, the Beylerbey palace, and most of all the vast Dolmabahce palace. The book began with a brief survey of the role of the Armenians in Ottoman architecture. When Fatih Sultan Mehmed captured Istanbul in 1453, he shipped in thousands of Armenian craftsmen, engravers, miniaturists, masons. Van Mour, a roving French painter reported in the eighteenth century that the architects of Istanbul were 'mostly Armenian' and that they 'need nothing more than an axe and a saw to build a house'. But the claim that struck me most was that Sinan, the greatest Turkish architect of all, was also an Armenian.

I telephoned the author and arranged to visit him later that day. But first I wanted to see for myself some of the Balians' work and set off for the Dolmabahce Palace. It was a bright day and the north wind swept down the Bosphorus, bringing with it the last of the Russian winter. The waters of the channel were a brilliant blue and Galata's shoppers were red-faced and impatient.

Beyond Galata was the new stadium of one of Istanbul's football teams. They were playing Konya – Ottoman capital versus Seljuk. I went in to watch for a few minutes. Konya played in the emerald green of Mevlana's *turbe* and I remembered the story an Armenian had told me of Konya's passage to the premier league. Before their qualifying match with Taksim, the only Armenian team in Turkey, a few of Konya's players had entered the dressing room and explained that if the Armenians did not allow them to win there would be some broken bones. Whether this was true or not, Konya were clearly not up to it; they kept falling over and when I left were already down by two goals.

Beyond the floodlight poles were the minarets of the Balians' Dolmabahce Mosque and beyond the mosque was the palace. Wandering around its 365 rooms, I felt I had stepped into an elaborate Disney set, something between Versailles and the Taj Mahal. In three days and three capitals – Konya, Bursa, Istanbul – Turkish rule had run its course before me. The buildings had swollen dramatically; piety had been shrugged off for pomp, Asia abandoned for Europe. Here in the palace throne room, the largest in the world, hung Queen Victoria's gift to the Sultan: a four-and-a-half-ton chandelier. In these marble halls, the last echoing halls of empire, I had the overwhelming sense of something falling. Looking up at the great glittering canopy of that chandelier, it amazed me that the whole thing had stayed up for so long.

Pars Tuglaci, author of the Balian book, lived in a smart, studious flat behind Istanbul's police academy. He was Armenian but had Turkified his name. He bubbled with an Armenian confidence that I hadn't seen since Beirut and had bold, bushy sideburns and the debonair looks of a proud dragoon. We sat around a low table covered in newspaper cuttings.

I told him I'd enjoyed his book and we turned to talking about Sinan. Sinan built prodigiously – more than 350 buildings are attributed to him; perhaps no other architect has ever built with such energy and panache. He was also a brilliant engineer and before he even became an architect, when still a soldier, he had dazzled his commanders with an ingenious bridge of boats across Lake Van. His work coincided with the brief apogee of Ottoman power and survives in a vast range of mosques, hospitals, *hamams*, palaces, bridges – spread from Bosnia to Mecca. He was enormously influential and it was he who, using Sancta Sophia as a model, developed the distinctive Ottoman style of mosques, which to me always look like something crustaceous – fat crabs brooding between the claws of their minarets.

The Turks claim Sinan as a generic Turk, like the Balians. But he was a member of the imperial guard, a janissary, and the janissaries were always Christian. It has often been supposed he was Armenian, but no one, as far as I knew, had been able to prove it. Pars Tuglaci leaned back in his sofa, one arm draped languidly along its back and explained the basis of his own theory.

'I consulted the Ottoman treasury archives, the *Hazine-i Eurak'ta*. There I found a decree dated 7 Ramazan 951 – that's 1573 in the Christian calendar. It concerned a personal request from Sinan to the sultan. Apparently the villagers of Aghrinas near Kayseri, were about to be banished to Cyprus for not paying taxes. Sinan asked for a reprieve and got it. Aghrinas was Sinan's home town.'

'And it was Armenian?'

'Not exclusively. But three of Sinan's family are mentioned by name. They are all Armenian names.'

That seemed plausible enough. But why did the Turks allow an Armenian to consult their archives?

Pars Tuglaci cocked his chin proudly. 'I have special privileges. When I went to Ankara to collect my medal from the President for one of my dictionaries, he said: "Mr Tuglaci, this is a magnificent work. We owe you much. What is it you are working on now?" I told him I was doing an encyclopaedia of Ottoman history. "How can we help?" he asked, to which I replied: "By opening up the Ottoman archives."'

He stood and leading me to his study, spread his arms wide: 'This room I call Pars Tuglaci's Wagon!'

There were three high cabinets containing drawers and drawers of entries for his Turkish encyclopaedia. There were wooden shelves for the dictionaries he'd compiled – his six-volume Turkish dictionary (fifteen years' work), his two-volume Turkish–English dictionary, his Turkish–French dictionary, his dictionaries of synonyms, antonyms, idioms, scientific terms, economic terms, legal terms, medical terms (in several languages). Below that were shelves for his historical works – several books on women in Turkey, three published volumes of a six-volume modern history of Turkey, and his twenty-three-volume *History of Turkey 1071–*, as well as the Balian book and an illustrated history of Bulgaria and several others.

I smiled and shook my head. 'All these words – very Armenian!'

'Ah yes, but come and see.'

Back in the sitting room he pointed to a row of cupboards. 'Some people do not believe me,' he said, opening them. They were bursting with countless files and typescripts.

I saw no reason now to disbelieve anything.

'I have another fifty-three works here waiting to be published.'


Walking back into Istanbul, I dropped down through Galata to the Golden Horn just as the sun dipped beneath the hills. I was beginning to recognize the silhouettes of Istanbul's prickly skyline. Perhaps it's the weight of sixteen centuries of imperial power, perhaps it's the senseless growth of the city in recent years, but here at its core the city's minarets and towers look strangely out of place. Istanbul appears unable to cope with the legacy of its past. Its people busy themselves around the feet of the monuments, perching at the entrance to sell you tickets, but do not seem to belong. Perhaps no one has ever belonged in Istanbul; even Constantine, the first of the city's great rulers, was a usurper when he, 'feeling glum, moved his capital to Byzantium'.

I don't know whether it's any consolation at all to the depleted Armenian community that a great number of the city's skeletal buildings, as I now knew, were built by their forebears – the mosques of Sinan, the palaces of the Balians, and countless other Armenians who worked with them. But none surpasses the miraculous shallow dome of Sancta Sophia, one of the architectural wonders of the world. That had been restored in 989, when a part of it collapsed in an earthquake. The architect was Trdat, the same Armenian who had built the cathedral at Ani.

Byzantium, Constantinople, Stamboul, *Istanbul*; many of those Armenians who remain in the city still call it 'Polis', like the Greeks, suggesting that everywhere else is simply provincial. In their hey-day that was true – the city has been a capital more often, and for more Armenians, than any of the other countless cities they have lived in. But it was never their city. They played an ambiguous, enigmatic role – as Armenian roles in exile always are. And never was it more ambiguous than during the Byzantine millennium. Throughout this period, some corner of Armenia was usually in revolt, yet in Constantinople, Armenians held key positions in the administration. It was Armenians more than anyone, for example, who generated the ninth-century Byzantine renaissance. Twenty-four Byzantine emperors were of Armenian stock. So important were the Armenians that the Byzantine Empire should, according to some, be named more correctly the 'Graeco-Armenian' Empire.

Steven Runciman, himself Scottish, has likened the role of the Armenians in the Byzantine Empire to that of the Scots in the British – providing the best soldiers, inventors and scientists, and just enough free, highland spirit to keep the whole thing fresh and dynamic. But in their time each, Scot and Armenian, has provided the centre with its share of problems. Deportation was the standard Byzantine prescription for the militant fringes; from the sixth century, a regular tide of belligerent Armenians was washed up in the Balkans.

And it was one of these Armenians who, in the ninth century,

The cave at Shadaddie, Syrian desert

ABOVE: The execution of Armenians in
Constantinople during the First World War

BELOW: Armenian deportations

St Sarkis, Khedzgonk,
Eastern Turkey. Built 1020,
abandoned 1920

LEFT: Enthronement of Archbishop Torkom Manoogian, Armenian Patriarch of Jerusalem at St James's Cathedral, Jerusalem

BELOW: Armenian quarter, Jerusalem

Bourdj-Hamoud, Armenian district of Beirut

The Bekaa valley

BELOW: The pass below Mount Lebanon

Easter, Bachkovo
monastery, Bulgaria

ABOVE: Kaspar and Magardich
Kasapian, Armenian painters,
Plovdiv

RIGHT: Near Gheorgieni,
Transylvania, Romania

Opposition rally, Sofia

ABOVE: Off-duty *fedayi*, Zangezour

BELOW: Survivors of the 1915 massacres, Meghri

fathered a boy named Basil. From Thrace, Basil trekked to Constantinople. There he picked up a job as groom. One day, challenged to fight a Bulgar champion, he threw the man across the stable yard. His feats of strength became legendary and even Emperor Michael came to hear of them. He called for Basil and employed him first as head of the Imperial stables and then, in time, as his bed-fellow. Basil exploited his position. First he murdered the Emperor's Chief Minister, then the Emperor himself. He took the throne and founded the greatest of the Byzantine dynasties. Later he went mad and was assassinated on the orders of his own son. But under this, the Macedonian dynasty, the twin Armenian strains flourished – the one in Constantinople, administrators, generals, architects and artists; the other defiantly Armenian in the east. And so it continued, off and on, right the way through the Ottoman period, until April 1915, when suspicion of the eastern Armenians led the Turks to arrest those in Constantinople and attempt to rid themselves once and for all of these truculent people.

I was always baffled that such a small people could accommodate these opposites. My initial image of an Armenian – a shifting, mercantile figure, shy and intense – was shattered every time I came across his pugnacious cousin. Each supports the other, and each in turn also threatens the other – but both do it in the name of being Armenian.

One evening after several days in Istanbul, I crossed the Golden Horn into Galata and discussed these things with an Armenian priest. Father Hagop was a wise-looking man with kind, hooded eyes and a long beard. We sat in his book-lined study and, overwhelmed suddenly by the extraordinary range of the Armenians, I said to him: 'How is it that it's all lasted this long?'

He smiled and buried his fingertips in his beard. I did not expect an answer and he didn't give one. He simply trotted through Armenian history, pointing out the eternal cycle of rebellions and reprisals, rebellion, reprisal, rebellion . . .

'And now the fighting in Karabagh?'

He put his hands together and looked up pensively at the ceiling. 'Yes. But you know, we all feel it. Somewhere we all feel the same. We just express it in different ways.'

Then he told me a story whose simple images stuck in my mind for weeks to come. Several years earlier the bishops and the old patriarch, a saintly man, had been granted permission to go to eastern Turkey to look at various ruined Armenian sites. On Lake Van the prelates took to a small boat. They were accompanied by a police guard. Gliding across the lake they gradually fell into silence, struck by the extreme beauty of the place and the mountains that ran 'like a chain around the horizon'.

Then came the sound, at first quite faint, of an Armenian folk song. They could just make out the words: a rhapsody to the lake. But the bishops could not see where the song came from. Standing alone near the stern was the patriarch. It was from him. He'd learnt the song in the Syrian orphanages and forgotten it until then. No one had ever heard him sing a secular song before. When he had finished he gazed across at the lake and the mountains and said, without bitterness: 'Who can say this is not Armenia?'

After a week in Istanbul, a week of cold winds down the Bosphorus, of evenings in kebab houses, of lying to Turks about the reasons for my journey, I concluded that these Armenians were among the most elusive I'd seen. I had not managed to break into the community as elsewhere and had the impression of skirting round the perimeter of something, looking for a way in. One morning I went to try and see the patriarch. His official residence was in Kumkapi, one of the old Armenian quarters whose fishermen in better days were the city's best.

I came to a heavy oak door and rang the bell. An old thin man pulled it open a few inches. His face was grey with ill-health.

'The patriarch?' I asked.

'Not here.'

'He will come?'

'Maybe he will come.'

He opened the door fully and I stepped into a dark, panelled hall. It smelt of age and under-use. I followed the old man down a passage to his office. He sat down slowly and put his hand to his eyes. His breath was strained and quick.

'Are you all right?' I asked.

He shook his head. Suddenly he seemed too weak to talk. He crept over to a day-bed and lay down. For a moment he was still. Then he whispered, 'Pills.'

A bottle of Ispodril stood on the table. I took two of the tablets and gave them to him with a glass of water. Swallowing noisily, he smiled and tapped his chest. 'Heart,' he said, and lay down again to sleep.

Out of the window, a sudden wind swept the gulls off the tower of the Armenian church. They dipped, then rose back against the wind and headed out to sea. The rain came in squalls, polishing the roofs, bouncing off the road in a grey mist. From behind the church screen an old couple stepped out, struggling with an umbrella. The old man began to snore contentedly.

A little later the patriarch's car pulled up outside. In the hall, he shook the wet from his pontifical robes and we went up to his office. For many years, he had been a monk in Jerusalem and I gave him news of George and Albert and Father Anooshavan.

'Anooshavan! How are his languages? You know, he used to speak the finest Koranic Arabic to buy tomatoes in the souk.'

'He is learning German now,' I said. 'He wants to read *Faust* in the original.'

'What a linguist! He must speak a dozen languages.'

'Fifteen. But he says the problem is that whenever he learns a new one, he forgets one of the others.'

The patriarch asked me to a lunch the following day in one of the presbyteries. There I met Father Manuel whose name I knew well as the central figure in the sad story of Doggy.

In Jerusalem, Doggy had been the guard-dog of the Armenian museum. He was a very large and very fierce Doberman pincher, so fierce in fact that only George, who owned and fed him, could get close to him. He had once escaped and mauled one of the Armenian school children; George had to appeal to the mayor to save Doggy from the slab. Doggy's presence hovered over the Armenian community who regarded him with something between affection and admiration, though for poor Father Manuel his very name was a curse.

Some ten years ago, Father Manuel was on his way to visit Jerusalem. He was stopped at Istanbul airport; the authorities had been waiting for him. 'You Armenians have a dog in Jerusalem,' they said. 'What is it called?'

Father Manuel said he did not know.

'It is called Ataturk! It is an insult to the father of our nation!'

Father Manuel was imprisoned. There were accusations too that he'd been involved with various Armenian political groups, but the dog remained at the centre of his case. A campaign was organized to lobby the Turkish government. Articles appeared in the world's press and thousands of letters arrived at Turkish embassies. Doggy became, as George put it, the 'most famous dog in the Middle East'. In Jerusalem he had to secure an affidavit from a Jewish lawyer to confirm that the dog was not called 'Ataturk' but 'Doggy'. Eventually Father Manuel was released. But the experience had left him severely traumatized. He had suffered severe beatings in jail and had been tortured. There was, I could see, something distressingly slow and tired in his manner.

On my last evening in Jerusalem, several months earlier, I had walked through the monastery to George's flat. I had come to say goodbye. But George was distraught. 'Doggy's very ill,' he said.

We went at once to Doggy's cell and he stood there with bloodshot eyes and the ribs showing through his sweaty grey flanks. We tried to administer some medicine but his jaws remained shut tight. Later that night, as I left Jerusalem, Doggy died.

In Istanbul I prepared to move on. I went to the Bulgarian embassy to secure a visa. I wanted to head west and north, up through the Balkans, where Armenians had always been a powerful presence. How many remained and in what state, I'd been unable to find out. The iron curtain had split the Armenian diaspora as it had done everything else. Thanking the patriarch, I left for the railway station and took a train across Thrace to Edirne, the last Turkish town before the Bulgarian border.

# II
# EASTERN EUROPE

If from the outset you recognize as the result
of scientific research only that which agrees
with your own point of view, it is easy to pose
as a prophet.

Karl Marx, Kölnische Zeitung no 179.

EASTERN EUROPE

UKRAINE

RUSSIA

MOLDOVA

Gherla • Suceava •
Sofia • Cluj • Iasi • Kishinev
TRANSYLVANIA Gheorgien
Frumoasa

Odessa

SEA
OF AZOV

CRIMEA Kerc
Novorossisk
Tuapse

ROMANIA

Bucharest

BLACK SEA

GEORGIA
Tbilisi

BULGARIA

Sofia

Plovdiv
Bachkovo • Edirne
Batum

ARMENIA

Yerevan

Istanbul

TURKEY

0 10 20  40 60  80 100 Miles

# 9

Navigare necesse est, vivere non necesse.

Pompey's exhortation to his crew.

Waiting to catch a bus to the Bulgarian border, I looked in on Edirne's Selimiye mosque, which, out of all his 350-odd buildings, Sinan named as his own personal masterpiece. From the back wall I sat and watched the young families and groups of women shuffle across the carpets. High above their heads, the perfect dome billowed out like a parachute. A dim, furtive light seeped through the mosque's 999 windows and gave a curious impression of someone watching.

A man in a black leather jacket peeled away from the crowd and sat down beside me. Over the back of his hand was a loop of prayer beads. 'German?' he asked.

'British.'

'You're a tourist?'

'Yes.' No! I was leaving the country; I thought I could push my luck. 'No.'

'You are studying?'

'Yes. The Armenians.'

I scrutinized his face; not a flicker.

'Armenians, yes,' he mused. 'An ancient people.'

'I've been studying their modern history, the time of the First War, the troubles . . .'

Nothing.

'I studied history at college,' he said absently.

'And now?'

'Now I am a police officer.'

I felt profoundly disappointed. This policeman had destroyed even the refuge of my prejudice. Perhaps it was this that inspired a last, rather petulant entry which I found in my notebook:

> I look forward to getting into Bulgaria. Not so much the thought of reaching a new country, as the relief of leaving this one. Turkey does not even have the appeal of being ex-communist; it is neither communist nor Western nor really Islamic, but a faceless mish-mash of the brutal and the mundane.

Crossing the border, on foot across the wide straits of empty tarmac, I felt better. Bulgaria reclined with an antique dignity; it was slow and sleepy and familiar. Striking out along the main road, I passed crooked pig shelters and red-tiled farm buildings the size of tithe barns. The yards were muddy and deserted. I followed a line of sad, bare poplars and then one of pollarded willows whose whiskery branches pointed to a grey sky. I squinted up to watch a stork fly north, its long beak twitching for the Balkan spring. On the edge of a small village, a roly-poly Bulgar offered to take me to Svilengrad railway station. The whole way there he was silent, not for one moment dropping the smile which hung like a sardonic banner from his face.

Sitting in the station restaurant, with its stained white tablecloths and a couple of meat balls swimming around my plate, I knew I was back in Europe – a broken and beaten Europe, but Europe nonetheless. I ordered two bottles of beer and drank to whatever threshold it was that I had crossed.

At the end of the sixth century, the Byzantine Emperor Maurice wrote in despair to his Persian counterpart Chosroes II. Neither of them, he suggested, could really run their empires effectively with the Armenians in between. He had a proposal to deal with this 'crooked and rebellious race': 'I will collect mine and deport them wholesale to Thrace. You do the same with yours and have them led away to the east. Then if they die, it is our enemies who die. And if they kill others, it is our enemies they will kill. And we shall live in peace. For as long as any of them are left on earth, we will have no rest.' Anticipating the solution of the Turks thirteen hundred years later, Maurice drove tens of thousands of Armenians from their mountain villages and marched them west, to the Balkans. Over the centuries, they were joined by others, subsequent waves of Byzantine deportation, the subversives, the militants and the heretics.

During the Ottoman years there was more deportation to the Balkans, whose towns were peppered too with Armenian adventurers, itinerants and merchants, and, finally, with the bedraggled survivors of 1915. It was the usual Armenian gallimaufry, but Maurice was wrong to suppose exile would tame the Armenians. Gibbon said this of them: 'The courage of these *dogs*, ever greedy of war, ever thirsty of human blood is noticed with astonishment by the pusillanimous Greeks.'

Ever since their arrival in Thrace the Armenians have made trouble for the authorities; they helped infect the Balkans with their heresies, taught the Macedonians to make bombs and, in the last few years, had been among the first to sound the death-knell of the communists. From the earliest years Plovdiv – originally Philippolis – had been the centre of the Armenians' Balkan community. Anna Comnena, the Byzantine chronicler, loathed the Armenians and their godless ways. She called them 'a brackish stream', making Plovdiv a 'meeting-place, so to speak, of all polluted waters'. In her day, the twelfth century, the city was dominated by Armenians and Bogomils and she couldn't see much to choose between them.

No one in Plovdiv station, a year on from communism, seemed interested in anything but keeping warm. They squatted in the underpass and gathered in huddled groups in the ticket office. They looked listless and gaunt. But the first person to approach me – a money-changer – shattered my illusions. And I thought I'd be doing him a favour.

'How much per dollar?' I asked.

'Fifteen leva.'

'OK. Here's twenty dollars. That's three hundred leva.'

'Twenty dollars?' He stared at me incredulously. 'Twenty *dollars?*'

He took a wedge of notes from his pocket. They were hundred dollar bills. 'Do you know how much I have here?'

'No idea.'

'Twelve thousand dollars! And you want to change twenty!'

Another student was more helpful. 'Armenians? I have an Armenian friend, just married. I will ring her.'

A plump, cheery girl came to meet me with her brand-new husband. I said I'd stay in a hotel but they would not have it. They said I was their first guest and made up a bed in their new sitting room, prepared a meal of soup and sauerkraut and phoned the Armenian priest. He was busy. But an aunt who taught English literature 'would be delighted to meet an Englishman'.

It was a staid evening. Forty-five years of communism had frozen Plovdiv and its view of the outside world in an age of net curtains and afternoon tea. The English teacher spoke Celia-Johnson English, adored George Eliot and asked about the Queen. Communism too had managed to Bulgarize these Armenians. In 1974, Plovdiv's Armenian school had been closed and now all except the oldest ones spoke Bulgarian as a first language. And many of the young, said the teacher wistfully, were now marrying non-Armenians.

But saddest of all was their ignorance of the rest of the diaspora. I had grown used to the urbane familiarity with which Armenians in the Middle East referred to communities in London or Paris or Los Angeles – as if they were outlying villages. Here, when I spoke about St James's monastery in Jerusalem, they looked at me quizzically. They shook their heads in disbelief to hear that Armenians occupied a whole corner of the Holy City and owned more rights to the Holy Places – where Christ was born, buried, prayed in the garden, suffered and died – than all of the Western Churches put together.

'We had no idea. No one ever told us.'

I felt I was announcing a legacy from some long-lost aunt.


My first morning in Bulgaria was almost warm. The frost cleared quickly and in the sun it felt like spring. I went to see Hagop Vardanian, described by my hosts as 'our grand Armenian expert'. Barely five feet tall, Hagop was a man of volcanic enthusiasm. He had brilliant darting eyes and talked incessantly. There was nothing he did not know about the Armenians in the Balkans; he leapt cat-like at each of my questions, teasing it, chasing it like a ball of wool and unravelling it with ever more intricate facts. Through him, I watched the familiar patterns of the Armenian diaspora spread up into Central Europe.

Hagop lived in one of the decrepit wooden houses that limped along beside the cobbles of the old town. His own family had fled Turkey at the time of the massacres. The only survivor was his ninety-year-old mother who sat outside in the yard, rocking back and forth and staring at the sky.

We ate lunch in an upper room. His wife creaked up and down the wooden stairs with vodka and bowls of soup, and plates of dried mushrooms.

'My first love!' grinned Hagop, and his wife turned away coyly.

But he didn't mean his wife. 'The mushroom!' he cried. 'All spring I hunt the mushroom in the Rhodope mountains!'

'They don't look like mushrooms to me.'

'They are very rare mushrooms.'

'Are you sure?'

Hagop winked. 'For ten years I feed them to my wife. She never gets sick.'

So I took one and flushed it down with the vodka and asked Hagop who he thought it was that founded the Bachkovo monastery. I had followed, in various books and journals, the wordy debates about Bachkovo's provenance, but was still none the wiser. All that had struck me was how much nationalism masquerades as scholarship in Eastern Europe. History is an extension of territory, to be claimed and defended with fortresses of facts. Who did what when, means nothing unless you know whether it was a Bulgar or Serb, Magyar or Romanian, Greek or Armenian who did it first. So, to the Bulgarians, Bachkovo is part of their own heritage; it is in Bulgaria, after all. Occasionally Greeks claim a hand in it – the monastery's original codex, signed by the founder, Grigory Paryukani, survives in a library on the Greek island of Khios. They and the Georgians would seem to have the best claim, for the text survives only in their two languages.

But, Hagop explained, the codex stipulates that there should be no Greek monks at the monastery (they were considered too sly and quarrelsome for a good monastic order). And it begins: I, Grigory Paryukani, come from Iberia in the eastern provinces of the Byzantine Empire . . .'

That appears conclusive – he was Georgian.

No, said Hagop, Grigory was Armenian.

Originally the codex had been written in three languages: Greek, Georgian and Armenian; that much is stated in the surviving texts. But in the Greek text are two mentions of something more convincing: Grigory signed his name with Armenian letters.

'But if you ask the Georgians,' shrugged Hagop, 'they would probably tell you another story.'

I had one more question, irreverent though it was. 'Why does it matter whether he was Armenian or not?'

'It matters only because the Armenian role is denied. It's our history. Don't you think we've lost enough already?'

# 10

Now what of that Church of yours, worldly man?

Tertullian, sometime Montanist

I had intended reaching Bachkovo before nightfall, but Hagop's medieval intrigues had stalled me. By the time I arrived in Asenovgrad, the last bus to the monastery had already left. For several hours I walked up a deep and rocky gorge. The river sighed against the cliffs. It sounded like cars approaching but there were no cars. When it started to rain I took shelter in an abandoned petrol station. The darkness crept out of the shadows and soon all that was left of the day was a silvery smear in the western sky.

The rain let up and I set off again.

It was Easter Saturday. For the first time in nearly fifty years the communists – now democratically elected and re-styled Socialists – had declared Easter a holiday. As one of Bulgaria's principal monasteries, Bachkovo was to lift the veil from years of bashful Easters and celebrate it properly.

The gorge closed in around me. There was a long tunnel and when I emerged from it, the clouds had lifted and the rain had eased slightly. A dim grey light shone on the cliffs and the road wound tentatively beneath them. It was late in the evening when Bachkovo appeared, its orange lights winking through the drizzle. In the courtyard of the monastery, a crowd milled across the cobbles. The children clutched painted eggs and looked cold and confused. At midnight something was going to happen; no one I asked seemed sure what, but they certainly didn't want to miss it.

Down in the restaurant was a ritual that the communists had not damaged. Condensation streaked the windows and the air was full of tobacco-smoke and laughter. In the middle of the room a great bearded man stood like an old oak, bellowing a Rhodopian folk song. A four-piece band in one corner struggled to keep up. Three girls staggered and hopped through a dance. Around the room were Bulgarians of every kind. Couples sat gazing at the singer, hand-in-hand, their eyes misty with sentiment, while crooked *babushkas* sat next to their ribald young, and one very drunk party in the corner which had collapsed on the table, all except a gypsy-like man whose hands slid under the skirt of a half-sleeping woman. A policeman stood at the bar with me, asking if I knew the American girl whose picture hung on the wall and who, wearing nothing but Stars and Stripes boots, was licking the barrel of a revolver. Elka Constantinova, opposition leader and Sofia's voice of the Far Right, stood sipping coffee with a strange woman in high boots and fishnet stockings and a skirt no bigger than a dishcloth. The Minister of Employment, Emilia Maslarova, came and stood inside the door for a moment, but soon left. I wondered idly what the monastery's codex would have to say about all of this.

As midnight approached, those still capable struggled back up to the monastery. The courtyard and both tiers of cloisters were full. Inside the pocket-sized church an aging abbot appeared blinking from behind the iconostasis. At once he was mobbed by the crowd who, stabbing their tallow candles at his, tried to glean its flame. His acolytes had to beat a way through. Outside, the abbot made a short, uncertain speech and at midnight precisely, everyone turned to each other and knocked their painted eggs together. Then they shuffled around, trying to keep warm, wondering if it was all over. Within an hour all but a few sleeping drinkers had left and the cobbles were littered with egg-shell and tallow stubs.

It was a bitterly cold night. I found a bed and a few blankets in one of the cells, but the mountain wind blew through its shattered windows and made sleep impossible. Soon after dawn I went down and sat in the church, where the candles and fug of worship had made it warmer.

All Easter morning a continuous stream of people filed in through the narthex to make votive offerings to the icons. The miraculous Madonna, buried for centuries in the forest during the Turkish occupation, received the lion's share: eggs, daffodils, wild hyacinth, a large round cake, a shoe, a pair of glasses, and a shirt in a cellophane bag. Two monks continually cleared the gifts to make way for more. Next to me in the misericords an old man collapsed, alternately wheezing and gulping at a bottle of slivovitz. Outside, beneath the campanile, a sheep bleated on its tether, awaiting slaughter.

As I left, the monks and abbot marched solemnly towards the refectory. A group of young people gathered to peer at them, these strange creatures in black robes and beards tied behind their necks. They edged closer, but not too close, and when some of them reached for their cameras, I felt I was watching some bizarre safari. On this first post-communist Easter, Church and people seemed far apart, and both a long way from God.

I gathered my things, left a donation in the box and went down the cobbled track just as a dirty grey van marked TELEVISION honked its way through the crowds. I longed for the quiet of the forest and found a track leading up into the Rhodopes. For hours there was no sign of human life. I followed a stream up its valley, crossed the watershed and pushed on through thick woods. The slopes were spattered with the egg-yolk patches of wild forsythia and my feet pressed into layers of rotting leaves. Above my head the limbs of scrub-oak twisted like serpents, but all I could see through them was the pale blue sky and more forest, more limestone outcrops, more hills.

None of the Balkan miseries had left a mark on this landscape: no bloody civil war or hated occupation, none of the concrete edifices – rest camps, picnic areas, statues – that I came to recognize as apparatchiks' way of dealing with nature. It appeared clean and unbruised. But it had not always been so still. When Anna Comnena wrote about medieval Bachkovo she threw in a description of the surrounding villages. The people of these villages, she said, were restless, fidgety, always moving – hardly the normal characteristics of peasant groups. Who were these people? Historians have suggested that the site of Bachkovo was chosen to offset a group of local heretics; a centre of Orthodox faith would help counter their heresies. The villages must have been peopled by Paulicians, the sect banished to the Balkans from Armenia in about the ninth century.

That would explain too Anna Comnena's observation – restless, pious exiles with no attachment to anywhere but the land they'd left behind. But there are none left now. By the nineteenth century the Paulicians and Armenians had all but assimilated.

Not long after midday I came across a man with a goat. I'd heard his tuneless whistling through the trees long before I saw him. He was standing in front of a simple homestead and his goat was pissing against the bare earth. When he saw me he started talking in low, unsurprised tones as though carrying on a conversation we'd interrupted earlier. But I couldn't understand a word.

'Niema Bulgarski,' I said.

'Turkski?'

'Turkski, yok.'

'Russki?'

'Nyet.'

We'd reached an impasse. I admired his goat in Russian and he smiled. Then we stood in silence and watched it nose through the leaves for food.

'Armenski,' he announced.

'Armenian! You speak Armenian?'

'I am Armenian.'

But before I could put any of my questions about how he came to be there, or to make any link, however tenuous, with the Paulicians, his easy-going manner suddenly snapped. He pointed into the forest. A figure was approaching through the trees.

'Oh! You must leave!'

'Who is it?'

'Wife – quick, go!'

He ran inside his house and came out clutching a broom and, as I left, was frantically sweeping the yard.

I carried on into the hills and soon the silence of the forest had cocooned me from this strange figure. I didn't envy that man and consoled myself that had he been a strict Paulician, he would not have married at all. It was a miracle – or rather a hypocrisy – that the sect survived so long.

Of all the things Armenians helped introduce to Europe from the East, none had quite the impact as the Paulician heresies. Unwelcome in Armenia, the Paulicians were exiled to the Balkans in the ninth century. There they persisted with their deviant beliefs, a continuing irritation to the Byzantine authorities. In 1130, the time of the first Gothic cathedrals, Christian heresy appeared in earnest for the first time in Europe. It spread rapidly, divisively, turning people against the Church, and Church against people. Anxious synods were called in Rome; whispers of heresy filled the markets and monasteries. Women who refused the advances of priests were branded heretics and tortured. The Papal authorities resorted to a sweeping campaign of inquisition and sponsored a series of crusades to flush out the heretics who named themselves Cathari, the 'pure'.

Unlike earlier crusades, these ones, which began in 1208, were not to some far-flung dusty land, but to southern France. In one purge, fifteen thousand heretics were slaughtered; many others were blinded, mutilated, dragged behind horses and lined up for archers to use as targets. For the first time, Europe was tearing itself apart over an idea. The idea was Manichaean dualism, and its progress can be traced from France back to the Balkans, back to Armenia, to a whole host of ancient roots. In Europe its success depended on two persuasive notions: the inherent corruption of any established Church, and the prevalence of demons whose wicked ambitions haunted the lives of every medieval peasant. For dualism addressed the question which has troubled theologians and philosophers from Job to Kant: if God is all-powerful and all-good, how can the existence of evil be explained?

The dualist world is classified by two elements, spirit and matter. Spirit is God's domain, and is good; matter is Satan's, and is bad. Everything that is associated with the visible world is therefore evil. The problem began when Satan and his rebel angels were cast out of Heaven. In retaliation they created the material world, the mountains and oceans, the beasts and the trees. But when it came to man, Satan found he was unable to breathe life into him. So an agreement was reached with God to share this creature: God provided the spirit, Satan the body. Because man combines both elements, his mortal life is a continuous torment. His corporeal desires vie constantly with the better wisdom of his soul. He is a divine spirit entombed in an evil body and the earthly duty of all is to do everything to end this devilish conspiracy. Fierce piety and iconoclasm were one thing, but dualists went too far for the Church authorities. These were people, after all, who scorned not only all images, but also any elevation of the Virgin. They abhorred the Cross which was the symbol of Christ's earthly suffering. And the Church itself, its buildings and clergy, was nothing more than a corrupt and worldly agency pandering to the whims of the devil.

For most dualists, eating and drinking were necessary evils. But marriage and all that encouraged procreation ranked as great sins: having children extended the domain of the demiurge, creating new bodies, new prisons for the spirit. Conversely, non-procreative sex was permitted and, by all accounts, indulged with vigour. Sexual orgies were standard practice; many dualists held that the body was intrinsically evil below the navel so it didn't matter what you did with it. The French called all heretics Bougres, after the Bulgarian Bogomils, and from this, with the suspicion that dualists also promoted sodomy, came the verb 'bougrire' and the English 'to bugger'.

The notion of spirit and matter, and the eternal conflict between them, is common to all sorts of religious traditions: Buddhist, Gnostic, Zoroastrian, Manichaean. In the early Christian years it emerged in dozens of bizarre sects, each adopting their own rites, antagonizing the authorities, but all having an essentially dualist belief. Among the more austere were the Montanists, famous for luring women from their husbands, who were known to receive their prophecies through dreams, to hate their own breath, eat radishes and actively seek out persecution. When the Emperor Justinian came after them, they burnt themselves alive.

The Borborites, the 'muddy ones' (so called from the Greek for 'mud'), considered any show of bodily hygiene as unnecessary pampering; they used both semen and menstrual fluid for their liturgy. The Carpocratians could not achieve salvation unless they had experienced every known sin. There were also the Helvidians and Paternians who were well-known for licentiousness. The Adamites were expected to pray naked, as if still in the Garden, and the Messalians required initiates to pray until the evil spirits bubbled out of their mouths; they would then fast for three years, after which, purged and pure, they could indulge again in all manner of bodily pleasures.

What really went on in these sects is hard to discover – to many of them written records were also evil, and those reports that do survive were largely put around by their detractors. The Paulicians, strict dualists though they were, appear to have been more temperate in their rites and did leave for posterity a curious Armenian text entitled *The Key of Truth*. Most of the sects had been whittled away by the seventh century; those that hadn't were swamped by the

Arab invasions, and many dualists became Muslim. But for the Armenians, ever the exception, clinging to Christianity in the mountains, the spread of Islam spawned a dualist revival and saw the rise of the Paulicians.

No less attuned than previous dualists to the mantles of the devil, the Paulicians' *The Key of Truth*, written in Armenian, identifies twelve guises of evil:

1. Serpents
2. Ravens (for their love of lewdness)
3. Beasts of the field
4. Calves (or seals – the Armenian word is the same)
5. Light
6. Women (who adorn themselves and chase men)
7. Men (who agree to things)
8. Teachers of the school
9. Clerics of the church
10. Apostles
11. Bishops
12. Monks (who love vegetables and damp places)

'We have only mentioned twelve,' warns *The Key of Truth*, 'in order not to be tedious to you, my loved ones.' But the list is enough to show the Paulicians' particular disdain for the Church. In Armenia that was hardly surprising – ordination was a hereditary right and dioceses were often run like little fiefdoms. For the laity, isolated and pious, Manichaean dualism was an appealing alternative.

Nowhere else were the two strands of early Christianity more evenly intertwined than in Armenia. From the west, from Byzantium, the creed had come wrapped in gold-threaded cloth, with gilded icons and teams of saints to honour. It was a pompous, authoritarian institution, dishing out Christianity from above. Such a faith was never any more than a gloss on the bucolic paganism of the Armenian peasants. They were steeped in less worldly beliefs, Zoroastrian and Manichaean among them. The Christian evangelists from the south impressed them more: holy men from Syria 'with words like honey'. The desert had nurtured a purer, more austere faith and it was this strand of Christianity that was closest to dualism.

The established Church in Armenia lashed out at the heretics: they must forfeit their land, have their foreheads branded with the image of a fox and be ham-strung if they relapsed, and, if all else failed, be banished to the far west of the Byzantine world. In Thrace, the exiled Armenians and dualists dominated Philippolis (now Plovdiv), the region's capital. It was a dumping-ground for Byzantium's misfits, Anna Comnena's 'polluted waters', a handy buffer for the Scythian invaders who would periodically sweep down from the north. And when the Crusaders passed through the town it was the Paulicians who alone did not flee.

The Knights Templar, with their esoteric traditions and strange rites, clearly had strong dualist leanings. One account tells how they were required, among other things, to spit on the Cross. They had encountered Paulicians and Armenians not only in Philippolis but also near Antioch – Templar and Armenians, as we have seen, even joined forces to take the castle of Baghras. It is popularly supposed that the Templars 'caught' their heresies from the Cathars in France, but in fact it may well have been the other way round. Cloth and rug merchants also helped spread dualism and, in Europe, heretics were often called 'weavers'. Already in the thirteenth century, the Armenians were selling carpets widely.

Many scholars contend that dualism spread not only from the Paulicians but also from Messalians and others. But it is telling that of all the various names used for heretics in western Europe, the only one with a specific Eastern derivation was Publicani, a Latinization of Paulician. At Vezelay, seven Publicani were burnt alive in 1167. Even in England a number of Publicani were discovered and had their foreheads branded.

The heresies didn't last. The Bogomils, Balkan dualists spreading from Paulician and Messalian roots, were crushed by the Turks. Rome succeeded in ridding itself of the Cathars, the Paterenes and the Albigensians. But the Paulicians survived in the Balkans as they did in Armenia itself. They survived in the same way the Armenians have always survived, and for which they have always been per-secuted: by doggedly refusing to conform. As late as 1717, Lady Mary Wortley Montagu rode into Plovdiv and wrote home that she had found 'a sect of Christians that called themselves Paulines'. And in the mid-nineteenth century, Plovdiv's Russian consul reported Paulicians in the city. Perhaps the hen-pecked goatherd was indeed a lapsed dualist.

\*

I arrived back in Plovdiv the same evening. The town was no longer a hot-bed of heresy, but Bulgaria's second city. I walked through the old town looking for Hagop Vardanian. The evening was dark and damp and the light spilled out of a small gallery breaking up on the cobbles. Two Armenian artists, Krikor and Magardich Kasapian, were exhibiting their work. They were identical twins. They wore the same overcoats, the same grey sweaters, grey shoes, had the same beards and the same piercing brown eyes.

Their work was mainly dry-point prints and each plate, they explained, took about a month to make. Things were a little easier now but under the communists they had had to mix their own inks and work the plates with re-cut dentists' tools. One of the prints – 'the Story of the Coin' – had won Bulgaria's major graduation prize.

I was talking to the twins about their work and about their parents' flight from near Bursa during the massacres, when Hagop Vardanian burst into the gallery.

'Ah good! So you found them.' He took me conspiratorially by the arm and led me away. 'They are good, these pictures, very good, don't you think?

'Yes. And very Armenian.'

'Why do you say that?'

'The detail – that microscopic detail. It's like the *khachkars* or the Armenian filigree smiths in Cairo or Beirut. Why is it, do you think, that Armenian art tends to be so intricate?'

'To try and stop the demons getting in!'

'Like the Paulicians.'

'Yes,' he smiled. 'Like the Paulicians.'

# 11

When I was in Patna four Armenians who had pre-
viously made a trip to Bhutan, came from Danzig.

Tavernier, *Travels in India* (seventeenth century)

From Plovdiv I took a train up to Sofia. Waking on the first morning
there, it was so silent that I thought I was going deaf. No more
mass of honking traffic, no more screeching bazaars and hemmed-in
buildings, none of the happy-go-lucky chaos of the east. Here was
a capital that was hushed and ordered. Inspection towers hung over
the traffic lights and trams hummed along pre-ordained routes. With
the order lingered a strange sense of anxiety. Beside runway-wide
boulevards, state buildings stared down from their neo-classical
façades: a thousand pompous windows beneath a thousand frowning
pediments. And under their gaze, under these stern cliffs, figures in
overcoats and blue berets criss-crossed the streets in a nervous tide
of activity.

But I liked Sofia. I liked its grey melancholy. It didn't matter that
it seemed stuck in an eternal, sleepy afternoon in the late 1940s. If
there was anger and tension, and I knew there was, it was hidden
discreetly inside the overcoats. The faces revealed nothing but a tired,
old-world charm.

The Armenski Dom was no different. Bulgaria's Armenian community, whittled down to about twenty thousand, was neatly rep-

resented in a compact four-storey building: the church somehow grafted on to the ground floor, the first-floor clothes exchange, the second-floor club (hard wooden chairs, Armenian tricolours, maps of the old country), and on the top floor the office of the Armenian newspaper, distributed to all of the fifteen Bulgarian towns where Armenians still lived.

The newspaper staff put me on to Sevda Sevan, an Armenian writer, and I arranged to meet her in the bar of the press club in the centre of town. The press club was decorated in regulation brown, Eastern European brown. The walls were dark, stained-teak brown, the curtains potato brown, the chairs and table-cloths tobacco brown. Even the red border of the carpet looked brown. A journalist sat alone at a table in this caramel saloon. Watching him, watching his chin sink slowly between the lapels of his brown suit, I imagined the whole of central Europe, from the Baltic to the Balkans, nodding off, falling slowly into a muddy-brown tide of post-communist torpor.

But beneath the brownness were centuries of ethnic hatreds and Sevda Sevan's Armenian anger was born of these. She burned with the bitter brilliance of the exiled and in her flat showed me at once some of a trilogy she was writing, named *Rodosto, Rodosto*.

'Rodosto was my grandfather's town. He had twenty-two farms but the Turks drove him out in 1915.'

'To Bulgaria?'

'No, south. He was marched south with his family. His wife was the first to die and he carried her for three days before she could be buried. He dug her grave with his bare hands. Bad water killed another three of his children on the way.'

'Did they reach Syria?'

'They got to Deir ez Zor. When he reached Deir ez Zor, my grandfather had only one daughter left. She found work with an Arab family, but died after she ate an infected egg. My grandfather had nothing more to lose. He escaped with two Rodosto friends. They walked at night, back up the Euphrates. First one, then the other man died. But my grandfather was always strong – he was born with all his teeth; all the males of his family have teeth when they are born. He walked all the way back to Rodosto and when he got there, when he reached his old house, he wept for the first time. "I will fill this house again with children." He had two daughters and when one was expecting his first grand-child, he died. I was that child.'

Sevda had hardly drawn breath. All the time she had been talking, sitting with her back to her desk, running through the horrors of her story, with her eyes feverish and her foot swinging against a chair leg, she clutched, in the long fingers of her right hand, a skull.

She glanced at it, as though holding a skull was nothing unusual. 'Oh yes, that. Someone gave it to me at Ras ul-Ain. You went there?'

'Yes. I went to Ras ul-Ain.'

'Look at the flat cranium – it is Armenian. When I write I have this skull always sitting above my desk.'


Before leaving London, I'd tried to arrange a Soviet visa for Armenia but had had no luck. On the day of my departure an Armenian friend arrived from Jerusalem and told me she knew someone at the Soviet embassy. I was to go to the Brent Cross Shopping Centre and meet there a lady in a dark overcoat. She would be waiting by the fountain. She would arrange whatever I required. She was, of course, Armenian.

I followed the instructions to the letter. Between the hot-house ferns of the fountain and Freeman Hardy Willis, I handed over a copy of my papers and asked for the visa to be telexed to the Soviet embassy in Sofia. I thanked her, then stepped back out into the North London snow. That evening I took the train to Venice.

In Sofia, the stony-faced Russian women shrugged and said 'Nyet'. They told me to fill in a form. I said I wanted to see the consul himself, and they said, 'Nyet, nyet!' But I went to see the consul anyway and he smiled and talked about Europe and the car industry and said, oh yes, he had received a letter about me; the visa would come in just a few days. So the experiment with the Armenians, of leaving London without any visas, had worked, up to a point.

I left the embassy with an Italian who'd been trying to get a visa to visit a girl in Kiev. We took the tram back through the park to the city centre. Sergio was also visa-less, but did not seem discouraged. He loved Bulgaria. The end of communism had opened up a whole new world for him; he now came here whenever he could. 'Cheap! Oh, it is so cheap!'

In the Black Sea resort of Varna he had discovered that, for a dollar a day you could take a room by the sea and for a dollar more you could ply the local girls with Bulgarian sauvignon and take them to your room and do whatever you liked. 'Look, I am over forty. In

Italy it is not easy for me to get young girls. Here it is no problem.'
We went to a canteen restaurant. A black student stood with us
at the counter.
'Where are you from?' asked Sergio.
'I am from Ghana, Africa.'
'That explains why you are so brown!'
I shrugged a mute apology to the Ghanaian, but he was laughing.
When we sat down, Sergio stopped talking and applied himself
wholly to eating.
'He must be hungry,' said the Ghanaian.
'Italians do everything very fast,' I explained. 'They walk fast,
speak fast and eat fast.'
Sergio dabbed his mouth with a napkin, and smiled. 'But when I
make love, I am verrry, verrry slow!' He turned to the Ghanaian.
'Look, maybe you can explain. Two weeks ago in Paris I was with
a girl from Cameroon. A cosmetologist. Twenty years old. Verrry
beautiful.'
The Ghanaian nodded eagerly.
'We are in bed, and it is good. It is delicious!'
'Yes?'
'But afterwards, all night she wants to hug me.'
'Yes?'
'I tell her – please! I must have a little freedom in the night, but
she wants to hold me. I think maybe she has psychological problem
or something.'
The Ghanaian frowned.
'Maybe she missed her family. So I say: "I think maybe you miss
your family in Africa." And she gets out of bed and says: "We will
not meet again." What happened? I do not understand it.'


Talking to various people in Sofia that week, I became aware that
the Armenians had been a much greater presence in the Balkans
than I'd first imagined. I had the name of an Armenian professor, a
linguist from Sofia University, and one evening sought him out
among the maze of apartment blocks on the edge of town. I spent
the whole evening with Professor Selyan in his study. He was driven
by that particular Armenian love of signs and codes and intricate
things. His imagination was mapped out with toponymic mysteries;
it echoed with the phonemes of at least four languages and was

scattered with the loops and tails of three different scripts. He had channelled his skills into developing a speed typing system which, using phonetic bites rather than individual letters, claimed the extraordinary speed of nine hundred and fifty characters per minute. But his real energies were put to tracing Armenia in his adopted region. He waved a sheaf of papers at me.

'Here – a list of Hungarian names of Armenian origin! Here – a map of dualist toponomy, Paulician and Bogomil villages!'

We spread the map out on the floor. The Bogomil symbols were scattered loosely over Macedonia, the Paulician ones concentrated around Plovdiv and in the southern Danube plain. I counted five Bogomil sites – but there were eighteen for the Paulicians. I had heard one theory that the Bogomils were simply Paulicians under a different name and told him about a group of half-ruined Armenian churches I had found near the Serbian–Macedonian border.

The professor's dialect studies had revealed even more Armenian clues, more of the Armenian motif. In western Bulgaria, many common words are of Armenian origin, including, in those mountains, one of the most common: '*andach*' or forest. On the Serbian border is a mountain named Vartanik Chemerneck – 'Vartanik lives on' in Armenian – after the Armenian fifth-century hero. And the professor had a bold claim about Vasile Levsky, Bulgaria's greatest national hero.

'He was of Paulician origin.'

'How do you know?'

'He came from a Paulician area, here, just north of Plovdiv. One of his ten secret names was an Armenian one. And he knew Armenian – in the Paulician dialect.'

'I'm sure the Bulgarians wouldn't thank you for that.'

'Maybe not. But it is the same with the Bogomils. Scholars here say: "Look how they influenced western Europe!" They never say that they were themselves influenced by Armenians.'

Even in the nineteenth century, there were one hundred and forty thousand Armenians in Bulgaria, despite most of the Paulicians having merged into the general population. By then the Armenians had become doctors, jewellers, architects, cobblers and, as always, merchants.

Armenian merchants travelled huge distances – between Persia and Poland, Istanbul and Amsterdam. In Plovdiv I had found the house of an old Armenian merchant, its first-floor living rooms painted with scenes of his commercial adventures: the Rialto bridge in Venice, Stockholm, Lisbon, the Pharos at Alexandria. The merchant's name was Hintlian, suggesting an origin even further afield, in Hindustan or India. No other people have plied these trade routes quite so extensively as the Armenians. For well over a thousand years they had been pushing through the Balkans on merchant ventures. But if the Middle Ages were the age of the Armenian mason – working at the highest level in Poland, the Levant, Moorish Spain, Seljuk Turkey – then perhaps the seventeenth and eighteenth centuries were the apogee of the Armenian merchant.

It was then that Armenians had sole rights to trade in Russia, when they dominated Polish and Ukrainian trade with Persia (where they enjoyed a complete monopoly on the silk trade), when Armenian ships sailed the Indian Ocean, when Armenians were powerful players in the three great Islamic courts of the age – Ottoman, Safavid and Mogul. At this time they also moved with ease around the Ethiopian throne, the Burmese throne, and were granted free passage on all the ships of the East India Company (who were so keen for Armenian favour that they agreed to build a church wherever more than forty of them had settled). When in 1707 Catholic missionaries limped up on to the Tibetan plateau, they found in Lhasa five well-established Armenian merchants. Armenians had been trading deep into China since the time of the Mongol khans. Even before Marco Polo, William of Rubruck arrived at the court of the Great Khan to find there an Armenian who'd travelled four thousand miles on foot, from Jerusalem. Armenians were in Calcutta before it was even a trading city. And in the seventeenth century pearls bought by Armenians in Java were sold by Armenians in Amsterdam.

Armenian caravans were famously austere. Though Isfahan merchants, for instance, lived in fabulous style, when they travelled for trade they travelled simply. They lived off smoked buffalo and biscuit, and took line for fishing in the rivers. If they heard of another Armenian caravan in the desert they would trek two or three days to meet them; then there would be wine and singing and stories. But otherwise it was days of flat horizons and camels' legs, nights in bare rooms in the *hans*. When finally they reached Paris or Genoa they would buy trinkets – mirrors or enamel to use for barter on the way home. Sometimes they would be gone for two years or more and if they did not recoup their outlay they would, out of shame, simply not return home.

The French traveller Tournefort recalled an Armenian making a deal in Erzurum. First the two parties place on the table their bags of money, the sight of which 'makes them sooner agree'. Then one by one the various goods are laid out. There follows a great deal of noise and shouting which mounts rapidly until they are pushing each other quite violently. Just as it seems they are 'ready to cut one another's throats', they squeeze hands – so hard that they both cry out. When an agreement is reached, the whole party – buyer, seller, dragoman, mediator – bursts into laughter. There is an oft-quoted Oriental adage about it taking three Greeks to get the better of a Jew, but three Jews to get the better of an Armenian. The Armenians traded in the same way that they do everything – with passionate intensity. The same questing spirit that sent them earlier burrowing into mathematics, into forging *khachkars*, into mounting a church dome on a square base, drove them, in exile, thousands of miles across Asia in search of trade. There was always something, some curiosity, some fearlessness that drove them on.

Professor Selyan sat forward in his armchair. His arms spun wildly. He was explaining how an atomic plant near Sofia was sited at an old Paulician village, as was the most horrible of the communists' concentration camps, Belyne, once Bely Pavlikian, after the Paulicians.

'When I finish my work at the university – this is how I'll spend my time, with these.'

The professor flicked a hand at the scholar's chaos around him, the stacks of books on the floor, the mass of information, the maps, the clues to history and its deceptive fossil patterns.


Tanya Markovska, who for a few days rented me a room in central Sofia, was a squat, kind old lady with ill-fitting teeth and a vermilion wig. She loved literature and had rows of leather-bound volumes – Dostoevsky, Tolstoy, Byron, Proust, Dumas, though I never saw her reading.

Long ago Tanya Markovska had been widowed; her husband had disappeared during some purge or other. Since then, the outside world had become a place of unimaginable horror. She never went out. The sun that reached her was diffused and grey, creeping through the fine mesh of her curtains. Her life was lived through others.

On entering the crepuscular flat, I would wait for her flame-topped head to bob around my door. 'So, you have come back, monsieur? It is very cold outside – yes? You will become ill!'

And as I left: 'You are going out? But monsieur, it is dark! You will become lost . . . attacked!'

'I'll be careful.'

'Where is the key?'

I would take it out of my pocket for her to see.

'No, monsieur! Never take her from the pocket. Back in the pocket!'

Several trips to the Soviet embassy that week yielded no more news from the Brent Cross Armenian in London. With my Bulgarian visa about to expire, I would have to leave the country, to continue north by train to Bucharest.

Tanya Markovska was appalled. 'Romania! You cannot go to Romania.'

'Why not?'

'Bandits! They are bandits and . . . and animals!'

'Don't worry, I'll be all right.' I bent down to clasp her hand and say goodbye.

But walking to the station, I realized that Tanya Markovska had coloured Romania with a little of her gloomy prejudice.


The train squeezed out of the Iskar gorge and into the wide Danubian plain. Bony limestone cliffs fell away to fleshy fields and a long horizon. We pulled in and out of the station at Pavlikeni, one of the old centres of Armenian Paulicians. At Gorna, slip-coaches were coupled to the train, marked for places that seemed impossibly distant: Minsk, Kiev, Moscow.

On the platform, a gypsy woman grappled with her drunken husband. She wore a dress of black and canary yellow and had about her a fierce beauty; the last of the sun lit up the wild fringes of her hair. Up and down she walked, gripping the man's armpit while his knee-joints flexed and folded beneath him. She yanked him, slapped him, shouted at him, but his head flopped puppet-like from side to side. He grunted like a pig. Soon, I knew, he would be asleep.

A frantic figure ran past them. Two leather bags flapped from his shoulder; a clutch of airline labels flapped from the bags. He wore a velvet-collared overcoat and had the kind of half-smart look of a Western journalist.

He looked up at the train. 'Bucharest?' he asked in a breathless American accent.

'Yes,' I said and helped him haul his bags into the compartment.

'Jesus, I thought I'd missed it, you can never tell with these trains in Eastern Europe, they're a law unto themselves. Phew!'

I asked him if he was a journalist.

'No, an attorney. In the adoption business.'

'The adoption business?'

'Yeah.'

Sitting down, he pushed his glasses up his nose and opened one of the bags. 'Got involved a few months back and was just swept along by it – see, here I got a lap-top and there a battery bubble-jet printer – that's brand new, seventeen hundred dollars. And there – a camcorder to video the kids.'

The train lurched forward, creaking out of Gorna towards the Danube and the Romanian border. The attorney took off his coat.

'So how does it work, this adoption business?'

'Well, I find the kids and fix all the red tape. In the US there's a real shortage of adoptable kids – five years and fifty thousand dollars in some states but I keep my costs down and do a link for three or four, maybe five. Most just want a white kid and Romanians, Hungarians, Yugoslavs are all Caucasian. Albanians can be a problem – some are a bit olive-skinned. Romania's closing up but next up I'm gonna try Siberia. Straight flight right over the pole . . .'

'And AIDS – isn't that a problem in Romania?'

'Yeah, but I got a pack: six and a half hours to test a whole orphanage for twenty-five hundred dollars, ninety-six per cent reliable.'

'And how many are positive?'

'Only about two or three per cent in the north but around Bucharest maybe thirty.'

By now he'd emptied most of his bags. In his enthusiasm to show me the tools of the trade he'd turned the compartment into what looked like a den of contraband: a video camera and a polaroid, computer paraphernalia, bags of ground coffee and cigarettes, and the strange phials of chemicals and the hypodermics of the AIDS pack. He looked content, surrounded by his hardware and supplies, like an angler checking his tackle before a day on the water. He felt good knowing that none of this stuff was available anywhere in the

Eastern Bloc, that soon he would be laying it all out in another Romanian orphanage, setting up another link.

He felt good until, clanging slowly over the Danube 'Friendship' bridge, the Romanian border guards pulled open the door. The attorney was a few dollars lighter by the time they left, stuffing their tunics with cigarettes. But he took it with a flick of his wrist. 'Par for the course. I done this trip so often I know how to deal with them.'

'So what do you plan for this journey?' I asked.

He picked up one of the files. 'I got into the handicapped stuff now, that's real satisfying, be seeing this lot tomorrow near Bucharest. Here's one, a real cutie, has a harelip but that's correctable. This one's a mess, had a fifteen-year-old gypsy mother and some sort of mental damage, won't be able to do much with him.'

'And you enjoy this work?'

'Enjoy it? Sure! I tell you there's nothing more satisfying than watching those kids get off the plane back home – of course I could work like a sleaze and bring back twenty in one go and charge maybe ten or more for a link, that's close on quarter of a million each trip.' He paused, considering that. 'But no, you gotta remember, I'm doing this for the kids.'


Bucharest was very dark and very cold by the time we arrived in the early hours. The attorney loaded his equipment into a taxi and headed for the Intercontinental. I stumbled across from the station and into the first hotel I could find. It was full of fun-loving Turks. They sat in the foyer with bottles of beer; their Turkish lira went a long way here. I found my room on the third floor. I could hear the banter of the Turks trickle up the stairwell. As I fumbled with the key, a woman came out of the shadows.

'You have madame?' she purred.

'I'm tired.'

'I very good madame for you.' She pressed against me and I felt her fingers flit lightly over the front of my jeans.

'No. Goodnight,' I said and closed the door.

I flicked the light-switch. Nothing. The basin taps produced only a distant, peristaltic knocking; a lump of fallen plaster lay on the bed. Through the window the sky above the city had only the lightest street-lamp glow. Romania seemed a lot more broken than Bulgaria.

# 12

Do not recall with grief the beautiful hair of the
convict's head.

Mullah Nasrudin

The first thing I had to do in Bucharest was to sort out my Soviet
visa. I went to the central post office to phone the Brent Cross
Armenian, to have the visa issued here rather than in Sofia. But it
was not so straightforward. In London they told me she was in
Moscow. In Moscow they told me she was in Yerevan, and there
were no lines at all to Yerevan. In fact, to secure any line out of
Romania was a battle in itself. After two fruitless days among the
phone cabins of the post office, I was getting nowhere. I went to
one of the big hotels. They had dozens of international lines and I
befriended one of their operators; for a couple of drinks she opened
up a line for me.

I left messages with Armenians in London, Moscow and Jerusalem. There was no sign of the Brent Cross Armenian. The whole
thing became absurdly complicated but at the end of day three, I
had done all I could. One of my messages must have got through. I
gave a carton of American cigarettes to my friendly operator and
settled back to wait. In the meantime I went to look for Bucharest's
Armenians.

During a long, lazy morning wandering round the city, I came across the Hotel Hanul Lui Manuc. Billed as Bucharest's 'most famous bar and restaurant', the hotel is in fact a converted caravanserai, dating from 1808, a time when Bucharest bisected some of the great trade routes. Manuc-bey, its eponymous owner, had been an Armenian. I spent a couple of hours in the courtyard of his old *han*, trying to imagine what it would have been like. But I found it hard.

Just outside I had been heckled by a crush of women at the state bread-ovens while inside two waiters dragged some zealous drinker into the kitchens when his hand had slid hopefully across the broad rump of his waitress. A narrow stream of blood ran down his cheek when he stumbled back out.

Perhaps, in the post-Ottoman years of Manuc, food was just as scarce and perhaps his staff had rougher customers to deal with. But at least the place then had a function, a slot in the Armenian network: cobbles ringing with the hooves of packhorses, store rooms full of spices and silks, whispered news of Odessa, of Vienna, of Isfahan. Epoca Ceauşescu had finally cut Bucharest off from that trade, driving the Armenians out or underground. Manuc's *han* was now little more than a cheap theme-bar.

But in the Strada Armeneasca was a more encouraging sign. A white Pontiac crouched outside the Armenian church. With its chrome wheels and Lebanese number-plates, it looked out of place in drab Bucharest. The priest told me it was the car of a Beiruti Armenian who'd driven up from the Levant, across four unfriendly borders, to open up an export deal for cigarettes. The Armenian spirit was seeping back into Romania. Strada Armeneasca has long been the hub of Romania's Armenians. Behind the cluster of Armenian buildings – the church, the library, the museum, the bishop's residence – stood a crumbling baroque villa, built by a long-dead Armenian merchant. The villa's lofty reception rooms (pale peach walls, chipped mirrors, garlanded cornices) were now the offices of the two Armenian newspapers, *Ararat* and *Nor Gyank* ('New Life').

Much of my time in Bucharest was spent in those rooms. I waited there for the distant, unseen wheels to turn and produce my Soviet visa – or refuse it. In frustration I waded through the office's Armenian books and the stacks of back issues and wrote an article for *Ararat* about Ras ul-Ain and Ani. But talking was what really filled the hours. Everyone talked. Like all good newspaper offices, people came in just to talk. Now I can scarcely even remember what was said. It was simply part of the slow rhythm of Bucharest and its stolen pleasures, the relief and anger of a shared complaint or a sudden coupling of hopes. All contact in Romania seemed to run with that same animal undercurrent, straining for consummation, threatening constantly to boil over into something either violent or erotic.

Varujan Vosganian, Armenian representative in the post-Ceauşescu parliament, also put in his hours at the old villa. He was an expansive talker and had the operatic gestures of a natural politician.

'Oh! I am late for parliament,' he exclaimed one afternoon. 'Come, Philip, come and help me fight the communists!'

'I thought you'd got rid of them.'

'If only we could.'

But the parliament was closed and his communists nowhere to be seen. Instead a rally had massed against them in the Piaţa Gheorghe Gheorghiu-Dej – in front of the government buildings. Demonstrators thronged in the square. They lined the scaffolding of the gutted university library and the Securitate office and perched in the boughs of the larch trees. The square itself, epicentre of the 1989 revolution, was a parade of bullet-scarred, burnt-out buildings. It reminded me of Beirut.

Over the sea of bobbing heads, the Romanian tricolour hung from various hand-held poles, flapping limply, like the sails of a becalmed ship. Only a week before I'd been to a similar rally in Sofia. It had been a much more orchestrated affair, the stentorian speeches synchronized with bursts of rock music. That too had been an opposition rally. Despite their revolutions, both Bulgaria and Romania still found themselves lumbered with the old order. The communists had hung on, keeping their support by holding up the head of their leader (in benign Bulgaria, Zhivkov, judicially arrested; in savage Romania, Ceauşescu, shot by a firing-squad).

But this was a mess. There were long silences between speeches. When they did come, the speeches were fanciful straw-clutching affairs: an attempt to cook up something from a political scandal, a call for the return of the king, and constant, lame cries for the resignation of the government. Ceauşescu's control had been so effective that no one but his henchmen had the first idea how to muster political support.

I had lost Varujan in the crowd, but stood with his sidekick, a world-weary Armenian from Bessarabia.

'Words,' he sighed. 'Just words. Some people are ruled by words.'

'But what else can they do?'

He shrugged. 'The parliament has no authority anyway. If it wasn't for the free canteen, none of them would bother going in at all.'

On Sunday I was invited to a memorial lunch in honour of an Armenian doctor.

There are little pockets of central Bucharest, with their rippling cobbles and caryatid doorways, that exist in a pre-Ceauşescu, pre-war cocoon. The doctor's flat, both inside and out, was in one of these. The main room was hung with lumpy oil paintings and dotted with the stick shapes of Art Deco figurines. The walls were painted in various shades of fruit – lemon in the dining room, pale orange in the hall, peeling apricot in the bathroom. Even the guests, none younger than seventy, with their pill-box hats and tweed suits, appeared to have been plucked from the early 1930s.

One old man regaled me with a rambling account of his time in England, four happy years at an English prep school between the wars.

'I loved cricket – could never quite get the rules, but goodness it was fun.' Taking up the fire poker he placed himself before an imaginary wicket. 'Now! Let's see: forward defence . . . on drive . . . off break. Is that right?'

'Very good,' I said. 'Though "off break" is what the bowler does.'

'Bowling – of course! I loved to bowl . . .'

His wife uttered a curt Armenian rebuke and the old man obediently put down the fire poker and said, 'Now, where is that priest?'

'He'll be late,' his wife told him. 'He's doing a wedding.'

'A wedding, eh? Can't remember when I last went to a wedding.'

Nor could I. I don't think I'd ever been to an Armenian wedding. All the gatherings I'd attended had concerned death in some way – funerals in Jerusalem, commemorations of the earthquake or the massacres, laments for Karabagh. And each carried with it all the others, so that each expressed that ever-present Armenian legacy and became a kind of well-rehearsed festival of loss.

When he did arrive the priest's dark, bearded presence filled the room. The old people fell silent and watched him flick open the catch on his suitcase and take out an emerald-green funereal sash. Placing it over his head, he then hurried round the table, boomed a series of prayers, raised a glass of Vietnamese vodka and thrust his fork into a slab of ham. The feast had begun.

Everyone began chattering at once. Within a few minutes I'd counted as many as six different languages: Romanian, Armenian, English, French, Magyar and Turkish. On my right sat an eighty-two-year-old man who'd been driven from Konya in 1915. He was being ribbed about his new wife.

'Given him a new lease of life . . .'

'. . . sends him to bed early.'

'Or an early grave if there's too much of that.'

The old man just smiled fondly and threw back his vodka.

'Is she Armenian?' I asked.

'No, Romanian. My first two wives were Armenian, but this one came along so I thought, why not? She's very pretty and only fifty-three.'

On my other side sat the cricketer, with his news-reel English.

'I'm sorry,' he said. 'You'll have to speak up. This is my bad ear. Stalingrad, you know.'

'Russians or Germans?'

'Germans, the cavalry. Hell of a campaign. Rode to Stalingrad, ate my horse and walked back. Two thousand kilometres, you know. Damned hell, that was. Then the Russians came so I fought for them.'

'And who did you prefer?'

'Didn't like either very much. But I loved the war – loved the horses, loved the danger. Know what the greatest danger was?'

'What?'

He leaned towards me, lowering his voice. 'Syphilis, old chap. Damned hell of a thing. Father died in the First War, no one to tell me. But I kept my hands well scrubbed.'

It was still Easter for the Armenians and intermittently, through-out the meal, the priest would cry the reassuring cry of resurrection. 'Christos hareav! Christ is risen!' at which everyone would raise their glass and drink.

When we had finished, the doctor's sister brought in a cake and placed it in front of the priest. The cake had coloured baubles on it and a single candle. The priest lit the candle and raised the plate. Then he started a long blessing for the life of the doctor. The old people stood and held the rim of the plate and those too old to stand clutched the hands of those who could, so that all were joined in a fragile, geriatric communion. I looked around the table, at the wistful row of faces and the diamond brooches and the silk gloves and hats and realized that this was something almost gone: the last of Romania's Armenians.

'Do you know what decides the character of a people?'

In the *Ararat* newspaper office, we were sitting round the table with the usual group of idle intellectuals, coffee drinkers, polymaths and theorists. Varujan – that is, Varujan the Astronomer rather than Varujan the politician – was expounding his ideas about race.

'Relief,' he explained. 'Relief, landscape and weather. Take the English,' he said, pointing at me. 'In England it is always foggy. In London it is so thick they call the fog 'pea soup'. Everywhere is fog. So what does this tell us?'

'That the English are foggy thinkers?'

'That the English like pea soup!'

'No, that the English are distant. They look at you as if through thick fog – through pea soup.'

'And what about the Romanians?' I asked.

'In Romania, there are little hills – no real mountains. So Romanians love little things. Neat packages. See how much they use diminutives – for coffee, it is *cafelutsa* more than *café*; for cake, *prajiturica* rather than *prajitura*, *cigarica* rather than *cigar*, and so on.'

'And the Armenians?'

Varujan smiled at me. 'You've spent time with Armenians – what do you think?'

I wasn't sure I subscribed to his deterministic theory. 'It's hard to say. Those I've met have been affected more by exile – by the loss of their land – than by the land itself.'

'But what does that do for the character? You must have ideas. Don't be a foggy Englishman!'

I told them that it seemed to me that exile, living in exile, had brought out a certain intensity in the Armenians and how much I admired that intensity. 'But perhaps it's just an attempt to preserve the memory of the land.'

Varujan nodded. 'But you have been to western Armenia – to Van and places – what does that land tell you about the Armenians?'

'Western Armenia is an empty place. It is haunted by the Armenians who have gone. I haven't yet seen Armenians anywhere living on their own land. That is why I want to get to Armenia. But

I can tell you that western Armenia is one of the most beautiful places I have ever been to.'

Varujan shook his head and sighed.

One of the women said, 'Some say that Van is the site for the Garden of Eden.'

'Yes, I've heard that. Do you think Adam was an Armenian?'

'Bound to have been!'

'So when the Armenians were driven from Anatolia, it was as if they were again being driven from Eden, from Paradise. Twice exiled – once by God and again by the Turks. Maybe that makes them twice as alive.'

Varujan countered. 'I think it goes back further than 1915, that intensity. Armenians have always been interested in ideas. Take astronomy—'

'With Varujan,' she teased, 'it's always astronomy.'

'Astronomy was an ancient Armenian art. You know why? Because Armenia is mountains, just mountains. So the Armenians saw only the sky and rocks – everywhere there are rocks in Armenia. So what did they do?'

'Threw them at each other!' said his neighbour.

'They studied the stars. They discovered laws of mathematics. They put the laws and the rocks together and built churches, beautiful churches.'


One day of that week in Bucharest, with no word yet from Yerevan on my visa, I managed to find a book which had eluded me since Jerusalem. There I had only skimmed it but here, in the flat of one of Bucharest's Armenian poets, I managed to give it the attention it deserved. I put aside a whole day to roam between its dusty covers.

*The Life and Adventures of Joseph Emin: An Armenian* had originally been published in Calcutta in the eighteenth century. Emin himself had written it and, were many of its fantastic tales not verified in contemporary sources, might easily be accused of liberal fancy. But instead his life remains an extraordinary part of the Armenian story. No one else, none of the other merchants, monks or military rogues I had read about or met, embodied the Armenian genius quite so well as Joseph Emin. That genius has manifested itself in all sorts of ways, but with Emin it was a kind of charmed bravado, an Armenian *chutzpah*. The world for him was a borderless place in which to move around at will, pursuing a given idea – in his case the emancipation of his own people. (He was, I believe, the model for the enigmatic Armenian in George Borrow's *Lavengro*.)

The story begins more than a century before Emin's birth with Theodorus, his great-great-grandfather. The year is 1604 and Shah Abbas has just defeated the Turks. Returning to Persia through Armenia, the victorious shah took with him every Armenian he could find. Thousands drowned crossing the Araxes river, another forty thousand died from malaria in Mazandaran. The column that wound across Persia's northern wastes, it was said, was three days march from tip to tail. But within a generation the Armenians had become an indispensable part of the Safavid empire. They won from the shah the monopoly of the silk trade. They helped build some of his finest buildings in Isfahan and fought loyally against the Turks.

Theodorus himself settled in Hamadan. His son joined the Persian army and, having been the first to scale the walls during an attack on Baghdad, rose to the rank of colonel. At the age of 110, he died defending his family against five janissaries; he'd disabled two with a club before he fell. A few years later, in 1722, Joseph Emin was born in Hamadan at a time of continuous strife. His mother took him to Calcutta.

Early on Joseph Emin became committed to the idea of liberating Armenia. At the age of seventeen, hoping to learn the skills of European warfare, he worked his passage on a ship of the East India Company and reached London. He was penniless and without friends. He began a miserable hand-to-mouth existence. He ate when he could, picked up odd jobs in the docks, drank porter with the Greenwich stevedores, and took long walks through the strange city. One of these walks led him to St James's Park and there he bumped into Edmund Burke. Emin had no idea who Burke was, but Burke, as he himself recorded in his journal, was so impressed with this Armenian boy that he gave him half a guinea. Later the historian visited him with a list of improving books. On another occasion, Emin met a fellow Armenian, from Aleppo, who was groom to the Earl of Northumberland (later the first duke). Emin was soon sitting with the peer in his drawing room.

'I see', said Northumberland, 'there is some extraordinary thing in your mind; conceal nothing from me.'

Emin recounted his story and his hopes, and by the time he had finished, at one o'clock in the morning, had won over his most loyal patron. (Emin loved his English dukes and, in the Caucasus many years later, fondly recalled the debt he owed the Duke of Richmond for providing him with the pistol that enabled him to blow away the face of a certain Lezgi.)

His military career began under the Duke of Cumberland in France. Billeted to begin with in some distant corps, Emin had soon brokered his way to the general's mess. There he used to dine and tell the officers of his plans to liberate Armenia. And in turn, from them, picked up what he could about the art of warfare. Once peace was made, he went off to join the troops of King Frederick of Prussia, and again was soon to be seen riding beside the king as he toured the camp. The Duke of Marlborough in Westphalia 'called him his Lion and kept him always with him'. For his part, Emin kept with him always the thought of Persia's occupation of Armenia. While prepared to grace the drawing rooms and mess tents of Europe, his heart had never really left the east.

But Emin's first trip to Armenia was a failure. The monks at Edjmiatsin locked him up when he killed one of their dogs. He returned to London a little dispirited. In the salon of Mrs Montagu (whom Emin refers to variously as Most Gracious Queen, Queen of the Universe, and Wisdom of Europe) the Earl of Bath spotted Emin and discovered the reason for the Armenian's dejection. His chief concern at this time was to get an introduction to the court of the Tsar, to seek Russian support for his Armenian campaign. Lord Bath got him the letter and with this began the planning of his next expedition. He obtained another letter from the Archbishop of Canterbury, money from Mrs Montagu, Lady Sophia Egerton and the Duke of Northumberland. The Armenians of Amsterdam pledged their support. He had an audience with Pitt. Even the Prince of Wales, hearing of Emin's efforts, offered help. But the Duke explained, 'He is already provided for. He can have any sum of money he chooses.'

In 1761 he set sail for Russia and, quashing a mutiny en route, arrived in St Petersburg early in 1762. He was soon a part of the court circle, had met Tsar Peter III, and won the support both of Catherine the Great and the Empress Elizabeth Petrovna. (Her father, Peter the Great, had greatly valued the support of the Armenians in his struggle to control the Transcaucasus. He had appointed an Armenian as his personal agent at the court of Isfahan, but the suspicious Persians expelled him when they found that his name –

Israel Ori – concealed a declaration of the Tsar's real intent: *Il sera roi.*)

In the middle of March 1762, Joseph Emin left Moscow by sledge, and headed south across the snowy wastes of Russia. Assured of an alliance with Prince Heraclius of Georgia, it seemed finally as if Emin had all the resources to fulfil his plans. But from here on his narrative becomes a sad catalogue of frustrations, of Caucasian treachery and Armenian in-fighting. His own circumstances fluctuate wildly. At one moment he is in command of twelve thousand men, at another he is wandering alone around the mountains, at night, 'like a cut-purse or murderer'. Sometimes he is welcomed by the Armenians like a prince, at other times his life is threatened. He left Armenia and returned, disillusioned, to India. Joseph Emin died in Calcutta, in 1809.

I have never discovered exactly how my Soviet visa was arranged, but on the sixth day of waiting I rang the embassy and they said, yes, it was there. The consul was baffled. He didn't like Armenians, and why should I want to go there, and why should I pick up a visa from Bucharest?

He stood behind his desk and thumbed the telex. He read out the conditions as if pronouncing sentence. 'In ten days you will fly Bucharest Kiev Moscow. Understand?'

'Yes.'

'You then will fly Moscow Yerevan.'

I nodded.

'On first day of arriving in Soviet Union, you will report to authorities. Understand?'

'Yes.'

'OK. Happy journey. Four US dollar.'

He shook my hand and gave me a small identity card. I could enter the Soviet Union. But I had no intention of going to Moscow, nor to Kiev, nor of taking a plane. Relief gave me a brief sense of omnipotence and, assuming papers would no longer be necessary within the Soviet Union, I set off in buoyant mood to catch a train to Transylvania.

# 13

'His majesty asks who you are?'
'I am a man.'
'What sort of a man?'
'My name is Emin: I am an Armenian.'

Exchange between the escort of King Frederick the Great of
Prussia and Joseph Emin, who became a favourite of the king.

I flicked up the blind and squinted at a grey, frosty morning. Transylvania rolled past the train: muddy homesteads, hobbled horses, the mossy turf of unfenced slopes, pine woods, beech woods, churches, curlicue towers, cement works, sleeper stacks, empty car parks, wide empty roads. During the night we had pulled through the passes of the Carpathian mountains and into one of those pockets of central Europe that defies description. That the loose, capricious mesh of current borders puts Transylvania in Romania means little. It is as much Hungarian as Romanian, as much Catholic as Orthodox. Its people are an exotic blend of Magyar, Romanian, Saxon, Jew, Slav, Gypsy and Székely. And for more than five hundred years Transylvania has been part of the Armenian world, the tip of a tentacle that stretched back to the Transcaucasus and the sacking of Ani by the Seljuk Turks in 1064. The Seljuk invasion created the first of the great waves of Armenian exile. One chronicle of the time records the perennial condition of Armenia lying as it does 'on the crossroads of all the ways, bare and dishonoured, and passers-by devour and abuse it.'

Two hundred years later, the Armenian monasteries had achieved

140

an extraordinary revival. Many of the greatest Armenian monastic buildings were put up at this time and the libraries were busy with scribes and scholars. This, Armenia's 'Silver Age', is one of the unsung glories of the medieval world. But then came the Mongols, and Armenia – innovative Armenia, with its own distinctive architecture, music, mathematics, literature, a thousand years of brilliance – was destroyed for good. Some fled to the Armenian kingdom of Cilicia in the Taurus mountains, but a great number of Armenians went north, spreading gradually around the eastern end of the Black Sea, to the Crimea, Ukraine, Poland, Moldova and eventually, escaping persecutions in the sixteenth century, over the Carpathians into Transylvania. And there were, I'd been told in Bucharest, just a handful left.

In Cluj, I had an Armenian name, a block of flats no one knew and a telephone number. All that day I tried to match them up. By mid-afternoon I'd still had no luck and elected to cut my losses and take the last train to the old town of Armenopolis. But at the station, as a final attempt, I asked a taxi driver who did know the place. He found the block of flats and I found the flat, but there was no one there. Across the landing was another front door bearing the name Oltean. Thinking it perhaps Armenian, I rang the bell. A woman answered. No, she was not Armenian, but what did it matter? I could wait for my friend there. Her husband poured me a large slivovitz.

The Oltean family was Romanian. They watched German satellite television and found Transylvania and its Magyars distressingly primitive. To make me understand just how primitive, Madame Oltean told a joke. Magyars, dumb peasants that they were, never went anywhere without a knife. To a Magyar, she explained, it is inconceivable how anyone else gets by without a knife like theirs. One day a Magyar couple is sitting by the road preparing lunch. A dog comes and steals the sausage from the man. 'Quick!' shouts his wife. 'The dog will eat the sausage!' But her husband is not bothered. 'It's all right. He won't get far.' He taps his pocket. 'I have the knife.'

The Olteans still found the joke funny and laughed heartily and we drank more slivovitz and the afternoon slid into evening. It was nearly nine o'clock before the Armenian returned. We went to his flat and there was more slivovitz and more German TV. He was a plastic surgeon; he'd trained in Rome and had operated once on a cardinal's nose. He had had word from Bucharest of my arrival and had booked me into Cluj's grand, communist hotel. I was too drunk and too tired to explain that I really didn't mind where I slept.

We parted on the hotel steps. He'd take me to Armenopolis in the morning. I muttered my thanks and wandered off through the maze of dimly lit corridors. Outside my room a woman in furs and short skirt was leaning against the wall. A Securitate officer was cajoling her; muffled music was coming from a room beyond them. A policeman lay in a chair on the landing, snoring. The whole place smelt of rotting privilege.

In the morning the desk clerk tried to charge me one hundred dollars for the room; I paid him five. I was probably the only one there who paid anything at all. The plastic surgeon drove me in his white Dacia out of Cluj, north to Armenopolis. It was a damp morning and low cloud swam around the wooded slopes. One or two cars swished past us and we overtook the occasional ox-cart, but there seemed in all little activity in that misty valley.

He drove every Sunday to Armenopolis, which had been renamed Gherla. His mother was buried there and on the back seat he'd wrapped four carnations in a cone of newspaper. The flowers were the same colour as the mysterious building which flanked the cemetery – an innocuous pale pink. 'Three storeys above,' whispered the plastic surgeon as we passed. 'Two below.' The building was one of Transylvania's most notorious prisons; below ground in damp, sunless cells, the Securitate had kept and tortured political subversives.

At his mother's grave he knelt to place the carnations on the ledger. For a moment we stood in silence. A prison guard gazed idly on us from his watch-tower and the drizzle shone like jewels on the mossy headstone. High in one of the scruffy larches a couple of crows squabbled noisily. We stepped back from the grave and wandered around the cemetery. The plastic surgeon trotted out the names of the Armenians like a roll of honour. Here was the bust of Dr Molnar Antol, barrister to the Hapsburgs; there the mausoleum of the wealthy Tuzeş family who had brought carpet-weaving from Anatolia. And scattered between the lines of graves were the sentinel shapes of juniper bushes. The whole place was unnervingly quiet and ordered. Perhaps in this uncertain country the only hope of order is in death – or in a regime that erects pink prisons to keep its people at bay. And perhaps for the Armenians, whose history has been no more than a continuous quest for order, a struggle against an unimaginable chaos, these marshalled plots are cherished more than most. 'To own a grave,' wrote Claudio Magris, 'is to own land.' This cemetery was all that remained for the Transylvanian Armenians; it was their Armenia, a little corner of a country they'd never seen.

Gherla, or Armenopolis, was the first wholly Armenian town I'd been to – not just a quarter or ghetto in someone else's town. In 1700, a group of Armenian merchants raised twelve thousand florins and bought the land from King Leopold I of Austria. It suited the Armenians well, lying on three trade routes – Cluj to Moldova, Braşov to Maramureş, Greece to Poland – and the merchants of Armenopolis prospered. Wine and Persian silks, and sacks of spices from India would stop in the courtyards of Armenopolis on their way north and west. The loads would be broken up and redirected and the footsore Armenians would exchange news about prices and distant wars.

The town grew. The merchants built large houses and Armenian churches and laid the streets out in a tidy grid. They lent money to Maria Theresa and she in turn gave them a painting from the school of Rubens, of Christ being lowered from the Cross. But under Ceauşescu, the Romanians had swept into the town in force. Many of the old villas had been torn down to make space for the workers of a furniture factory. The Armenians' Rubens was now sitting in a vault in Cluj. All but a few of the families were gone. Only in the centre had the old toy-town baroque survived, and nowhere more obviously than in the Armenian cathedral, a lime-green basilica swollen out of proportion by the pious enthusiasm of the merchants.

Evensong was just beginning. A dozen elderly Armenians were scattered thinly among the pews. Near me sat an elderly woman with cotton wool in her ears. I could see her wince at the alien language of the creed, but when it came to the Armenian liturgy, she took out the cotton wool and her shrill responses rose like an aria towards the peeling stucco of the ceiling.

Outside the church I asked a woman about the Armenian priest. She said she'd take me to the presbytery, but first I must be her guest and eat with her family. She was half Magyar, half Armenian and kept reminding me of the Romanian Madame Oltean in Cluj.

'I speak five languages. The Romanians don't speak any except their own. And look' – she pointed through the window at the new housing opposite – 'look what they've done to our town.' She lived in one of the old merchant's houses, with its high ceramic stove and tent-vaulted rooms. She had no German TV, no TV at all, but instead shelves of books on science and literature in three or four different languages. Both these dark-haired women, Romanian and Magyar-Armenian, were about the same age, had a tacit control over their gentle husbands, had good jobs, loved their children, hated the communists, pickled their own vegetables, filled their own sausages, were bright, friendly and amusing. But put them in the same room and I had the impression they'd tear each other to pieces.

In twenty years, the portly Father Saşka had watched fifty-four of Gherla's Armenian families die out. Now there were not enough young people even to marry each other. No, he could not see the next generation being Armenian. All around the hall of the vicarage, his predecessors stared down accusingly from their gilt frames. Where once there'd been a dozen or more Armenian priests in Transylvania there were now just two. I asked him how I could find the other and he pointed on my map to a town some way to the east.

Last year there'd been a third. Father Ferents Diarian had tended to the small Armenian congregation at Dumbraveni. But in March he'd given a mass in honour of the Magyar demonstrators who'd been killed in Tirgu Mures. The authorities came for him the same evening. They burst into his house and took him by the arms. They sat him in a chair and tied his hands and gagged him. They pulled out his nails. Then they beat him with a heavy object until he was dead.

It took six hours to get from Gherla to Gheorgieni, from one Armenian town to the next, from Father Saşka to Father Fogolyan, six hours and four trains. You must take the gypsy train, he'd said. The gypsy train was all there was, the only way across this bumpy, pastoral country. Men with saws lumbered on and off it; women clutched knotted scarves of food, and the Carpathian foothills stretched their mossy tongues towards the mountains.

It was almost dark when the gypsy train finally pulled into Gheorgieni. I walked to the Armenian presbytery but there was no sign of

Father Fogolyàn. I left a note and took a room in an old Austro-Hungarian inn. Downstairs was one long bar, full of smoke and men with crab's-claw moustaches. One sat down heavily at my table. His fingers were yellow and he had floppy, drunken gestures. He leered at me and his eyes slipped in and out of focus. Then, grunting, he settled his head on the table, and started to snore and the girl with him sighed and ran her fingers idly through his hair. Quite suddenly he slumped from the table and his head cracked on the stone. I went round to kneel beside him; the blood was already dripping from his scalp. The girl gave me her neckscarf and I tied it around his head. A car came and took them away, and all the while, among that hazy archipelago of tables, the gypsies had not for a moment interrupted their silent card games.

Next morning I went back to the presbytery and found the elderly Father Fogolyan in his library. He was hunched over a book with a broken binding. The early sun fell through high windows and made tidy oblongs of light on his carpet. The Armenian presbytery had a magnificent library. Shelves and shelves of buckram spines ran up the walls. The whole place was a reliquary for the Armenians' most holy remains: thousands of pages of St Mesrop's script. The word as prop, collected by generations of priests; the word as code, carried in calfskin saddle-bags from one Armenian quarter to the next; the word as thick as blood, binding the strands of the diaspora.

I spent some time looking at the books. Father Fogolyan showed me Abbot Mekhitar's Armenian dictionary of 1733, an Armenian-Turkish dictionary of 1846, titles from Dolian's press in Gherla, the Venice bible of 1687, a hand-coloured Mekhitarian bible of 1733 and the famous Amsterdam bible of 1666. For Fogolyan these books made the whole thing worthwhile; they made him feel he belonged. Only a few months earlier he'd arrived from Venice.

'And how do you find it here?' I asked.

He nodded towards the window. 'See, just across the road? The police station?'

'Yes.'

He bent towards me. 'They tap the phones, you know.' He came away from the window, nodding grimly.

I said, 'You must miss Venice.'

'Oh, no.'

'Why not?'

'The air. I love the mountain air here. I love the crisp mountain air. Venice is such a *damp* city.'

The vicarage was about as damp a place as you could imagine, damp as a cave. Moisture streaked the walls and hung in the air. It settled on the musty boxes of clothes sent for poor children by Fogolyan's friends, the Venetian nuns. It spotted the pages of the books and cultured fungus on their covers. In one corner a tin bucket sat beneath a leak in the ceiling. Father Fogolyan looked sadly at his books and ran his fingers along their spines.

'I need a mackintosh,' he muttered. 'But I don't think the diocese will pay.'

'It can't be that expensive.'

'Oh, but it is – the government charge very high duty.'

'On raincoats?'

'Coat? Not coat! Macintosh – Macintosh computer! To catalogue the books. These are very rare books, you know. They must be catalogued!'


Father Fogolyan had heard about Armenians in the village of Frumoasa. I took the train on down the valley to Miercurea Ciuc and spent the evening in the dining room of a small hotel. A group of fat, anxious men sat at one end, huddled near the radiator.

'Communists,' whispered the waitress. 'Listen to them talk: "We must have good German telephone system. Telephones are the first step to recovery." Telephones! They think German telephones will save them. Nothing will save them. Not now . . .'

The morning was frosty again, the sky a wide expanse of milky blue. I walked out of town and found a straight road avenued by plane trees. It was good to walk in such country. The mist thinned and the sun crept up over the ridge. One or two carts creaked past me, rattling towards market; beneath the silhouette of a church tower two horses hauled a plough through the loamy furrows. Leaving the main road, I took a track towards the hills.

For some days I'd been trying to work out what it was that gives Transylvania's landscape its strange beauty. Something to do with the low hills and their crowns of wild forest, and the way one or two trees always strayed down the lower slopes, like grazing deer. It was oddly seductive and I found myself being pulled unconsciously past the straggling trees, up the spongy slopes and into the forest. In the shadow of the conifers, I crested the hill and found a small clearing. I sat and pulled out the last of a stock of spiced sausages I'd bought in Istanbul. Originally meant as gestures of goodwill, these sausages had begun to take on an intrinsic value. What use were my hundred-dollar bills in beaten Romania beside this sausage? Beautiful sausage! I pulled out my knife and began to feel like a true Magyar.

Across another valley and another ridge and round the frayed skirts of a larger forest and there below was the mossy orange patchwork of Frumoasa's rooftops. Like many of the villages in the area, Frumoasa was made up largely of Csángó, a sub-group of the Székely people. Meaning simply 'wanderer' in Magyar, the Csángó were religious dissenters, outsiders, persistently hounded by the Church for their non-conformist beliefs. They had a lot in common with the Armenians.

Peter Zakharias had been Frumoasa's tailor. He was now an elderly man with slow movements, and tired eyes that had squinted over too many seams. He had just finished shaving when I tapped on the pane of his garden door. He let me in and packed away his badger brush, his soap stick, his strop and blade, patted his cheeks, smoothed down his moustache and poured some coffee from the stove. For forty years he had cut the cloth for the good burghers and farmers of the valley. He had tailored in Cluj and as a boy had spent a few terms at the Armenian school in Vienna. But otherwise his entire life had been spent here in Frumoasa. Two years earlier his wife had died and now he lived alone.

Everything in his house was ascribed its place. There was something compulsive about his neatness: drawers divided into compartments for his shaving kit, for his sartorial props – thimbles, needles and shears; the unused parlour with the curtains closed, the clean antimacassars, the seven treasured Armenian books and the squared-off stacks of Armenian newspapers – *Nor Gyank* posted up every week from Bucharest. The whole place had the air of somewhere tidied before a long journey.

'I have a picture of English!'

'Show me.'

He went to the seven books and pulled out an Armenian history.

'Mr Lud is his name.'

'Lud?'

'Yes, Mr Lud. Here it says he was "a good friend of the Armenians".'

'Show me.' The picture showed a fine figure in frock coat and lion's-mane sideburns. 'Lord Gladstone,' read the caption; the Armenians had ascribed him a peerage.

'Yes, as you say, Mr Lud!'

Peter Zakharias returned the book and reached into a drawer. From it he pulled a small box, and from the box an envelope containing a more recent, dog-eared photograph. It showed a young couple. They looked happy and full of life, he in homburg hat holding an ox on a chain; she with loops of dark hair and a dress of white cotton. Peter Zakharias looked at it and sighed. 'We were digging the well in the garden.'

'Tell me, how did your family first come to be in Transylvania?'

The question muddled him for a moment. Too big a question, too long a story; he looked away, muttering. Then he took a piece of paper and emphatically drew a small circle: ANI 1064 – then a sweeping arrow up to: CRYM, POLONA, MOLDOVA 1595, TRANSIL-VANIE 1663. He drew another emphatic circle round the last and prodded the paper. 'There – that is how we left Armenia, that is how we came.'

The 'we' hung in the empty house like something shameful. Peter Zakharias gazed through the garden door at his fruit trees and at the well. He was the only one left.


If I move my arm just a quarter of an inch, I will lose it, this last pocket of warmth. I don't think I could bear that after ten hours – ten hours of slow trains and cold waiting rooms, of creeping fatigue and no food, of dark-eyed gypsies eying my bag, covetous Magyars waiting for me to sleep, ten hours over the Carpathians into Moldova to this: two-thirty a.m. and an unlit train in the Siret valley.

The night air rushes through two broken windows, orange lights flit across the seats. Everyone left the train hours ago, everyone except me and a soldier skewed asleep on the floor. I am hungry. Weeks of snatched meals have chipped away at my strength and it's been days since I ate properly, days since I felt warm. Earlier some American cigarettes elicited a lump of cheese and a shot of vodka from the soldier who has now emptied his flask and finished the cigarettes. He is snoring. I'm too cold to sleep, too tired to sleep and if I move my arm just a quarter of an inch . . .

The lights of Suceava fill the windows and the train slows and shudders and stops. I climb down and the station is oddly quiet. There are people huddled together who blink and stare. I wake a taxi driver and sit by the heater in the front seat and doze off. He elbows me awake: the hotel I asked for doesn't exist; another is closed. There is nothing for it but the state hotel, and I am too exhausted to mind. At the night desk is a woman with sultry good looks. She quibbles my papers and says there are no rooms; I know there are rooms.

'I know there are rooms.'

She shrugs.

I know too that anger won't work. But something about the glass cabinets of Moldovan handicrafts, the cigars and whisky and the dollar price tags, the breezy tourist posters of painted monasteries and sun-stabbed woods in summer, conspires with my fatigue and snaps the last thread of self-control. I lean towards her. 'Did you not hear about the revolution they had down in Bucharest?'

She smiles for the first time. She must be used to it. 'You seem nervous.'

From a drawer she pulls a bottle of whisky, pours two large glasses and draws up another chair. OK, she can find a room and there is food if I want it. I ask for a sandwich and we toast the fall of communism. She shows me pictures of her children and we part friends.

Moldova suited the peripatetic world of the Armenians. It was flat and easily traversed, open to the Russian steppe and the underbelly of Poland, to the Balkans and the Alps. From the thirteenth century trade flowed freely. In carrying it the Moldovan Armenians displayed their normal disregard for distance and hardship, the traditional equivalent of cold trains and communist hotels. At one time in Moldova and neighbouring Wallachia, it is said that as many as seventy different currencies were in use. In such borderless conditions, the Armenians thrived. Twice in the second half of the sixteenth century, Armenians sat on the Moldovan throne: two Johns – John the Horseshoe, and John (variously) the Armenian, the Brave, the Heroic, the Bad, the Mad, who in the end was deserted by his own boyars and killed by the Turks. Yet just before these rulers, there had been pogroms. Those Armenians who refused to convert to the Orthodox faith were tied up and bundled into tents, which were then set alight with flaming torches. The Armenian story was acted out in Moldova as everywhere else; in Suceava I came across the now familiar epilogue.

A woman was on her knees in the church in Strada Armeneasca. She was scrubbing the floor. Straightening her back, she said, 'Cemetery. Today they are all at the cemetery.'

Moldova's only Armenian priest was doing his rounds – yesterday was mass in Botosani, today the blessing of the graves of Suceava. A group of widows trailed behind him as he passed from plot to plot, muttering prayers for their dead husbands. It was raining gently and his velvet hat was soon spotted with raindrops. One woman had baked some biscuits and a rice cake which she laid out neatly on her husband's grave; there was a gap on the headstone for her own name. She pushed a candle into the cake and tried to light it but the rain put it out. She lit it again and arched her hand over it, but when she stood up, the rain fell on it again and it went out.

'Oh!' she cried in frustration. 'You see now even the candles won't work.'

In the nineteenth century, she said, Suceava had been half-Romanian, half-Armenian. Before that Armenians were the majority. An Armenian town! She shook her head at the thought. But now? Perhaps twenty families, no more than twenty.

The priest swept from one grave to the next, like a hospital doctor on his morning round. The woman with the cake eyed his progress and when she saw him come close, took out the matches and bent again to light her candle.

In 1565, some thirteen years after the Suceava pogroms and only six years before the reign of John the Armenian (or Brave, Heroic, Bad, Mad, etc.), Moldova's capital was shifted south to Iaşi where it remains. Many Armenians moved too. But there is little left except the earlier fourteenth-century church and the priest's quarters and the graves. An elderly Armenian was tending the graves but I saw no others. Iaşi is now known chiefly for its powerful and savage mafia. There is a wealth of weapons in private hands and they were used frequently to re-establish the boundaries of power. Behind a parade of modern blocks, and the crumbling older blocks, was the whispered lawlessness of a frontier town. Ten miles to the east is the 'accursed' River Prut and the Soviet border.

Another cold, ill-lit train from Suceava to Iaşi delivered me, later that night, to another decaying communist hotel. On a hunt for food,

I ended up on the fourth floor, in the room of the stores manager. He had cheese, ham, bread, and I gave him two dollars for a little of each. A young couple came into his room. She had long dark hair and wild, flashing eyes. She opened the buttons of her coat and underneath wore a lace slip. She had a laugh like a tractor. Her pimp took a bottle of whisky and left her with the stores manager. I took my bag of food.

Outside he said, 'Very good damski. You want?'

I told him what I wanted was to eat.

'Ten dollar, maybe eight for you. Yes?'

'No.'

'Maybe you want gun? Very good gun, man like you need gun, paf-paf-paf! Big danger for Western man.'

I told him I would be happy just to eat and sleep and, tearing off a corner of bread, walked back through the darkened corridors to my room.

# 14

Our tracks which I wish all the more to be continuous and without gaps, since I know full well that
these tracks will soon be blown away by the wind.

Gregor von Rezzori, *The Snows of Yesteryear*

To buy a ticket across the border to Kishinev proved something of
a problem; for once I could find no Armenians to help. At the railway
station I was told I must have a currency form. The currency form
came from a bank and the banks were closed for the weekend. I
found the station manager and a student to translate. Perhaps a bribe
would help: I flashed a few dollars at the manager . . . No! No form,
no ticket.

The student said, what does it matter? Spend the weekend here
in Iaşi, lots of fun in Iaşi. I did not doubt him. But if I had stopped
at every such hurdle I would still be in Cyprus. I told him I had to
get to Armenia and left him looking a little bewildered.

At the bus station, they said there was nothing until after the
weekend. They told me to take a train. But as I left, I saw a Cyrillic
newspaper jammed down behind the windscreen of a bus. A crowd
of Moldovans was waiting to get on: special bus, they said – Kishinev.
I slipped aboard with them and they told me that every weekend
they made this journey – to see their families which had been split
apart by Stalin's border. The driver agreed to take me to the border.

We pulled out of Iaşi in the mid-afternoon and entered a series of short hills. The Moldovan villages were exuberant beyond anything in Transylvania. The simplest bungalows were filigreed and finialed and painted bright blue, or lilac, or deep olive green. Barge-boards looped and curled below the eaves, and in muddy paddocks apple trees paraded their blossom like over-dressed brides. Even the wellheads were adorned like miniature cathedrals.

At the border, everything was glass and concrete. A Soviet officer in a cake-dish cap sat me in his office and prodded me with questions: why this border, where family, why British, what dollar, what weapon? But in the end he waved me through. I rejoined the bus and we carried on – on into the crumbling mess of the Soviet Union and the miles and miles of cars queuing to get out. Women crouched beside them cooking food, washing clothes, their fat arms spilling from sleeveless frocks, while all around them sat tight groups of vested men.

Then came the low hills again and the forest, and the bright villages just a little brighter than those in Romania. If crossing from Bulgaria to Romania had been going down two pegs, leaving Romania for the Soviet Union seemed like stepping back up one. But these last thousand miles to Armenia daunted me. I planned to go through the Crimea and Georgia but my papers said otherwise. I could not use hotels or ticket offices or anywhere else they would check papers. I had three words of Russian and not a single rouble. (No one could change my hundred-dollar bills and the banks would need papers.) I was tired and hungry. I wondered how many of those thousand miles I could cover before being put on a plane for Moscow.

It was dark by the time we pulled into Kishinev. A Moldovan family on the bus offered me a bed. I gave them three packets of American cigarettes. They lived on the fourteenth floor of an apartment block which was still being built. They had a very large Alsatian chained to a radiator. In the morning they took me to the bus station and bought me a ten-rouble bus ticket for some more cigarettes. They stood waving at the bus as it pulled away, the four of them: kind, plump Moldovans, baffled by the way our two worlds had merged in an evening of pidgin French, only to spin apart again.

All morning the Dnestr plain stretched away to the east, fenceless and unending. Teams of tank-like tractors advanced across it. Villages stood in the emptiness of the steppe like shy oases, their fringes of trees already in leaf, their blossom already tired. Here spring seemed about two weeks ahead of Romania. Perhaps the state farms had learnt to induce it.

I reached Odessa soon after midday and tried to find a boat down the east of the Black Sea; but there were no boats for a week. I tried to change some money, find a room, but failed on both counts. I tried to gather information – but information was as scarce as everything else. If I took a train, for instance, how could I get across the Sea of Azov: did it mean going round by Rostov-on-Don, or was there a ferry across the Straits of Kerc? And the fighting in Georgia: were the buses and trains running? Nothing – no one could tell me anything; no one seemed even to know. When I showed them a map, a map of their own country, they stared at its web of lines and shadings as if it were some devilish cipher.

As the day wore on, my priority became finding a place to stay. I had tried some hotels, but they all asked to see my papers or said simply: 'Nyet.' Some students had tried to help, but gradually dropped me when they realized there was nothing they could do. Late in the evening I found myself – and how I got there I'm not sure – sitting in Odessa University's theatre, watching the rag-week review between two professors of English literature. I couldn't quite squeeze my rucksack under the seat, so it sat on my knee like an overgrown child.

'Socks,' whispered the professor on my right.

'Socks?'

'Socks,' he nodded at the stage. 'There is a lamentable shortage of socks in Odessa. This modest little drama concerns socks.' His English had suffered from too much reading of classics.

A group of bare-footed students shuffled around the stage. A man in high boots pranced among them. One of Odessa's last socks was stretched over the top of his head. He announced he was Lenin and all the students fell on the ground and waved their toes in the air. Lenin made a short leap. After that he threw down the sock and jumped up and down on it. Everyone laughed.

'Odessa', said the professor, 'is the capital of humour.' When the lights came up, he asked, 'Who are you? Are you a tourist?'

'Yes.'

'A queer-looking tourist.'

'Perhaps he is from Scotland,' suggested the professor on my other side. 'Like Burns.'

'Or from the Lakes – like Wordsworth . . .'

'Or a bard from Stratford-Avon!'
I said I just needed somewhere to stay.
'He is a hobo!'
'A Beat!'
'A carpet-bagger!'
'A ne'er-do-well!'

At the rag party afterwards, one of the professors introduced me to a student who had his own flat, adding darkly, 'I'm afraid he is half-Jewish, half-Armenian. It is the worst combination!'

'Or the best.'

Tigran was in fact a God-send. He had a large flat in one of the old Jewish tenements. We drank Armenian brandy and ate a tin of Baltic mackerel. His Georgian girlfriend joined us and we talked of the Caucasus which they both missed, and missed more with each brandy. Tigran broke up a hundred-dollar bill and changed forty dollars into roubles – enough to get me to Armenia. (In fact when I left the old Soviet Union a couple of months later, I had been unable to spend any more than half of these roubles.)

In the morning I went for a long walk around Odessa. Tigran had spoken of Odessa's independence, how different it was from any other Soviet city. But I knew it only from books as a place of misfits and commerce, of Jewish gangsters and Italian architects, of Turkish mullahs returning from Mecca, Armenian merchants with bales of Persian silk, of Isaac Babel's Odessa stories, and Mr Trottyburn the English trader who comes ashore and announces his wares: 'Cigars and fine silks, cocaine and files, unbonded tobacco from the State of Virginia, and dark wine from the Island of Chios.' But now the docks were listless; Odessa languished in a post-Soviet daze. I sought out Isaac Babel's old house and found it above a bare-shelved state supermarket. I came across a church converted to an 'Olympic training centre' and another whose onion domes housed a planetarium. Tigran's parents had joined a flood of exiles from Odessa, to Israel and the United States, and the whole city seemed choked by its own decay. I wondered if Armenia would be the same.

Before boarding a train that afternoon for the Crimea, I asked Tigran if he knew the situation there. He didn't. The authorities were different there. Everyone had their own rules now. I had the sense of trying to pull myself up on to a raft that was breaking up; bits kept coming away in my hands and I couldn't tell yet whether I was on board.

Having bribed the concierge for a berth, I joined a compartment with a young merchant seaman on leave. His waif-like fiancée clung to his arm. He had two silver front teeth which he flashed in grinning recollection of English ports: Hull, Liverpool, Lowestoft, 'bitter beer and fog'. He had just returned from the Far East and while we talked gripped the hand of his fiancée so tightly that his bronzed knuckles turned white.

I woke the next morning to the low hills of the Eastern Crimea. Swamps filled the hollows and their brackish pools fused with a grey dawn. I thought of the countless hurdles between here and the Armenian border. If I could not cross the Straits of Kerc, it would mean a four-day detour around by Rostov. Armenia was getting no closer. I leaned back in my berth and, with the others asleep and with the Crimea slipping past the window, I settled down to read.

Contemporary with Isaac Babel, also Jewish, also to die in Stalin's purges, was Osip Mandelstam. Between them these writers give an extraordinary sense of Russia's timeless horror. Mandelstam spoke of its 'watermelon emptiness' and, stifled by post-revolutionary Moscow, looked constantly to the south for relief. He visited the Crimea a number of times during the 1920s. And from the Crimea he pushed further south. Each visit saw him cover a little more of the eastern Black Sea coast, down to the Caucasus, until, in the spring of 1930, he reached Armenia. Here he stood on what he considered 'the world's edge'. For him, this isolated republic, the remnants of an ancient civilization, had come to represent the far outpost of the classical regions which he so revered. He marvelled at Armenia's stubborn resistance to Islam and how it had 'turned away from the bearded cities of the East'.

Armenia, in her stone ruins, had the noble antiquity for which Mandelstam had been searching. But his Armenian cycle of poems and his *Journey to Armenia* are filled with something else. Folding away his map of ancient cultures, Mandelstam was swept along by the present. His prose is charged with a sense of the mountains and the unchanging villages. Before he came to Armenia he had written hardly a word for five years; by the time he left, he had begun some of his finest work. In Armenia he 'saw men who loved life', 'women of leonine beauty'. He was overwhelmed by the 'rude tenderness' of the Armenian villagers, by 'their noble inclination for hard work'. And their 'splendid intimacy with the world of real things' forced him to conclude to himself: 'You're awake, don't be afraid of your own time.'

But Mandelstam's own time caught up with him. The year of his Armenian journey marked the beginning of the worst of the Soviet decades. Three years later, in 1933, he revisited the Crimea. This time he was horrified by the starving refugees from the Ukraine. Nadezhda Mandelstam, his widow, reflected later that even Tamburlane and the Tartar invasions could not have caused the destitution they saw that spring. Mandelstam returned to Moscow and, privately, denounced Stalin as a slaughterer of peasants. Soon afterwards he was arrested for the first time. Several years later, hounded and broken by the state's nameless henchmen, Mandelstam died in transit camp 3/10 USVITLAG, near Vladivostok. His *Journey to Armenia* was one of the original spurs to my own journey. Re-reading it on that train in the Crimea, I was struck again by its zest, by its infectious celebration of life.

It was in the Crimea's traditional capital, Stary Krim, that he witnessed the refugees in 1933: 'Cold spring, in starving Stary Krim . . . Nature wouldn't know her own face.' And in this town too, he must have encountered Armenians, perhaps sharing with them tales of his own from Armenia. For Stary Krim had one of the oldest Armenian communities anywhere in the diaspora. Eight hundred years earlier, Armenians fled the Seljuk Turks and the smouldering ruins of Ani. The Crimea was the first real refuge for these northbound exiles. In quarters of Stary Krim and Kaffa and Kherson, they kept their traditions. They built caravanserais and churches, and their influence spread up into the Ukraine and Poland. They trekked across Central Asia in search of trade and, by the fifteenth century, there were as many as two hundred thousand Armenians in the Crimea.

In 1475, the peninsula was taken by the Ottoman Turks. The local Armenians had aided their victory, hoping it would overcome the local hegemony of the Greeks. The new pasha invited the Armenians to a celebratory banquet. They ate a fine meal of pilau and shashlik and sweetmeats. Afterwards the pasha reclined on his divan and the Armenians came to bow and take their leave. Outside stood a janissary who held his sword high in the darkness and, one by one, beheaded them as they left.

*

At noon, the train came to a halt in Kerc. I still did not know whether it was possible to get across the Sea of Azov. An Armenian woman at the station promised to help. She wore a strange electric-blue raincoat and dismissed my questions with a flick of her wrist: maybe there is boat, maybe bus, maybe taxi – maybe, maybe, but now you come to lunch. We crossed a cheerless copse of tower-blocks to her flat. Bustling off to the kitchen, she pointed me to a garish, Soviet-style sitting room. Everything in it shone and swirled and clashed. I was suddenly exhausted and, leafing through a book of Armenian architecture, was soon nodding off into the harmonious curves of Sanahin's rib vaulting.

'You are tired, English. Eat.'

I was so tired I hardly had the energy to eat. There was soup and sausage and I dealt with them mechanically; later we drank coffee and vodka and I felt a little restored.

The Armenian woman hummed absent-mindedly as she wandered around the flat; the tunes followed her from room to room like a scent. She had a loaf of dyed, blonde hair and was sad and still beautiful in an Armenian way. But her family had deserted her: there was a son in Moscow, a daughter in Kiev, and a husband no more than a derisory flick of the wrist. She showed me her photograph album. She showed me her plants. She showed me the souvenir plates of Yerevan, the framed picture of Ararat which hovered above her bed. She threw open her cupboards where stacks of boxes and packets and jars were racked like arms against a militant future. This was hoarding on a grand scale: there were hairdryers, cases of Armenian brandy, Russian vodka, several televisions, Turkish coffee, socks and shoes – dozens and dozens of pairs of shoes.

The afternoon was slipping away. I could have slept for eighteen hours, but I knew I had to keep going, to press on for Armenia. I could not stay too long in one place and invite questions.

'I must go,' I said.

She sat down beside me. One hand rested on my thigh. 'English-*djan*, stay.'

'I cannot stay.'

'But you are so tired – look at you. Stay with me. You must rest here, English-*djan*. Why don't you stay?'

'I cannot.'

She withdrew her hand slowly and stood up and went to the

window. The sun was bright and she blinked towards the sea. 'Very well, English. But leave now.'

A few miles to the east of Kerc there was a ferry across the straits: why couldn't anyone tell me before? A brisk wind swept down from the Sea of Azov. At the guard-rail was the merchant seaman I'd met on the train. He smiled his silver-toothed smile and his fiancée leaned against his chest.

'Look at this old ship,' he scoffed.

'I'm glad it's here at all.'

'In Turkey, they have now *two* bridges on the Bosphorus. Here just one old ship. And no fish – all the fish are dead! Polluted! That is Soviet Union!'

On the ferry the merchant seaman introduced me to a doctor, and the doctor was driving to Novorussisk. There he knew someone who worked in the state hotel. We reached the town at dusk and I was given a room with no questions asked. Be on the dock at five tomorrow morning, said the doctor. Maybe you'll be lucky – sometimes there is a boat to Sochi, although usually there is no boat.

That night in the hotel dining room, while a troupe of Russian dancers shed their clothes for the party bosses, the chandeliers rattled and in Georgia there was a violent earthquake. With that and the fighting in Ossetia and the strikes and the fuel embargoes, the Russians in the hotel abandoned any hope of knowing what was going on; Georgia was just too confusing and too noisy – too much fighting, too much problem.

Long before midnight, I left the dining room and took the lift to my fifth-floor room. I stared closely at the fittings of the hotel. I tried to work out how it was done, how such lavish blandness was achieved. Blandness like that required a special talent. No expense had been spared: the best marble facing, the best brass lights, the best Ukrainian furniture, and Kazakh tapestries for the landings. This was a palace of the Planned Economy, a faceless temple to the State.

I packed up ready for an early start; I would give the five o'clock boat a try. I went out and stood on the balcony and watched the ships at anchor in the horseshoe bay; above them were the dark, outstretched limbs of the upper Caucasus. It was a clear night. Reports of the earthquake crackled on the BBC: twenty dead, a number of villages destroyed . . .

What was it? What was that sense of disintegration that haunted this Armenian journey and intensified the closer I got?

I had been asleep a couple of hours when there was a knock on my door. I ignored it.

'Police, police. British, open please!'

Damn. I rolled out of bed, picturing at once the questions and confusion and the plane to Moscow and God knows what other impediments. Somehow I dreaded most losing the opportunity that now confounded me: the freedom to travel this last stretch, through Georgia to Armenia.

'Police! Police!'

'I'm coming.'

Outside the door was a man in a brown suit. He had deep, lancing eyes. Over his brown suit he wore a black leather jacket in the manner of the KGB. One of the dancing girls hung on his arm. Smiling lazily, he swung a bottle of vodka at me.

'Come and drink – drink with girl and policeman!'

When he told me he was Armenian somehow I wasn't surprised.

Early the next morning I walked round the bay to the docks. The sun had not yet cleared the mountains. Smells of spring resonated in the still air: blossom and buds and pine resin – and new paint slapped on the Soviet monuments for May Day. The Sochi boat was there, but going only as far as Tuapse. At Tuapse I got off only to be told it *was* going to Sochi, but there were no places. A crowd teemed around the foot of the gang-plank and filed on board. I watched them for a while, wondering again how to get down this coast. There was nothing but the boat.

I took out a five-dollar note and climbed back up the gang-plank.

'Da,' the deckhand nodded and stretched out his hand for the note but the wind caught it and suddenly it was spinning away, rolling and somersaulting along the deck, lodging against a stanchion before waltzing off again. Then it slid over the gunwale and stuck in the water. All eyes stared at this rippling sliver of paper and I felt a sudden shame at my own clumsy wealth: two months of their salary floating in the harbour. I was glad to see it disappear between the timber piles of the pier.

The passage to Sochi was spent playing backgammon with the crew, being plied with tea, then vodka. 'Russian service,' they explained ignoring various complaints from the passengers. At Sochi, they said the boat would be carrying on.

'To Sukhumi?' I asked.

'Sukhumi problem.'

'What problem?'

'Fight.'

'Poti?'

'Poti problem. Earthquake. We go to Batum.'

So we would cover the whole troubled coast in a single hop. I'd thought it would take days.

All afternoon the Black Sea shone with a blue-grey brilliance. Silver-backed waves lunged and flopped towards the shore, there to prostrate themselves at the feet of the Caucasus. Nothing of the panic and disorder could be seen in the coast's wooded slopes, nor amidst the strutting pantheon of its snow-capped peaks.

Towards evening, stretching my legs on the upper deck, I overheard a couple speaking Armenian and greeted them. They both had deeply bronzed faces and peered at me closely. 'You speak no Russian, but you speak Armenian? You are a strange man!'

The Minossians had been camping for a few days near Sochi. They pressed me to stay at their flat in Batum but I needed no pressing. I helped them carry the tent up the stairs to the ninth storey and a studded leatherette door which burst open on crowds of children. The Minossians had ten children. They had so many children that the oldest ones had children who were older than their aunts and uncles. They leapt out of the warren of rooms and swarmed around us in a mass embrace, jumping and screaming and chattering, pointing to the place the ceiling had buckled and cracked during last night's earthquake.

In the morning the house was quiet. I whispered goodbye and tiptoed to the front door. Ten pairs of shoes were arranged in ascending order in the hall. I had some chocolate from Odessa and left it by the smallest pair. By the largest I left my last packet of American cigarettes. Silently I pulled the door closed and did up my boots on the landing.

Walking down through Batum's dusty streets that morning, I felt for the first time that Armenia was attainable. Soviet authority had effectively ended at the Caucasus and with it my apprehension about papers. At the docks they steered me towards the railway station and there I crossed the concourse with a sense of liberation. But there were no trains. The only way to Yerevan was via Tbilisi and all the trains in Georgia were on strike. At the bus station I found a bus, but pulling out of town it burst its radiator and ground to a halt.

For several hours I sat by the roadside waiting for a replacement bus and watching the other passengers act out a parody of the Caucasus's bellicose peoples. The Azeris squatted on their luggage, arguing with each other; then they lobbied the Abkhazian driver, who was furious with an Armenian, whose wife pleaded with the colossal Lezgi conductor who stood stony-faced and still no bus. The Lezgi glared at the Armenian; the Armenian glared at the Azeris, before forming an alliance to pester the Abkhazian together. A neat Russian colonel scowled on the side-lines, convinced the Motherland would be much better off without all these tiresome people.

The next bus took us up out of the jungly hinterland of Georgia's coast, into country of plunging valleys and dashing streams. Then that one broke down. Tbilisi was shrouded in an ominous, war-like darkness by the time we arrived. I found a room in the Armenian quarter, but had to hunt for food. The streets were dark and full of wind-chased rubbish. A large rat ran down the escalator of the metro. The streets were empty and, searching for food, I found everywhere closed out of respect for the earthquake casualties.

But downstairs at the Tbilisi Hotel the restaurant was open. The Kiev correspondent of the London *Times* was there, forking cubes of shashlik around a swampy plate of rice. A bottle of Georgian wine stood at his elbow and he had only two complaints: that there was no toothpaste in Tbilisi and no helicopter to take him to the earthquake zone.

The next morning was cool and damp. Swollen clouds still clung to the mountains above Tbilisi and at the railway station I found the first signs of Armenia. A squad of Yerevan taxis waited there with open doors. They gleamed with the fresh zeal of enterprise and bore stickers of Ararat and Edjmiatsin and Lake Sevan. Six of us gathered in one of these taxis: an Armenian spiv (in the customary shiny black shirt and gold chains), an Armenian couple from Bukhara

The Armenian alphabet

ABOVE: The mason's hut, Haghartsin

LEFT: *Khachkar* at the monastery
of Haghartsin

ABOVE: Mount Ararat

BELOW: Funeral of *fedayi*

LEFT: Tenth-century stelae, Odzun

BELOW: Father Vasken, priest of Kapan and Meghri since 1921

Refugee from Getashen

ABOVE: Damage from the 1988 earthquake, Gumri (formerly Leninakan)

BELOW: Survivors at the earthquake epicentre, Gogoran

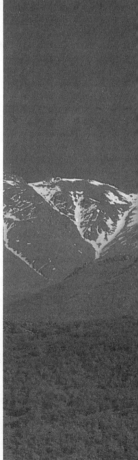

ABOVE: On the island at Lake Sevan: Writers' Rest Home (circa 1932), and church

LEFT: *Khachkar* at Noradouz cemetery

Sarcophagus of couple clutching the symbol of perpetuity

RIGHT: Masons restoring the monastery of Vahanavank (circa 911)

BELOW: Near Tatev, Zangezour

ABOVE: Armenian tailor, Frumoasa, Transylvania

RIGHT: The Armenian church of the Holy Trinity, Gherla (formerly Armenopolis), Transylvania

BELOW: The Armenian church of Sfînta Maria, Iași, Moldova

BISERICA CREȘTINĂ ORTODO
ARMEANĂ
CU HRAMUL SFÎNTA MAR
DEȚINE CEL MAI VECHI DOCUME
SCRIS PE PIATRĂ
DE ATESTARE A MUNICIPIULUI IA
ANUL 1395.

(blue eyes set like jewels in their desert-creased faces), and a Lithu-anian girl who turned out to belong to the spiv. At that time Armenia was under siege. For three years Azerbaijan had blocked all routes to the east, including the gas pipeline and main railway. The track through Georgia was now cut off by strikes and there were no links along the Turkish or Iranian borders. Only the airport and two narrow, frost-scarred, earthquake-torn roads linked Armenia with the rest of the world. One of these roads wound up through a bright morning into the forest. The beech leaves dipped and fluttered on their sappy stalks. I felt suddenly elated by the thought of Armenia. I looked around at my fellow passengers to see if they felt the same. The spiv was asleep and his girlfriend was sulking. Only the Bukhara Armenians showed any enthusiasm and when, still in Georgia, we stopped to wash at a spring they gazed like gold-panners at the water in their cupped hands.

It was past midday when the trees thinned at the top of a long valley. Clusters of wooden houses straddled the road. In their shadows were the last crystals of frost. Apple trees blossomed behind the houses. Goats picked at the new grass and in the sheep-folds were bleating lambs. Up this narrow combe winter was thawing fast, like the old communist guard, and spring was squeezed into a single day.

At the pass was a cob-built guardhouse and two soldiers. One of them leaned on the back legs of his chair. His tunic was unbuttoned to the sun and his eyes were closed. A rifle lay across his knees. The other shuffled out of the hut and yawned. Seeing the taxi, he waved slowly before tugging at a cord and raising the wooden barrier into Armenia.

Six months and twenty countries had led me to this – this high frontier and these sleepy guards, to the tiny state of Armenia and its bald hills. This was all that remained of the old country, the ancient Armenian nugget; behind me, the diaspora was no more than a scattering of its dust. Through the barrier the land levelled off. The upturned bowls of distant peaks swelled from the horizon. Everything looked too small on that high plain: the towns were like flocks of sheep, the flocks of sheep like stones, and the stones – Armenia is famous for its stones – you couldn't see at all.

# III

# ARMENIA

'Do you see that, the white thing yonder? High
   up? Do you know what that is?'
'No,' replied the other sleepily . . .
'That is Ararat.'

James Bryce, Transcaucasia and Ararat

GEORGIA

Alaverdi  •Haghbat
Gogoran  Sanahin
         Haghartsin
Spitak       •Goshavank
Leninakan  Dilijan
                Sevan Island
Noradouz    Lake
            Sevan
Yerevan

AZERBAIJAN

KARABAGH

Shiraz  Sovetashen

Mt.Ararat
△

TURKEY

NAKHIJEVAN
ARMENIA   Tatev
ZANGEZOUR

Goris

David
Bek

Ghapan

Meghri

I R A N

0  10  20    40    60    80 Miles

# 15

Accept me tenderly, my new country, and with
wisdom –
I come to you singing my song, beneath your
Octobrist flag.

Aram Arman, 'The Chant of the Returned Poet' (Trans. from
Armenian by Aram Tolegian.)

Behind one of Yerevan's countless grim blocks of flats, in which
people seemed less housed than packaged, a slab of wasteground
stretched anonymously towards the next grim block. In the middle
of this empty acre was a wooden hut. In the hut was a cobbler.
Somewhere in Transylvania I'd first noticed the split. One evening I'd bent to unlace my boots and there it was, a two-inch tear
along the instep. At the time it had struck me with a kind of mute
horror, like the first shivers of a fever. These boots were all I had,
the same boots I'd pulled on every day for months, my most valued
prop.

Each day I had watched the split grow. It grew both ways, towards
the toe and backwards towards the heel. I tried to find someone to
mend it, but got only shrugs and 'Nu!' and 'Nyet!'

By the time I entered the Ukraine, the creeping fissure had stopped
creeping and I felt confident about reaching Armenia. There I was
sure they'd be able to fix anything.

The late sun streamed into the cobbler's hut and fell across his
apron in crooked shards. He wore half-moon glasses and worked
swiftly, planing over a spongy leather template. Opposite him, on the
salvaged back seat of a car, sat a donnish-looking man. One of his

stockinged feet rested on a cardboard box. I undid my boot and handed it to the cobbler. He pressed and fingered the wound, scratched his stubbly chin, and shrugged. Behind me were dark mutterings about Russians and the cobbler handed the boot back to me. I turned to the donnish man and told him, in Armenian, that I was not Russian.

'Polski?'

'British.'

'I'm sorry, I thought you were Russian.'

The cobbler accepted the boot. The donnish man made room for me on the car-seat and pulled out a bottle of vodka. 'You have been here long in Hayastan?'

'No. I just arrived.'

'Ah, from London!'

'Yes.'

'How is the weather in London? Rain, I think.'

'I came the long way.'

'Long? What long?'

'Through Georgia, Russia, Ukraine, Moldova, Romania . . .'

'Romania? That is long!'

My boot was now inverted on the cobbler's last. He gripped the sole with a pair of pliers and began to peel it back. I winced and turned away. Pinned to the walls of the hut was an improbable medley of images: a print of a tempest by the Crimean Armenian Aivazovsky, a plastic cast of the poet Paruir Sevak, a calendar featuring His Holiness the Catholicos of All Armenians, and a Russian girl with agricultural breasts. Secular communism had left a strange iconography in its wake.

Some political intrigue was being unravelled beside me. 'You see, I am a scientist. I know these things. You heard of the earthquake in Georgia?'

'Yes, I did.'

'Russians. The Russians did it.'

I looked at him sceptically.

'It's true. The Georgians were fighting in Ossetia, so the Russians made the earthquake. The same thing in 1988: the Armenians make trouble for the Russians, the Russians make earthquake at Spitak. Paf!'

'Nonsense,' I said.

'You don't believe me? I am a scientist. I have seen the place they make these special bombs. They put the bombs in the fault-lines and make earthquake where they want.'

'Let's have some more vodka.'

The sole of my boot now curled away from the heel like a flap of torn skin; the cobbler was stabbing a needle through the leather upper.

A woman leaned round the door with a broken-heeled court shoe.

'Come in! Come in!' urged the scientist.

We made room for her on the car-seat and she propped one stockinged foot against the upright. Soon we were talking about meat shortages and the Azeri embargo and then, quite naturally, about Vartan and the Persian wars of the fifth century, and the Arab invasion in the seventh. And of General Andranik, the hero of Armenian resistance who led a whole series of guerrilla bands against the Turks and is buried in Père Lachaise. We talked of Armenian poets and each of them quoted lines from Sevak and Siamanto and Charents. We drank more vodka and the scientist fed me more improbable stories: he'd worked on a nuclear detonator, Armenia had the bomb, the Turin Shroud had belonged to an Armenian.

For a moment there was silence. The sun fell like a rug on the dusty floor and ruffled up the weather-boards of the back wall. The cobbler tap-tapped with his hammer and I felt Armenia slide in and out of focus.

The woman sighed. 'They are still there, by the Opera.'

'Many?' asked the scientist.

'Very many.'

'I saw them.' The scientist turned to me. 'You saw them today, by the Opera?'

'Yes, I saw them.'

They had come down from the mountains in a slow cavalcade of black Moskvichs. Yerevan's streets were cleared and they crept towards the opera house, the hub of the republic. Seven coffins; seven *fedayi*.

A local journalist told me the story. In Karabagh the Soviet generals were trying to flush out the Armenians. They were meeting some stiff resistance from the local forces, the *fedayi*, who were defending them. One of the villages had proved particularly intransigent and the Soviet commander had called a ceasefire. He went himself to negotiate with the Armenians. Seven *fedayi* had stood with the commander. Each clutched a hand grenade, should anything go wrong. But an agreement was reached and the colonel turned and headed back to his own lines. Before he got there, however, he dropped suddenly to the ground and shouted at his men to open fire; only one of the *fedayi* had been sufficiently intact to be put in an open coffin.

I stood on the steps of the opera house and watched their coffins bob above the heads of the crowd. Ten, fifteen, twenty thousand Armenians were massed there. They were silent and each held up a clenched fist. On the steps beside me was a guard of half a dozen *fedayi*. I couldn't believe these people. They had mythical faces: blue-grey eyes, teak-brown complexions, and sprigs of black hair which burst from their scalps and from their chins. Criss-crossing their chests were cartridge belts, and their assault rifles seemed grafted to them like an extra limb. The head of General Andranik was stencilled on their black fatigues.

But one woman overshadowed their Stygian presence. She stepped up to one of the coffins and stared down at its bevelled lid. It was that of her husband. She spread her hands across it and threw back her head. I thought she would scream, but instead she just tightened her lips and crushed her palms into fists.

It was true what was said about Ararat; all the cliches I'd scorned were true. For a couple of days I resisted it. I saw the mountain lurking at the ends of the avenues, filling spare bits of sky between the Stalinist blocks. I watched it pose against the orange backdrop of the evening. It had tried so hard, so obviously, to impress that I reserved my admiration for its shorter neighbour, the more perfect cone of Little Ararat. But early one morning, I stood on the steps of the Madenataran, above Yerevan, and for the first time saw the mountain in full. It was magnificent. It rose above the city's tumbling sprawl. It rose above the hackneyed, reproduced images of the diaspora. It sat impossibly, unnaturally high. Though more than forty miles away, I felt I could simply step across and amble over its leathery slopes. In the early light, the snowy peak shone like a crown. I could not ignore it again. Within a week, it had crept up on me and I found myself sneaking glances at it, looking for it down west-facing streets, sad when I couldn't see it. Like all good Armenians, I too had developed a passion for the mountain.

Second only to their love of Ararat, of Massis, is the Armenian passion for their language. 'These are people', wrote Mandelstam, 'who jangle the keys of their language even when they are not using them to unlock any treasures.'

The Madenataran is a shrine to it. Set into the upper slopes of Yerevan, with its full view of Ararat, it is home to about ten thousand bound manuscripts and one hundred thousand historical documents. At its entrance, sits Mesrop Mashtots who made it all possible, who devised the so-called regiment of letters and its thirty-six warriors.

It would be hard to overestimate the importance of Mesrop's script. The Armenians and their script have become inseparable; the survival of one would be impossible without the other. A whole popular mythology has grown up around it and its works. There are stories from 1915 of women scratching the letters in the sand at Deir ez Zor as they died, so that their children might learn it; there were the damaged manuscripts of medieval Armenia buried like knights with full honours; and the *Homilies of Moush*, an enormous thirteenth-century manuscript of six hundred calf-skins, brought out of Turkey in 1915 by two fleeing women who found it so heavy they had to cut it in two.

And early on in the Soviet years, so the story goes, the Bolsheviks approached a well-known Armenian philologist. They wanted him to revise the script to aid the assimilation of the Armenians. He refused. They tied him up and burnt his face with cigarettes, but he still refused. So they approached a second philologist and burnt his face with cigarettes. In the end this man gave in. Years later he became ill and lost the power of speech. He wrote to the first philologist pressing him to come. When this one arrived he found his old colleague was dying. He was handed a note. Please, begged the sick man, will you forgive me?

'Yes, I will forgive you,' said the first philologist. 'But it is not enough. Soon you will be going up there. When you come face to face with St Mesrop himself, what will you say then?'

Antoine Millet, a French philologist, applauded Mesrop's script as 'a masterpiece' and Margaret Mead suggested Armenian as the most suitable of all the world's languages for a *lingua franca*.

Behind the Madenataran, drilled into the mountain, is a tunnel which leads to a bunker designed to withstand mould, fire and nuclear attack. The whole library can be wheeled in there at a moment's notice, a poignant reminder, if one was needed, that words outlive us all.

Is this the very heart of Armenia? Perhaps it is. If it is the Armenian language that pumps through the distant limbs of the diaspora then, yes, the Madenataran must be the heart. Or is Ararat the heart? Untouchable Ararat. Ararat stolen by the Turks. Ararat where the demon *yazatas* chained up Artamazd who will one day break free and save Armenia . . .

Or is it Edjmiatsin? 'Light of the Lord descended to earth,' seat of the Catholicos of All Armenians, the holiest site of Armenia, where every visiting Armenian comes to light a candle, where the chrism is blessed for the baptism of every Armenian child. Here is where the fractured notion of Armenianness is united with its emblem: Armenian Christianity. Never during the Soviet years did the Catholicos and his vartabeds not celebrate the Eucharist here, nor in the sixteen hundred years before that. Beneath the central apse is a gilded ciborium, and beneath that the host and beneath the host is the velvet canopy of the altar. This is the still-point of the spinning Armenians, their *ka'aba*.

But buried underneath the altar, older by far than anything else above, older than almost every other known place of formalized worship in the world, here at the very centre of Armenia is a fire-temple. The heart of Armenia is Christian but the heart's core is elemental, pagan, Mazdaean – and preserved.


It was warm that week in Yerevan. I had chased spring round the Black Sea and now it was here, filling the air with its warmth and the white floss of poplar seed. I stayed with a young family in a flat with a vault-like door and several mortice locks. Outside were concrete stairs and peeling paint; inside was a priceless collection of paintings, Russian icons, sunny Russian landscapes and bronze Sukhothai buddhas.

It was not Yerevan itself but the sense of arriving that lulled me into a state of torpid ease. I ate and slept properly for the first time in weeks. I had things to see, people to look up. I had no anxieties about papers or borders; I felt among friends. That lasted about three days. Then the questions that had driven my journey rose again. Certainly I hoped that Armenia itself, what survived of it, would help explain the diaspora and its survival. But Yerevan was more Soviet than Armenian. Its squares and municipal buildings – even its bus shelters – have transformed the motifs of Armenian architecture into an oddly charmless pastiche.

I arranged to leave Yerevan. Someone I had met tugged at the old Party strings and secured a cottage for me in the woods near Dilijan. On my last afternoon I walked up to the monument to the massacres of 1915. The paved approach was unimaginably bleak. Two structures, like a lance and a shield, rose from the concourse: a slender obelisk and a concrete henge of inward-leaning blocks. An eternal flame burnt beneath these blocks. Around it was a waist-high hedgerow of wilting carnations: each one had been brought separately by mourners two weeks earlier, on 24 April, the annual day of commemoration.

Of the three parts of the monument, the flame, the henge and the obelisk, two of them, the latter two, the most visible, stand for the land and its loss. The twelve concrete blocks are the twelve stolen provinces of western Armenia, while the obelisk is in fact split by a fine hairline into two parts, representing the split between western and eastern Armenia.

For me that confirmed the pervasive truth behind the massacres: that the loss of the land was as deep a wound as the loss of life. That truth had haunted all the exiles I'd spoken to in the diaspora, all the tales they'd told me. It did not diminish the atrocities. Rather it deepened them, helping to root the whole episode, to make it more accessible, almost tangible.

Of all the old Soviet republics, Armenia was the first to introduce land reform. The villages were now no longer arms of the state machine. The thought of those villages, Armenian villages, made me want to shake off the months in the town-houses of the diaspora. I crossed Yerevan on foot and boarded a bus for Dilijan.

# 16

He wrote that every living being is subject to decay, and the seeds of life emerge from decay; the world continues to exist as a result of this contradiction.

Gevork Emin (twentieth-century Armenian poet) on Ananiah Shiragatsi (seventh-century Armenian scientist)

Out of Yerevan and its misty heat, only Ararat rises through the haze. It hovers and swells like a vast projected image; there is something proprietorial about it. The afternoon is heady and bright, and the furled spars of poplars line the road up from Yerevan. On the plateau, the bus pushes past the abandoned greenhouses of the old state farms, the tangled net of cables and pylons, the silly statuary, the awkward monuments, the bus shelters in the shape of fish.

Lake Sevan is mirror-smooth. The peaks and ridges of the mountains snake across its surface. A woman hoists herself on to the bus and her bag of trout drips blood on to the floor. The mountain sun is very warm and heats the inside of the bus like a tin. Thick woods now cover the slopes as far as the ridges on the dim horizon. The road bunches into a series of impossible switchback bends and at the bottom a cement-mixer lies on its side.

Off the main road a track burrows into the woods, winding up to the cottages of the Composers' Rest Home, a curious, crumbling legacy of the communists.

*

I idled away the best part of a week at the rest home. Each day the woods became greener and the meadow grass grew higher. On an oak table in my cottage, I spread out all my notes and papers from the diaspora and settled into the slow, convalescent rhythm of the place. Behind these artists' rest homes, scattered in pleasant spots all over the old Soviet Union, lay the notion of 'Culture', with its prescribed function in the state machine. Put your composers here in the mountains with the bird song and the bubbling streams; give them meals in the refectory; free them from the wearing concerns of normal life, and let them turn out fine music to stir the people.

The Composers' Rest Home was part of the Party's now-collapsing economy, the parallel economy, which dispensed favour and terror in equal measure. But the whole system was now in limbo. Some of the rest homes had fallen into the shadowy underworld of the mafia. In the next valley was the Cinematographers' Rest Home, no longer anything to do with film, but a convenient venue for Yerevan's hoods to take their prostitutes.

The Composers' Rest Home maintained some sense of its original purpose. There was still a piano in my cottage and in others, in other corners of the woods, composers worked and re-worked their scores. One day, tired of the confines of the cottage, I joined some musicians and their families for a picnic on the grassy alps above the complex. We scraped together some food: the kitchen staff gave us bread and cheese; someone had some apples; I had a big bag of almonds from the town. It was a beautiful spring day. We lay on the grass and looked down the wooded valley towards Dilijan. One or two clouds drifted in the bay of blue sky between the mountains; buzzards coasted around the tree-tops. The children picked harebells and chased each other and fought, and I talked to Ashot, a quiet, bearded composer, about the peculiarities of Armenian music.

A lot of traditional music, he explained, relied not so much on melody but what he called a 'tonic home', a motif or series of notes. 'That is what gives much Armenian music a continuous quality. The music has no beginning or end, but just this tonic home which it revolves around.'

'Like the Armenians themselves.'

He smiled and nodded, and we went on to talk about the great unsolved mystery of medieval Armenian music. A great deal of sheet music has survived from Armenia's golden age – church music, requiems, sung liturgies, hymns (the Armenian for hymn, *sharakan*, means literally 'row of gems'). They were supremely intricate pieces, with their microtonic blend of Persian and Armenian traditions. But no one has been able to work out what they sounded like. All that survives is a mass of folio pages, covered in the long-forgotten Armenian notation system. Some say that Father Gomidas had managed to crack the code and breathe life back into these mute notes. But in 1915 he was arrested in Constantinople during one of the first purges. The secret went with him into the interior and the massacres drove him mad.

In Yerevan I'd tracked down a scholar who claimed to have worked it out. He'd published four volumes of work on the subject but having talked to him, I was none the wiser. He skirted round my questions, and his answers were obtuse.

Ashot too was sceptical. 'Yes, I've read his work. I can't make any sense of it.'

'He said the key to it all will be in the fifth volume.'

Ashot shrugged. 'Well then, let us wait.'

What interested me was not so much his promised solution, the mystery itself, as the existence of such a system at all. Medieval Armenians, it seems, had reduced their whole world to a series of linked abstractions. In codes intelligible only to themselves – numbers, letters, musical notes – they had captured their slippery cosmology, tied it to the page, and taught it to perform certain tricks.

St Mesrop was the master of the plan. His script had proved more durable than the land and went a long way beyond its purely phonetic function. The first letter Ա is the initial of Astvadz, or God, the last letter Ք for Kristos. So Father and Son, united in Armenian christology, stand like sentinels at either end of the system, the same system which transmits, through the Bible, all the laws and subtleties of their Word. And that system too, St Mesrop's band of warriors, with its neat four rows of nine symbols, doubles up for that other code of divine law – mathematics. Juggling with these symbols, translating the movements of the heavens into geometric principles, the Armenians used numbers, their Promethean fire, to build churches. The brilliance of those early churches! But how many are now abandoned and no one knows the songs that filled their domes.

I said, 'And the stone crosses, the *khachkars*. They too seem to be celebrations of order and pattern.'

'Yes,' said Ashot. 'But if you look closely, you find that they are never quite symmetrical. From a distance they look symmetrical, but up close they're not. And no two are ever the same.'

It was the same with the churches. The cathedral, for instance, at Ani – a miracle of order and proportion. Yet none of the dimensions quite fitted. And early Armenian poetry shows the same elliptical sense of order. Stanzas vary in length, feet swell by one or more syllables. Yet overall there is a powerful sense of pattern. It is as if they were saying, these medieval Armenians, this is the way of the world. You may think there are patterns but there are not. Patterns are what we want to see. Patterns keep us clear of the darkness, but they are imagined. If creation seems a benign, ordered place, look again, look more closely.

I took a stone and tossed it down the slope. It rolled and bounced through the grass before splashing in the brook. The clouds had thickened above the mountains. Their high bulbous folds looked like some swollen fungus. A sudden wind shook the tree-tops and hissed in the grass.

'The rain is coming,' I said.

The first thunder bellowed from Sevan. It bounced off the peaks and half-drowned the *thuk-thuk* of the helicopters. I watched the wasp-like silhouettes push across the valley and bank towards Karabagh.

'We talk,' said Ashot, 'while they fight.'


They came that evening in four yellow buses. It was raining heavily. In the refectory they gathered beneath the strip-lighting with wet hair and bundles of clothes and bedding. The old men sat in one corner, huddled and beaten. The women were stony-faced and tired, but when they started to talk, their voices cracked and they wept.

'Oh, we knew the soldiers were coming . . . For fifteen days we fought, but then came the tanks and helicopter . . . so many tanks! Ten a.m. and there were twenty, thirty tanks for our village . . . We killed our sheep and said to the soldiers: come on, eat our sheep . . . Even enemies must not refuse a gift! But the soldiers were drunk. They said: "You have two hours!" And we thought the Russians were Christian.'

The kitchen staff had gathered around them. They bubbled with questions, echoed the sudden curses and dabbed their own tears on their grimy aprons.

'Oh dear God, then they burned the houses . . . the children killed
. . . the sick burned in their house . . . we were not able to find them
. . . we could not even find them to bury . . .'

The next morning the refugees milled around the cottages. They
looked dazed and lost. In the orchard a group stood up to their calves
in the spring grass, chewing on dandelion stalks. One old man sat
on a bench and stared at his hands. Grey stubble covered his chin
and on his lapel he wore a campaign badge, the Order of Orlov, a
hammer and sickle in a double star. He had fought under Marshal
Baghramian in the Second World War but now the same Soviet
army had come to drive him out.

'Look at my hands. You see? Working hands. What can I do without land? I had six cows, twenty sheep and bee-hives . . . In my
cellar were five hundred bottles of vodka, one thousand of wine.
And the fruit – last year raspberries alone brought five thousand
roubles! Always my family lived in that home . . . You know, those
old Armenian houses, with the books and rugs and old things . . .'

A crowd had gathered around us and I could feel its brooding
shadows push closer. One woman elbowed her way through. She
thrust a photograph at me: of her standing in a doorway with a willowy young man squinting at the camera, head and shoulders taller,
wearing combat fatigues. 'Look! It is my son!' She tore the picture
down the middle and the two pieces fell to the ground. 'Dead!'

The old man pushed deep into his pocket. He held his fist out and
opened it. Some dried apricots fell into my palm. 'It is the last of our
village, the last of Getashen.'

'You must keep it.'

'No, no. For you.'

Each day for the refugees pushed Getashen further away; they soon
knew they would not be going back. The women's anger was quickest
to pass. They were soon spending their mornings bustling around with
buckets of water and loaves of bread; they went on expeditions into
the forest and came back with pinafores filled with fruit and berries.
The men, by contrast, slowed down, became indolent. Without land
they were lost. They spent less and less time in angry huddles, more
and more time shuffling knee-deep through the orchards, in silence,
chewing herbs. I could hardly bear to watch their decline.

Refugees of a different generation arrived at the end of the week.
I'd met one or two of them in Yerevan. They were overseas students,
the grandchildren of 1915, and had come to Dilijan to visit a young

composer from Syria. But really their visit was an excuse for *khoravats*.
'Leave your books, Philip. We make *khoravats*!'
In the boot of a rusting Moskvich were three trussed chickens and
two fuel cans filled with wine.
'*Khoravats* chicken, *khoravats* wine. Now we need *khoravats* fire!'
They were an eclectic group, gathered like a random sample of
the diaspora: an actor from Beirut, a writer from Cyprus, a play-
wright and his wife from Paris. A Uruguayan musician had brought
her Californian boyfriend, and in amongst them all was a little old
lady who everyone called *Mets-mayr*, Grandmother. Mets-mayr came
from Buenos Aires. I pointed the others to a place in the forest where
there was wood and stayed to talk to Mets-mayr.

She was a music therapist. She'd trained under a great Swiss, who
had explored the power of certain harmonies and rhythms to rid his
patients of anxiety. She said it worked, and worked well, if you
tailored the music to the patient. I asked her how she had ended up
in Buenos Aires and she smiled and looked up into the trees.

Mets-mayr's wandering life began like those of Getashen, fleeing
Azeris and Russians. Some years after the Bolshevik revolution there
were pogroms in Baku. With her brother and father, she fled to Berlin
and there met a young Armenian journalist. The two of them spent
several years in the capitals of Europe before he was posted to Buenos
Aires. But her brother stayed on in Berlin. 'During the war I heard
they hanged him. But many years after I had a letter from Canada. He
is living there with a Canadian wife. He said, yes, they hanged him,
but by the foot and the hand and he managed to escape.'

The *khoravats* went on long into the night. When the wine was
finished, we turned to vodka. The cottage's baby grand hammered
out Caucasian sword-dances. No one really noticed when the electricity was cut. Mets-mayr sat on the bed throughout, watching the
dancing like a dowager. When the candles were low and the dancing
became disjointed, she simply flicked the switch on her hearing-aid
and lay down to sleep.

Early the next morning, after the best part of a week, I left the
rest home and the Getashen refugees, and the sleeping students and
Mets-mayr, and headed for the north-eastern corner of Armenia. I
hoped for another step back from the Soviet republic, away from
the cracked, pre-fab façade of Communism. It was a region of old
monasteries and high villages. Perhaps here would be an end to the
rootless sagas I knew so well, some sense of Armenian continuity.

# 17

Were they to ask me where one can meet the most miracles on this planet of ours, I would name Armenia first of all . . .

Rockwell Kent, nineteenth-century American painter

After the Seljuk Turks overran Armenia in the eleventh century, there began, paradoxically, a period of intensive monastic activity. Hidden away in remote valleys, on high cliffs, Armenia's monks built and wrote on a scale not seen for four hundred years. Known as the Silver Age, this period coincided with the age of the great monasteries of medieval Europe. It was a feverish, innovative time but finished not, as in Europe, with a renaissance but with the Mongol invasions. So ended a thousand years of Armenian civilization. Never again did they achieve such brilliance in their own land. No better examples of the Silver Age exist than a group of four monasteries here at the top of the Armenian republic: Goshavank, Haghartsin, Haghbat and Sanahin. It would take several days to see them all.

From the rest home, I crossed the meadows above the concert hall and ducked into the forest. Shafts of sunlight fell between the leaves and bathed the undergrowth in a flickering, subaqueous light. The stalks of young ferns tilted and waved like stiff kelp. I found a track which cut through the trees and for several hours followed the river down to Dilijan.

Picking through the scrappy remains of Dilijan's shops and stalls,

I retrieved some bread and apples for lunch. I sat on a low wall beside the market and spread out my modest picnic. Out of the mass of swarthy Armenians gathered among the stalls, emerged a woman who asked me what I was doing. She had long fair hair and pale skin and large, sad eyes. I asked her to join me and she perched on the wall and took out a lump of cheese wrapped in a scarf. She was Russian, she said, a Molokan, the sect of non-conformist Christians. I hadn't realized there were any left. She said that her own family had been banished to Armenia in the 1840s. There were, she explained, three types of Molokans: Common Molokans, Constant Molokans and Jumpers. She was a Constant; she didn't like the Jumpers, they were too demonstrative.

She explained too about the name. I gathered that it could have something to do with *moloko*, 'milk' in Russian, or perhaps a connection with the Moluchnya river. But I preferred the theory that it comes from *malo kyatse*, meaning 'little confession', because the Molokans had so little to confess to the Russian priesthood.

She took me to see her friend in Dilijan's museum who had stored, away from the public rooms, shelves and shelves of earthenware pots. Most of them, he said, dated from early in the first millennium BC. They had all been found in the hills around Dilijan. He was a great enthusiast and, perched on a step ladder, handed me down a whole series of objects, pointing out the symbolism of each one. The terracotta lamps were shaped like turtles, because the earth rested on a turtle's back. The handles of the small urns were fashioned as goat's heads for thunder, or snakes for wisdom. And there was a motif of strange spinning segments, known as the 'whirligig' motif, which ran round the rims of many of the pots. This type, he said, is the most common of all – it stands for the eternal process of regeneration.

By the time the local bus pulled out of town it was late afternoon and almost dark when it arrived in Goshavank's village square. Around the square, the homesteads jostled between broken picket-fencing; bright-painted balconies loomed out of the dusk. The air was still and sharp, and columns of smoke curled out of the cannon-barrel flues. A woman leading a goat directed me to the house of her cousin. There, she said, they would have a room for the night.

Behind a muddy yard, I found a large stone-built house; a crack from the last earthquake snaked up the sitting-room wall. The old man had died only a few months before and his two sons and their families now shared the house. One was dour and the other wild-eyed and charming. Over the whole family hovered the presence of the old man's widow, an indomitable Armenian matriarch. The evening passed in a homely haze of high spirits. I played chess with the quiet man and drank vodka with his brother. We toasted Armenia; they cursed the Azeris. And I imagined thousands of households like this one, scattered through the Armenian mountains, briefly shaking off the shadow of perils past and the threat of perils to come. It was almost midnight when I climbed into the old man's bed and sank into the steep, deserted valley of its mattress.

Against the pale pink cliff behind it, the pale pink ashlar of Goshavank monastery almost disappeared. Its tight cluster of buildings seemed hidden, camouflaged. But nothing could disguise its austere genius. I spent a whole morning there, alone, under its spell. Completed in the thirteenth century, Goshavank was among the last of the great Armenian monasteries. Its eponymous vartabed, Mekhitar Gosh – 'he of little beard who comforts' – spent years up here in the lull between the Seljuk and the Mongol invasions. Hunched over manuscripts, he mapped out his own comforting vision of collective order, which became the text of Armenia's standard Code of Laws.

Empty though they were, the buildings had remained intact and ordered, an oasis of calm in a dangerous world. I'd half forgotten the power of Armenian architecture. I'd half forgotten its strange spirit, the spirit of Ani and Digor and Aghtamar. Too long in the diaspora had cast doubt on my impressions – too many miles and too many books. After several years' gap, I was now back within sixty miles of Ani, convinced now that there *was* something extraordinary about these churches, that in them burned the same fuse that coursed through Armenian history, both brilliant and explosive.

Goshavank is a higgledy-piggledy group of chapels, a library, a gavit, some bitty outer walls. Not a curve or angle is out of place; every block of pink masonry is cut to precision. The structures are still as solid as the bed-rock beneath. Even the stone furrows of the roof fitted like a jigsaw, and all the curving blocks of the central drum were joined by no more than hairlines.

Beside the ogee entrance of the marriage chapel stood Armenia's most famous *khachkar*. I ran my hand over its surface. There are thousands of these stone-crosses all over the highlands; their intricate woven patterns are reminiscent of the Celtic crosses of north-western Europe. Scholars have toyed about with the idea of possible links, citing the Armenian bishops who reached Ireland in the eleventh century. But I suspect the similarity stems more from a common impulse – the impulse to forge patterns from the shapeless rock – than a common historical root.

No *khachkar*, and no Celtic cross I have seen, can match that here at Goshavank. Chiselled from a single slab of tufa, it looks from a distance like lace or some vast clay filigree, but close up, you can see that every inch of its lattice has been chipped away. It is a Gordian knot of a stone. But it's not beautiful. Such passionate precision seems vaguely unsettling. Something anxious lies behind it, perhaps the persistent anxiety of invasion, for the *khachkar* is dated 1237, the year after the Mongol hordes arrived on Armenia's borders.

Examining the knotted course of the *khachkar*, trying to work out whether it was true that a single stone thread linked every corner of the six-foot sculpture, I thought of Yerevan's Edward Ghazarian, a micro-sculptor, whose work has the same vertiginous effect. Ghazarian's micro-sculptures are the smallest in the world. He can only work using a powerful eye-glass or microscope. Once, arranging a group of dancing girls in gold, he accidentally inhaled ten of them and now always wears a mask when working.

His chosen settings are such things as grains of wheat and the eyes of needles. But it is his sculpture of Gulliver that is the most extraordinary. Based loosely in the land of the Lilliputians, Ghazarian placed a micro-Gulliver on a human hair and suspended him between two tiny houses. In each hand Gulliver balances a ball. On one ball are two martial artists. On the other an acrobat stands on a bar one hundred times thinner than a human hair. The slightest touch charges the whole sculpture with static and sets its performers spinning and fighting. They say that no two movements of this microscopic circus are ever the same.

And I remembered too the prodigious mnemonic feats of Samuel Gharibian, a Yerevan lawyer. During the earthquake of 1988 he had committed to memory the names and addresses of thousands of families in order to reunite children who had been lost. He was found to be much more efficient than the computers. His gifts too have earned him a place in the *Guinness Book of Records*: during five hours, one thousand words were dictated to him, at random, in a dozen languages. He then recited them back, flawlessly.

I couldn't help feeling that there was something cathartic about the Armenian passion for details and very small things – small things and patterns. Ghazarian's gold dancers and corn-kernel paintings seemed products of the same genius as Mesrop's alphabet and the web of medieval systems. The world must be divided and divided and divided, the chaos stemmed. Armenian art, when it is not austere and monumental, is obsessively reductionist.

Michael J. Arlen, son of the author of *The Green Hat*, travelled to Armenia in the Seventies. As an American Armenian who had been brought up to forget Armenia, to avert his eyes from the Armenian tragedy, he had become intrigued by it. His journey was a marshalled, Intourist view of the Soviet republic but his book, *Passage to Ararat*, is full of good things. One reflection in particular had struck me. I had thought it referred to 1915 but I now saw it as having a much wider application:

> I realized at that moment that to be an Armenian, to have lived as an Armenian was to have become something crazy. Not crazy in the colloquial sense of quirky or charmingly eccentric . . . or even of certifiably mad. But crazy: crazed, that deep thing – deep where the deep-sea souls of human beings twist and turn.

After the *khachkar* I longed for something smooth and unadorned. I went into the dank interior of the main church with its plain walls and the dim light falling through its plain, slit windows. The church was full of house martins. I startled them as I entered and the air now trembled with their wingbeats. Their twittering sounded like running water in a cave. Somehow their exuberance made the stone seem even deader. But the walls that I'd thought were bare were not. Out of the semi-darkness, beneath the spatterings of guano, came something alive. The walls were covered in them: the carved patterns of prayers and *grapar* texts, hundreds and hundreds of Armenian letters.

I walked down from the monastery into what Mekhitar Gosh had called Tandzot, the Valley Full of Pears. Now there were no pears but there were steep cliffs that hour-glassed the valley's entrance. Perhaps it was these that had kept the Mongols out.

The next monastery, Haghartsin, I imagined to be about four or five hours' walk. I set out along the main road. It was warm and the edges of the puddles were ringed with dry mud and dust. Azerbaijan was not far to the east and the road was empty. But after an hour a man in a black Volga pulled up and said that it was not good to walk when he had a car and with the problems, and that if I didn't come with him at once he would make trouble for me with the authorities. But almost as he said it, his stern exterior cracked and he grinned. 'I like to make joke!'

It was a sunny day and he wore a raincoat. He was director of a raincoat factory. Fingering his own quilt-lined, top of the range, Europe-style coat, he trotted out a litany of raincoat statistics: hem lengths, gusset depths, button size, man hours, production levels, deadlines. Then he cursed the Azeri embargo for slowing production. How could he get materials? How was he supposed to export his coats? And the electricity always going off – on and off like sun and cloud! I shook my head and commiserated and soon we were splashing down a track to his home. In the kitchen he poured two glasses of brandy and proposed a toast: 'To peace.'

'To peace,' I said. 'And more raincoats.'

He took me in to see his elderly mother. She sat on the edge of an iron bed and her short stockinged legs dangled towards the floor. She wore black and I could see she had been weeping. Her son leaned forward and put his hand against her forehead.

'One hundred and four,' spluttered the old woman through her tears.

'Oh, mama-djan. It is high temperature.'

She jabbed a crooked finger towards a large wireless. 'No, fool! One hundred and four, in Karabagh – killed. Oh, oh, dear God . . .' She tugged a handkerchief from her sleeve and, spreading it flat in her palm, pressed it to her sobbing eyes.

The raincoat man urged me not to go to Haghartsin. He said that it was dangerous in the woods and that I should stay. The forest was full of Russians and bears and Haghartsin was an old, dull place. I should come and see his factory and his stitching machine from Italy with built-in computer. All afternoon in the forest I kept my eyes open for bears and Russians but saw neither. The wooded valley was deserted. The beech burrs cracked beneath my feet and I could hear the fast-flowing river below.

Close to the monastery was an abandoned cable-car station, the carcass of another ill-conceived Party plan. In calmer days visitors could stop their own cars and travel the last one hundred yards to the monastery by funicular. (In truth the road was much quicker – even, I imagined, to walk.) But I was struck by the pathos of this short-lived scheme and spent some time just wandering around it. Built to look like a sixth-century church, its secular shell was now useless. The wind blew through its cables and the trees seemed to shy away from its rotting corpse. Some way off, its heart, a massive six-cylinder engine, lay bleeding into an oleaginous pool.

The three or four monastery buildings stood alone on a grassy bluff above the river. Nearby was a cabin of green weather-boards. It was the home of a stone-mason. No one else lived at the monastery or for miles around. It was as remote a place as I'd been to in months. I spent a couple of days there and for the first time since arriving in Armenia, looking up to the ridges, I had a feeling of space.

The mason had two dogs and a single rank of bee-hives. He had dug neat trenches for his radishes and potatoes. He had cherry trees and kept a sheep with haemorrhoids which hobbled around the glade. At night the dogs crouched in the space beneath the floorboards. Sometimes, if they heard a bear or a wolf, they would bark. Hornets had hollowed a nest out of the walls above my bed. Between the barking of the dogs below me, the hornets above and the distant howling wolves, there was little chance of sleep.

Nowadays the mason didn't do much but weed his vegetables, tend to his bees and collect wood. His work at the monastery had come to a halt. There was no gravel for cement and no benzene to fill the generator to drive the saw to cut the stone. He'd given up asking and simply went about his daily tasks like an ascetic.

During the Silver Age, Haghartsin had been the great centre of Armenian ecclesiastical architecture. For three hundred years successive generations of masons had added their pieces of cut stone to the jigsaw. The buildings they left were brilliant and somehow boastful. On the drum of the main church was one of the symbols I had seen in Dilijan's museum: a circle of spinning scalloped segments, the Aryan symbol of eternal life (and, perversely, the origin of the swastika). But for now the place seemed no more than a fossil reminder of a better age. Then the monks had commissioned building on an exuberant scale; now the mason was idle. The shelves of Dilijan's shops were now bare and this spring most people were relying on the land for food and fuel, even medicine.

Who could claim that the 'superstitious nonsense' of medieval belief had been sacrificed for anything worthwhile? Post-Soviet Armenia seemed pre-medieval. There was no talk of ideology any more. No more banners professing the liberating benefits of a utilitarian age. There was just a dull confusion.

On the way to Haghbat and Sanahin, the last two great monasteries of this corner of Armenia, I spent a night in an out-of-the-way village near Alaverdi. There was a certain similarity to the people in this village. They fell roughly into two types: short and stocky with billowing chests, and short and thin with scarecrow shoulders. Most of the men were called Ludwig.

It was already late when one of the stocky Ludwigs had found me on the main road, trying to get to the town of Alaverdi. He offered me a room. His village was perched high up the cliffs and he had driven through the hairpins with a kind of defiant fury. Ludwig was young and wide-eyed. He had the unquestioning enthusiasms of a true nationalist, occupying as he did a black-and-white world of Good men and Bad men, Armenian and Turk, where violence was the only common currency between them. His views had never been sullied by direct experience; other than a recent spell of national service near Yerevan, he'd never left the mountains.

He showed me into a bare room and left. I was tired and kicked off my boots and lay on the bed. I was soon asleep.

Ludwig returned a little later. 'Look, Philip,' he said, handing me a book about the *fedayi*, the early *fedayi* in the years before 1915. 'Good men,' he said. 'Good, brave men.' Then he reached into his boot and pulled out a knife. 'See my knife, Philip. It is a good knife, yes?'

'Yes, it is a good knife.' It was a huge knife.

'A good knife, you think, for Mussulman?'

'It looks a good knife for anything.'

Its fat, fish-shaped blade flashed in the dim light; Ludwig ran the pad of his thumb across its blade and leaned toward me. 'Show me your knife, Philip.'

I produced a rather waif-like stiletto, used strictly for peeling fruit and sharpening pencils. 'It's Spanish,' I said. 'Espagnol.'

'Espagnol?'

'Yes.'

'Espagnol. Oh, Philip.'

He looked at it closely, then grinned and pumped the knife backwards and forwards. 'Espagnol!' (Only later did I discover that *spanel* is the Armenian verb 'to kill or murder'.)

Outside there was a sudden commotion of dogs. Ludwig pressed his face to the window.

'Oh, they come. Look, my friends have come!'

His wife showed in two men and slipped away.

'We are three together,' said Ludwig, clapping his arms around their shoulders. 'Philip – Shahan, Ludwig. Shahan is Hunchak, I am Dashnak, Ludwig is communist.'

'Not communist!' This Ludwig glowered at Dashnak Ludwig.

'You have Party card!'

He reached into his coat and pulled out his card. 'I spit on card.'

'Communist!'

'I hate communist! Look, English, I tear card!'

'Keep it,' I said.

'Why keep? I tear. Not communist!'

'Keep it to show to your children.'

He looked at it, at his own laminated communist face staring out from it, then slipped it back into his pocket.

Dashnak Ludwig shouted for brandy. His long-suffering wife shambled in with a tray and glasses. She didn't say a word. Ludwig poured four glasses, and distributed them. 'To Hayastan!' he cried.

'To Hayastan!' echoed not-communist Ludwig and Shahan.

'Come on! Let's go!'

They whooped and cheered and Dashnak Ludwig slapped my shoulder. 'Come on, Philip, the forest!'

The forest?

'*Gernank! Gernank*, Philip!'

I pulled my boots back on and followed them to the car. We rattled off through the darkened lanes of the village, picked up two others, bucked and slid up a track and into the trees. I was gripping the door when the car spun off the track and into a thicket. Laughing, everyone tumbled out to push and Shahan sat on the bonnet while Dashnak Ludwig revved it out.

There was a darkened glade beneath a cliff. A cold wind blew down from the mountains. Shahan lit a fire with some old tyres. Dashnak Ludwig pulled out his knife and stuck it in a tree. One of the others had a pistol and pumped a few rounds into the fire, grinning silently as he did so. This was a brutal place. I watched the flames make pagan shadows on the group's reeling forms. I wondered how much of the Armenian code was written here, in these glazed faces. I marvelled again at the range of the Armenians. In how many corners of the world, by how many different Armenians – Beverly Hills millionaires, Parisian scholars, stubble-chinned *fedayi* – are glasses raised with that same toast, 'to Hayastan'?

A bottle was passed around. I took a swig, buttoned up my coat and wandered away. The stars were very bright but there was no moon. Far below I could see the speckle of lights from the village. Above them were the mountains, the shadowy, silent mountains. Their jagged ridges ran across the night sky like the cardiograph of a sick old man.

In the morning Stocky Ludwig said he'd drive me to Alaverdi but I said I'd walk. I was very keen to walk. I had to insist and left the village feeling irritated at my own ingratitude. Down below the village, the river had done strange things to the landscape. A deep gorge had sliced down through the valley floor and left a shelf hanging on either side. On this shelf were most of the medieval villages and churches; in the dark gorge below crept the railway and the road and all the tattered steel and concrete of the Soviet years. This was Lori, Armenia's black country. Walking along the main road, I felt the gorge grin down at me with the blackened teeth of its basalt blocks. The distant ridges hung from the sky like torn black-out screens and there was a strange dark quality to the light. I felt the blackness pressing in, filling my head with dark thoughts.

But shortly after midday I found a bus which pulled up out of the gorge. In Haghbat, things brightened up. The afternoon was sunny and the village slow. In the main square a woman sat in the shade of a rowan tree while her children kicked a ball about in the dust. From behind the houses a mattock chinked on the rocks. Above the square were the monastery buildings. They were spread out like an eccentric family portrait, spanning the hardy generations of Armenia's Silver Age. Goshavank and Haghartsin had been the same, a collection of monuments built up over the years. And each collection was a testimony to the priorities of the monks – the predominance of chapels, the meeting hall and refectory, the library – but never any sign of cells or living quarters.

While those at Haghartsin had concentrated on masonry and architecture, here at Haghbat they devoted themselves to the Word. Their scribes were the most dedicated of all. They endeavoured, during the eleventh and twelfth centuries, to make their monastery a repository for all that existed in the Armenian language, a former Madenataran. Monks tramped the mountains searching for manuscripts, digging around in the dusty vaults of monasteries from Van to Urmia, transcribing those they could not keep. And when, during those turbulent years, news came of another Turanian wave or Mongol horde, they would bundle up their work, run up the hill and hide the vellum sheets in caves. Now the buildings are empty. Their thick walls are shiny with damp and the stone is stained black from centuries of tallow smoke.

Squatting against the rear wall of the chapel, which was built like the cathedral at Ani and the restored dome of Sancta Sophia by Trdat, and watching the sunlight squeeze through the narrow chink of the windows, I thought of Mandelstam's iconoclastic outburst at the Armenian church in Ashtarak:

> Whose idea was it to imprison space inside this wretched cellar, this low dungeon – in order to render it homage there worthy of the psalmist?

Many Armenians would share his disapproval. In these mountain villages pre-Christian traditions have died hard. Just as at Edjmiatsin, buried beneath the surface here are traces of ancient Persian beliefs – Zoroastrian, Manichaean, dualist. The Persians were loath to lock their gods in temples; they felt closer to them in the open air and worshipped outside. Herodotus recorded their preference for prayers in high places. The Zoroastrian prayer-book, the *yasna*, even contains a special prayer to be recited 'on seeing a great mountain for the first time'. The Armenian devotion to Ararat is a part of this tradition and a number of mountains in Armenia are named after Zoroastrian deities. Until quite recently, Armenian villagers would perform their morning ablutions, then go outside to pray to the east.

*Khachkars* and stelae and *vishaps* show too how closely the Armenian land is tied up with belief – something that sets more sacerdotal Christians mumbling about heathens, pagans and animists. But in such a climate, dissident groups like the Paulicians found followers easy to find; to many Armenians, dualism was always more persuasive than Christianity.

The dank chambers of churches have always vied with the Armenians' earthier, more oriental beliefs. But in one respect these extraordinary buildings are defiantly Armenian. Nowhere else do churches – nor, to my knowledge, buildings of any kind – look so different outside as they do inside. What outside is angular and pointed, inside is round; where outside there is a sharp cone, inside is the cupola; outside triangular blind niches, inside tubular alcoves and apses; outside a pitch roof, inside barrel-vaults or arcing rib-vaults. Looking at the ground plan of these churches, they appear almost like two buildings in one. By using walls in-filled with rubble the Armenian masons seem now to have been presenting some sort of deliberate enigma.

Often, alienated in a group of Armenians or grappling with some Armenian paradox, I thought of these churches and forgave myself for not understanding. I'd become used to surprises. Every time I saw a pattern – some symmetry in the Armenians – it would be thrown out, offset like a glimpse behind the church door.

That night I stayed in Haghbat's burgeoning seminary. The term was over and only the vartabed and two pupils remained. After supper, Father Vartan excused himself to go and pace up and down the garden. I dipped into his library while the two boys sat testing the Armenian font for their Apple Mac computer. In the morning I left for Sanahin.

The monastery of Sanahin was visible from Haghbat, but to reach it, I had to descend again into the gloom of Alaverdi, and there I became waylaid by two rotund restaurateurs.

They were well-connected, these Armenian gourmets, having what in Romania were called 'good relations'. In the Soviet Union these clandestine channels were simply the mafia. The mafia wore a smiling face and an imitation Rolex on its wrist. Not a night went past when the inside of its raided flat was not shown on the television news: stacks of US dollars, guns, imported liquor. Sometimes the mafia was violent but at other times, and this was one of them, it showed a talent for unctuous bonhomie.

'English, more brandy. Drink! This brandy the very best!' We were having breakfast, seated at a long table in their sitting room. I'd become used to the habit of early-morning drinking.

'And here, English, caviar from Caspian Sea.'

'Caspian caviar? I thought there was a blockade.'

'Yes, blockade. Azeri blockade. Terrible, very terrible.'

I found Sanahin monastery tucked into a wooded slope above a concrete-and-glass settlement of the same name. Its monastic halls were dark and empty. Beneath a series of colonnades, the mud floors were paved with tombstones. Here, as at Haghbat, medieval scribes had battled with summer fleas and winter cold. Here they translated Euclid and Plato, spinning together the twin threads of Classical and Oriental traditions that characterized the Silver Age.

Some half a millennium after the Mongol invasions, with Sanahin still just about ticking over as a place of learning, the young George Ivanovitch Gurdjieff arrived to study. The son of an Armenian mother and Greek father, Gurdjieff was also a product of eastern and western traditions. But the real source of his ideas remain, by his own intention, obscure. They defy all categories. But there are clues. One of Gurdjieff's first adventures, as told in *Meetings with Remarkable Men*, was to go to Ani. There he built a hut among the ruins and spent his time, as most of his early life was spent, reading obscure texts and hunting for esoteric secrets. One day at Ani he discovered an underground passage. At one end of the passage was a room in which he found a few scraps of parchment. To his delight, these scraps, inscribed in classical Armenian, referred to the re-location of a lost school of ancient Babylonian teaching somewhere south of Lake Van. He set off to find it.

Whether this story is true or not, it holds a considerable symbolic weight. For Gurdjieff the Arab invasions of Mesopotamia in the eighth century made Armenia the sole keeper of the flame of ancient belief that pre-dated the monotheisms of Islam and Christianity. In rooting around in the ruins of Ani he was beginning to uncover the dualist, Zoroastrian and Mithraic traditions that remain in Armenia. From there his quest spread outwards, to the south and to the east. For twenty years he wandered around the Near East, central Asia and the Himalayas before turning up in Moscow. There he began to teach the ideas he had gathered and which, frequently misunderstood, have inspired, bewitched, charmed, angered, emancipated and confused the minds of the West ever since.

His great work, in the *All and Everything* Series, is entitled

*Beelzebub's Tales to his Grandson.* Twelve hundred pages of virtually impenetrable stories present a cast of allegorical characters as diverse as Blake's. He wrote it, in pencil, partly in Russian and partly in Armenian. He chose Russian as it was more widely known. But he found it limited, 'like the English, which language is also very good, but only for discussing in "smoking rooms", while sitting in an easy chair with legs outstretched on another, the topic of Australian frozen meat or, sometimes, the Indian question.' Armenian had been his favourite language, being utterly unlike any other, and corresponding 'perfectly to the psyche of the people composing that nation'.

Gurdjieff belonged to no tradition. But to me his own particular rootlessness could only have been bred in this region, in old Armenia and the Caucasus where the traces of antiquity could still be found among the ruins, and where the clash of ideas – dualist, Zurvan, Sufi, Christian, Islamic, Bolshevik – has made it more diverse, more dynamic, more dangerous than perhaps anywhere else on earth.

At midday I left Sanahin and walked back to the main road. Down in the valley it was hot. In Alaverdi, I found a lift to Leninakan where Gurdjieff had been born one hundred and twenty years earlier.

# 18

It had been well known for twenty years that the distribution of large and small earthquakes followed a particular mathematical pattern, precisely the same scaling pattern that seemed to govern the distribution of personal incomes in a free-market economy.

James Gleick, *Chaos: Making a New Science*

The city of Leninakan had gone through the usual turncoat charade of renaming. Now it was called Gumri, its ancient Armenian name; before Leninakan it was known as Alexandropol, and it was under this Tsarist banner that Gurdjieff spent his early years. I wasn't sure what I'd find in Gumri; not his house, certainly, but perhaps some traces of the Greek quarter where he'd lived. There was nothing. The Soviet blocks had swallowed the old city as they had most Tsarist cities; then the blocks themselves had been destroyed, scythed like high grass by the 1988 earthquake.

From Alaverdi, I'd hitched down through the mountains with a brooding man and his taciturn mother. She'd sat in the back seat and knitted with a curious desperation. The car was filled with a heavy silence. Only when we stopped at a remote graveyard did they unwind. The old woman set down her needles, took a bag of apples and led us up through the wafer headstones to the twin grave of her husband and elder son, killed by the earthquake. There, in the Armenian way, the context of death and its certainty made her relax. She sat on the low parapet and gnawed at an apple, her red cheeks swelling with its shards. From the other side of her mouth she chatted away, saying how pretty the other graves looked with their red and white carnations and how next time she would bring flowers if she could find any . . .

She convinced me to change my plans. Having established what I could about Gurdjieff's birthplace, I'd intended heading south, to Lake Sevan. I had not thought to look into the earthquake; it was a natural disaster, arbitrary, not part of the essential Armenia. But I was wrong: precisely because of its arbitrariness the earthquake came to reveal a good deal about the Armenians.

In Gumri I had lunch with the widow and her son. They lived in a makeshift home which was so diligently kept that it was not easy to see that the whole thing was little more than a large wooden box.

I spent an afternoon kicking around the muddy ruins of Gumri. I thought of Revolution Square in Bucharest and of Beirut. I looked at the grieving stumps of tenement blocks, of second-floor bedrooms with their fronts ripped away and the chipboard doors still intact. I stood before the shattered façades and tried to imagine the moment it all happened: 11.41 a.m., 7 December 1988.

In Yerevan, in one of the sleepy academic institutes, I'd spoken to an eccentric Armenian polymath who had urged me to look at those numbers.

'Do you see?' he had said. '11 and 41 – what do they say to you?'

I could think of nothing.

'Prime numbers!' he had become quite animated. 'And not just prime numbers, but you see they are clearly out of sequence with the quinary system of minutes. Not 11.40 or 11.45, but 11.41!'

I said that in Skopje, Macedonia, the railway clock had been left as a reminder to the 1963 earthquake. 'And the hands point to 5.17.'

'You see, again! Prime numbers! Irregular. Think of a man-made disaster – Hiroshima, for instance: 8.15 precisely!'

I liked his theory. I was interested in the way the horror of the earthquake appeared to demand the consolation of pattern, of any explanation, however improbable. The only pattern for him, for this numerologist, was in the very randomness of its timing. To others earthquakes are acts of God. In His inanimate world God abhors patterns. Rocks have no symmetry until worked by man, or unless in fossils they bear the imprint of vanished life. Earthquakes strike at random, at unpredictable times, in unpredictable places. They reduce cut stone to shapeless rubble, lashing out at those who dare to create order.

But Soviet Armenians were brought up in a godless age; they'd been fed on different truths. There *is* a pattern to history, and it *can* be made to work in our favour. For seventy years the Marxist-Leninists taught that a benevolent State replaced the need for God, glossing over the fact that the benevolent State, like any deity, could also be vengeful.

And so to the man in the cobbler's hut in Yerevan who'd told me, as others had, about the controlled subterranean explosions. The earthquake was the work of the Soviets. An act of God meant little, but an act of State, well, that made more sense: they wanted to punish us. Since the beginning of that year, 1988, Armenia had been stirring up problems, as if there weren't enough problems for the Kremlin. First it was a chemical works, belching out poisonous fumes; they wanted it closed down. Then there was Karabagh. From late February on, the Armenians had been for unification with the enclave. Border changes, pollution – new headaches for Moscow from the union's smallest republic. On one day alone a third of Armenia's population, an estimated one million people converged on Yerevan's city centre. It was to be the largest display of anti-Soviet feeling in the whole seventy-year history of the Union.

Then, in the last days of February and in response to Armenian claims on Karabagh, the Azeris conducted a pogrom in the Caspian town of Sumgait. The Armenian quarter was surrounded. For three days the Azeris rampaged through the town, burning houses, using hatchets on the inhabitants and throwing their bodies, living or dead, from the open windows of tower blocks. No one knows how many were killed. The Armenians never forgave Gorbachev for not sending in the troops earlier; they assumed it was retribution.

During that summer the two republics polarized. Two hundred thousand Armenians left Azerbaijan for Armenia and about one hundred and fifty thousand Azeris left Armenia for Azerbaijan. The Armenians were billeted wherever there was space, in hotels, assembly rooms, and doubled-up in apartment blocks. Many ended up in the cities of northern Armenia, Leninakan, Kirovakan and Spitak. There, after a few months of hardship, shortages of food and fuel, problems with water, no jobs and little to do in the desperately cramped conditions, the earthquake struck late on a grey snowy morning. Within minutes an estimated twenty-six thousand people had died.

Now in Gumri, more than two years later, the town still seemed dazed. It had lost its head for heights. Everything went on at ground level. Trucks full of stone lumbered through the broken streets and mobile cranes, operated from the ground, stretched their remote limbs over the building sites. Among the *yurts* and the Portakabin shanty were schools and offices and clinics, and somehow things seemed to work. Of all the shops, most of them little more than lean-to shacks, the most popular were those selling home adornments – gilded plastic swags, ersatz chandeliers, garish icons and countless little trinkets to brighten the hardboard blandness of this refugee city.

'Of course, it's different in the villages,' a vegetable-seller explained. His tufted carrots lay on the roadside like fallen knights. 'In the villages, they have nothing.'

'Where are these villages?'

'In the hills. I came down from the villages. I have not been back. I had no home after *yeghashar*.'

*Yeghashar* – the Armenian has the cadence of direct experience; it trembles and shatters and falls. 'Earthquake', by contrast, sounds as cold as a physician's diagnosis.

I gave the vegetable-seller some roubles, refused his carrots, and set off to try and reach the villages. Spitak had been the closest large town to the epicentre. In Armenian it means simply 'white', but it was now grey and broken. I went to find some aid workers whom I'd met in Yerevan.

I reached them in the early evening and they invited me to stay on their compound. They were diaspora Armenians from France and Canada and the United States. They lived in a strange Swiss-built capsule which they had installed, just above the town, in the ruins of the Communist Youth Camp. The forest had begun to take over the camp and had colonized the collapsed concrete with a vanguard of ash saplings. But around the capsule itself was a layer of dark new asphalt. There were two beds of petunias by the door and inside everything was meticulous and ordered.

Much of the evening I spent with Michael, an Armenian Buddhist from Boston. He was the only Armenian Buddhist I'd met. He wore Ivy League spectacles and a Lacoste shirt, but could not disguise his Armenianness. Coming to Armenia, he explained, was his karma. He'd been planning to go to a Zen monastery in Japan but, at the airport, had suddenly decided on Armenia instead. He was now married to a girl from Yerevan.

197

'Shall I tell why the Armenians can live anywhere in the world?'

'Please do.'

'I have been all over this country. It is very small, but there is something distinct about this place. Know what it is?'

'I have my own ideas.'

'Here in Armenia you have every type of climate and landscape imaginable. People are used to extremes. So we Armenians can go anywhere in the world and not mind. Wherever we go we can adapt.'

I tried to explain that what interested me was that the Armenians had *not* adapted, but had, like him, remained Armenian however far they'd gone. But his theory seemed so neat that he was unwilling to enter an argument.

At the Aralez Psychosocial Rehabilitation Centre in Spitak, set up for orphans of the earthquake, I spent a happy few hours the next morning waiting for a lift into the mountains. It was a bright day and the sun played on the heads of the children as they entered the centre's courtyard.

In the process of psychosocial rehabilitation, music played an important part. The aid workers kicked off with an exemplary display, singing impromptu Armenian folk songs to a flute and guitar in their cramped main office. In another hut, a puppeteer was rehearsing a sung sketch with his wooden wolves and pigs: sly grinning wolf lollops after long-lashed pig, pig flees, wolf dies. Then the orphaned girls filed into the assembly hall in their pom-pom shoes and red pinafores. They had pink top-bows in their hair. Each girl in turn stepped forward, curtsied, pulled up the stool and played a four-finger piece on the piano. We all clapped, vigorously.

It was almost over when my lift leaned round the door, gesturing to me that she was about to leave. Isabelle was half-French, half-Armenian. She had dropped everything in Paris to spend two years with the earthquake victims. I warmed at once to her dedication, her slightly scatty manner and the complete lack of concern she had for her own comfort. We left the main road and joined a muddy track that led up towards the villages. The slopes of the valley were smooth and rounded, and there were few trees. In places were small outcrops of rock. Several miles away, at the valley head, a sponge of cloud was squeezing its moisture on to the mountains.

Isabelle loved this bleak terrain. 'There's still life in this land – the communists can't take that.'

'Nor the earthquake?'

'No, nor the earthquake. They're so tough, these people. My God, they are tough. You know, it's incredible. Every two or three generations, something happens: the earthquake, Stalin, the Turks. Sometimes I wonder why the Armenians are not crazy.'

'Maybe they are,' I said.

'Why do you say that?'

I told her about Michael J. Arlen's idea that the Armenians were, at some very deep level, crazy.

'So why do you want to come to this crazy country?'

'Maybe for much the same reason as you.'

'But I am Armenian.'

'You could have stayed in Paris.'

'Paris! It is so unreal!'

'Exactly.'

'But why Armenia particularly?'

I told her about Anatolia and Lake Van. I told her about Ani and the church at Digor. I said I wanted to find out why the Armenians had survived so long.

She smiled. 'Are you sure you are not Armenian, not even a little bit?'

We stopped off in the village of Sarahar. Isabelle had a class to give at the school and I wandered up through the ruins. The stone-bearing trucks had transformed the road into a quagmire. There was a bench in the graveyard and I sat there with a book; but the book lay unopened beside me. I listened instead to the chatter of larks and finches, and the wind in the poplars by the cemetery fence, and the bees in the grass, and the dry statement of a crowing cock, and the perpetual tap-tap of a hammer. And beneath it, more imminent than all of this, was something silent and shapeless. I recognized it from Deir ez Zor and a dozen other places on my route. I could not avoid it. It was squatting here at the frayed corners of the village. It lingered in the puddles. It was prodded and scraped by a woman bending to clear a drain of mud. It was spelt out by the hands of a clock on the headstones, 11.41, and by the dates: 1932–1988, 1961–1988, 1974–1988, 1957–1988, 1982–1988.

We drove on up the valley, further towards the epicentre. Gogoran was the last village on this road. Beyond it the mountains disappeared featurelessly into a bank of clouds, and the grey-white of the snowy slopes merged with the grey-white of the clouds. In Gogoran the signs of rebuilding were scarcer. Half a dozen pre-fab houses stood primly among the ruins, but that was all. A couple of women in rubber boots shuffled through the mud, another threw a bucket of potato peel at her goat, another sat on a large block of broken stone, knitting.

After the earthquake, this small corner of the Soviet Union was pledged so much money from around the world that the survivors assumed it was only a matter of time before they lived like the Armenians in California, with tiled kitchens and patios and picture windows. In Gogoran and the remote villages, they saw out that winter beneath plastic sheeting and tarpaulins. In the summer, when it was dry and warm, that's when the rebuilding would start, that's when the money would come.

But no convoys trickled up to Gogoran. Most were too busy in Spitak and Kirovokan and Leninakan. Pledged money remained in Western banks, or disappeared in Moscow; the Azeri blockade and the Soviet system put dampeners on the rest. They waited all through that summer. Still numb from the earthquake, the survivors did little but graze their flocks. In late August the first cold wind blew out of the mountains and it was the women who, according to Isabelle, broke the spell. It is us who must rebuild, they said, and galvanized the men to build shelters for the winter.

Isabelle took me to see her favourite family. They lived in a bucolic fug in one of the new houses. It had two rooms that opened into one another; the walls were plasterboard tacked to the wooden frame and their old furniture looked out of place. There were five of them: two sons – Arthur and Saro – a father who was in Spitak, a devoted mother with a sad smile and a mongrel puppy named Lassie.

Coming into the village we'd passed a monument – two sections of broken concrete raised on their ends. Between them was suspended a clock with its hands jammed at 11.41. The clock was the school clock, and the concrete a part of the classroom floor. It had been a three-storey building. When the earthquake struck, the children of Gogoran were all at school. Built, as most were, on the cheap, with corners cut to bolster Party perks, the school collapsed instantly. All but a dozen or so died.

Walking with Saro on the slopes above Gogoran, he told me what he remembered; he didn't like to talk about it at home. That morning his class should have been physical exercise. But the physical exercise teacher had not bothered to come in, so it was maths. Saro hated maths and he was bored. He was bored and only half concentrating when the first tremor struck. He recalls, in the split second afterwards, seeing his teacher running to open the door. Then Saro found himself upside down. The ceiling had gabled over him and saved his life. Only one other boy survived in his class. For several hours they shouted at each other through the dust before they were rescued. Saro was virtually unscathed.

His brother Arthur had not been so lucky. He was in a physics class, reading aloud a passage about Newtonian thermodynamics. He recalls a moment of surprise and weightlessness, and then one leg was shoved against his stomach and the other round his neck. The dead body of his teacher was pressed against him, and he could see another limb in the rubble. In that position, with his back broken, Arthur waited an hour and a half before the debris was cleared by hand. (You can still see people in these villages with their fingers worn down to the first knuckle from clawing at the rubble.)

Arthur was wrapped in a mattress, but passed out on the way to Kirovokan. Since then he had been to France to have spinal surgery. The operation was a success and he could now move the upper half of his body. In France he'd been given a mini pool table, which now occupied a large part of the house. He spent much of the day spinning round it in his wheelchair, with a shortened cue.

We came back from the mountain. Arthur was waiting for a game of pool; his mother was knitting a pair of stockings. She put aside her knitting and watched us playing pool and sighed. She loved her two boys, who'd survived. She stood slowly to fill the kettle before sidling up and leaning over Arthur's wheelchair to kiss him.

'No, Mama-*djan*. I'm playing.'

'Oh, Arthur!'

Arthur was laughing, using his cue to fend her off. 'Ma! No!'

She managed to plant her lips on his forehead before she fell, also laughing, on to Lassie, who was lying on the bed. 'Oh, Lassie-*djan*!'

'Careful, Ma!'

Saro chalked his cue and studied the table. His mother nestled Lassie like an infant and started to sing.

'Mama-*djan*,' shouted Saro. 'Quiet! We're playing.'

'Oh, games. Always games! What can I do, Philip-*djan*?'

I smiled, bending to play my own shot. 'I don't know.'

'Oh, you boys!'

Arthur manoeuvred his wheelchair around the table and Saro grinned at his mother. 'Don't worry, Mama-*djan*. Soon I will be gone. Two weeks and then the army.'

'No, Saro-*djan*! Not the army.' And she hugged Lassie even closer.


All night the sleet pattered on the tin roof. In the morning, a cold wind chased it out of the pass above the village. It streaked the bevelled barge-boards of the new houses; it hung in the body of a shirt on the washing line. It had turned to snow before eleven o'clock. I played pool with Saro and Arthur and waited for it to clear. From time to time I glanced through the window, but the cloud had come right down. It was early afternoon before the far side of the valley became visible. Over there, they said, there you'll find the epicentre.

Saro walked part of the way with me. The wind was still fiercely cold and the mud on the track was brittle with ice. We were joined by a wild country boy with staring eyes and a skull-like face. He was an advocate of the Earthquake as Soviet Conspiracy.

'There were strange things just before.'

'Strange things?'

'A few days before, many trucks on the road. Then all the Russian soldiers suddenly left. I was in the fields in the morning, and there was a flash all across the sky, and then – boom! *Yeghashar!*' The flaps of his woollen hat beat against his hollow cheeks. 'Bomb explode! Buildings fall!'

I didn't find it any more credible. But I knew that in the mythology of the mountains – those stories that would roll down the generations like snowballs – the earthquake would forever define the Soviet age. It was the swan-song of autocracy, the last act of the dying empire. It was all too neat a pattern to be chance.

We rounded a low spur and Saro pointed across the valley. 'The villages: Geghasar and Nalbend. Just follow this path.'

We embraced and shook hands. I told Saro to be kind to his mother. I told him to look after Lassie and his brother Arthur, and that if he wanted to beat him at pool, he must get his chin right down on the cue. There was more embracing. There was clapping of shoulders and more hand-shaking. For a long time afterwards when I turned around they were still there, standing beneath the grey sky, against the snowy slopes, hands raised and waving, their breath floating like veils around their heads.

The epicentre of the 1988 earthquake had been established as a line that cut across the valley between two knuckles of high rock. It was an imaginary line, but once it had been pointed out it emitted a strange force. One of the two rocks towered over the semi-ruined village of Geghasar. After another night in the corner of another hardboard home, I walked around beneath the rock and up its lower slopes. In places here the soil was still torn from the earthquake, short six-foot scars like stretch-marks.

The mountain grass gave way to rock, and I scrambled up the last thirty feet and out on to a high ledge. Geghasar lay almost immediately below, about five hundred feet down, and beyond it the river and the main road and beyond that the village of Nalbend. Above Nalbend, about three miles away, was the other rock, the partner in this grim tectonic crime; the two rocks faced each other guiltily, like dyarchic despots.

Something strange happened up there. Perhaps it was the climb or general fatigue or the cumulative effect of malnourishment; it might have been all three. Or perhaps it was just too much thinking about the earthquake. It lasted only a short time and was accompanied by a sense of vertigo. The whole landscape became suddenly fluid. The clouds stayed still and the ridges and hillocks moved like waves. The valley swayed like a cradle. Everything that shouldn't shift, shifted; everything that was dead became animated.

I leaned back against the rock. Light snow curled over it and I squatted down in its lee. I pulled the collar up around my neck and looked down. There had, until the earthquake, been a shrine built on this ledge. It was revered as a sacred rock. Far below it, like a smashed vase, I could see the pieces of the building scattered in a narrow gully.

Quite suddenly I felt tired, profoundly tired. I felt tired from all the half-destroyed places, from the paradoxes and un-solid things, from the thousands of miles and the borders, tired of keeping going. I was asleep no more than a few minutes. When I woke the valley had disappeared. Geghasar was nothing but a faint shadow beneath the snow. When I stood up, the flurries beat at my face and streaked past my ears. Already the snow had collected like dust in the crevices of the rock. Cursing my foolishness, I felt my way back along the ledge. The rock stretched down vertically until it faded into the storm. I half closed my eyes to stop them filling with snow and kept them fixed on my feet. When I reached the grass below, I felt hot and sweaty inside my coat, but my hands were numb with cold.

By the time I got back to the house, the snow had eased. The women were sewing, picking at the stitches of an old folksy dress for the summer.

'Look! How cold you are. Come, sit by the fire.'

'Thank you,' I said and pulled off my boots.

Their four-year-old son giggled at the steam rising from my shoulders and my trousers and from my socks. Behind him was a home-made shrine to his grandfather and two aunts, killed in the earthquake. One of the women pulled up a flap in the floorboards and reached into the potato-clamp below and filled her apron with vegetables. Her husband, Manouk, came back from a morning's work at the Russian camp. He uncorked a bottle of vodka and grinned.

'To you,' he said, raising his glass.

'No,' I replied. 'To you. To all of you.'

Having had lunch, I went with Manouk to the edge of Geghasar to find a lift down from the mountains. A group of cars had shunted up against the doors of a long shed and the men were cramming their boots with meat for the towns.

'One of these cars will take you,' said Manouk. 'Where do you want to go?'

'South. To Lake Sevan.'

He frowned. 'It is far, but maybe you will find someone from Kirovakan.'

I shook his hand and paused to watch him walk back up the hill. The village made a strange, messy sight beyond him. Late snow merged with the early blackthorn, the abandoned shells of the old houses mingled with the new, and over it all, piercing the blanched skin of the mountains, was the earthquake rock, now in exact alignment with where I stood and the rock opposite. This old co-operative cattle shed was placed precisely over the epicentre, the very heart of the 1988 earthquake.

I stepped into its gloomy interior. There was a smell of meat and excrement. At the far end cattle were leaning over their stalls, tugging at strands of hay. The cow-herds led them one by one to a butcher who slashed their throats. Their blood wound its way towards the drain, which was half choked with dung. All around me men and women were hacking at the carcasses. One old woman alternately sawed and pulled to try and free the bone from a haunch, while lashing out with her other hand at a woman who was working on the shoulder. Others stood around some scales, exchanging fistfuls of roubles for various pieces of cow. At my feet a man worked on a body with its head already missing. His hand was buried deep in the beast's entrails. Goaded by his wife, he yanked out the liver and slapped it on the concrete beside him. Then he took a knife to the stomach. He failed to remove it intact, and it split open and slopped half-digested dung over his hand. The only thing that bothered him, that made him grunt and curse with anger, was that it had extinguished his last cigarette.

I found a young sausage-maker and his wife who were going to Kirovakan. I shared the back seat with two tongues in newspaper and a head; the boot wouldn't quite close on the other two heads they'd bought and we'd had to tie them down with cord. I wound down the window and let in the mountain air.

The man was fairly drunk and took the roads with a kind of floppy gusto; there was one moment when he lost it on a bend and the car slid into a gravel bank. The cow heads in the boot knocked against each other, but the man hardly interrupted his monologue. Laid on for my benefit, almost the entire journey was spent on a story about the local communist hoods who'd had a Party function in Yerevan and ate like fat animals and drank so much that some slept on the table: 'See how they much they drink and the country all in a mess . . .'

I felt in no mood for argument. Already I'd seen two or three wrecked vehicles on the rocks below us. I didn't want to anger him by pointing out his own drunken hypocrisy. So I shook my head and shamelessly tut-tutted in all the right places.

# 19

I reap the harvest of the vine
My garden treats me with its wine
I drink in shade beneath the fence
Then hear: 'Your garden leave – go hence!'

Grigor Aghtamartsi, sixteenth-century Armenian poet

I felt at once uplifted by the sight of Lake Sevan in the late afternoon sun. A carpenter had driven me over the high pass from Kirovokan and dropped me off beside the lake. I was glad to see water after so much broken rock. Down at the shore I propped my bag against a tree-trunk and slipped off my boots. I hobbled over the rocks and thrust my feet into the water. It felt cold and slimy where the minerals left a residue on the skin.

Near the shore the surface was a clear metallic green and still. Further out, it was furred by a light breeze which blew down from the mountains. The mountains themselves rose along the eastern shore in a row of bulging spurs. Somehow they made me think of the story of the dissolute communists at their Party function in Yerevan, cheek-down and drunk on the ruffled tablecloth of the lake. Just over their dozing, snow-dusted shoulders lay Azerbaijan. To my right was the island of Sevan, now not an island at all, but joined tonsil-like to the mainland. Away to the south – thirty, forty miles – the far shore lay beneath the horizon and the lake simply disappeared over it.

I returned to my bag and sat down on the pebbles. Pulling out the travel-scarred volume of Mandelstam's *Journey to Armenia*, I trekked for the umpteenth time across the undulating steppe of its first sentence:

> On the island of Sevan, which is distinguished by two very worthy architectural monuments of the VIIth century and also by the mud huts of some lice-bitten hermits who recently died off, now thickly overgrown with nettles and thistles and no more frightening than the neglected cellars of summer houses, I spent a month enjoying the lake water standing at a height of four thousand feet above sea level and schooling myself to contemplate the two or three dozen tombs that lie scattered about, a kind of flowerbed among the dormitories of the monastery, which repairs have made young again.

That was in 1930. Mandelstam carries on to describe the island as a crucible of the new Soviet life: the fading elements of the Church, whose dormitories have been made 'young again' to provide sleeping quarters for a youth camp; the Armenian archaeologist Khachaturian who is too involved in Urartian antiquity to bother with communism; the communist Karinian who is too idle to bother with anything but the new Soviet literature; and Gambarian, a youthful sixty-year-old chemist who seems ambivalent to it all. He takes on a model Soviet youth in a swimming race around the island but has to be rescued, half drowned, by Karinian, the ideologue. The epilogue to this farce was being acted out that evening: Soviet Armenia was dying on the island of Sevan.

As I walked across the isthmus to the old seminary building, a car pulled up and a young priest offered me a lift. He was grinning from ear to ear. 'I must tell you the good news. In Armenia we say when you share good news with a stranger, it is twice as good!' He pointed to a semi-derelict building, once part of the seminary but commandeered by the state in Mandelstam's time. If the Church wanted it back, the order was, they would have to pay – three hundred and seventy-five thousand roubles. But the Committee had just told the priest he could have it for nothing. For nothing! Not only that, but he had been to see that day some factory directors. These men, once the bastion of communism, had switched their loyalties. One had pledged to provide lights for the seminary and his finest chandeliers for the main hall and church, and would replace all the pipes that irrigated the gardens. Another had agreed to give a million roubles for the restoration of a seventh-century church in one of the villages.

Magnanimous in his worldly victory, the priest offered me a bed for the night. In return I gave a class to the seven seminarians. They each had a new Bible and at the back of each Bible was a map of Jerusalem. I pointed out the Armenian quarter and the monastery and all the Holy Places to which the Armenians had rights. Later, eating soup in their new kitchen, they explained how when they had arrived six months before there was no electricity or water. After their Bible classes they would go outside into the snow and cook on an open fire.

I rose early the next morning and set out to find the Writers' Rest Home where Mandelstam had stayed. The sun rose over the mountains and gilded the lake's flat surface. In a few hours it would be hot. 'What is there to say about the climate on Sevan?' asks Mandelstam rhetorically. 'The golden currency of cognac in the secret cupboard of the mountain sun.'

That, perhaps, and the tendency to set admiring visitors reaching for elaborate metaphors. To Maxim Gorky the lake was a section of sky inserted in the mountains. Colin Thubron spent five nights here in 1981 and 'the water lay in a trance – less a lake than a huge, unblinking eye of glass, sated and colourless: the eye of the earth itself.' Even at a distance, the lake has lured travellers into enthusiastic excess. H. F. B. Lynch, empirical and taxonomic as only the Victorian explorers could be, spent months in Armenia, counting and measuring and mapping things. He never reached Sevan, but that didn't prevent him gathering information for his wonderfully exhaustive: 'Tabular Statement of the Evidence of Travellers in Respect of the Fluctuations in Level of the Three Great Lakes (Van, Urmia and Sevan)'.

Lake Sevan made Marco Polo credulous of the claim that here the world's 'finest fish' rise to the bait only during the forty days of Lent. Simone de Beauvoir, on a Soviet tour with Sartre, was rhapsodic about the Sevan 'Ishkhan' fish – 'as long as one's arm, pink as salmon and so delicious'. Their meal, and the lake, clearly moved Sartre to relax his guard and soon afterwards he rose to make an ecumenical toast. His comments about Franco-Armenian relations, made to a group of Armenian ministers and Party big-wigs in the full flush of Soviet hatred for the West, were met with icy silence and a table of grim stares.

But in his unbridled response to Sevan, Mandelstam remains the master. On the lake he let loose some of his wildest images – tenuous, invigorating, and always coloured with his own wry poetic vision. The island's grasses 'were so strong, juicy and self-confident that one felt like coiffing them with an iron comb'. At the near drowning of the chemist Gambarian, 'the island became nauseated like a pregnant woman.' When early one morning he hears a boat's motor across the lake, its rhythmic chugging whispers to him: 'Not Peter not Helena, not Peter not Helena' – a cryptic reference to the Armenian Church's shunning of both Rome and Constantinople. And – my favourite – as he walked on the beach during the sudden evening storms 'the incunabular surf would hasten to publish by hand in half an hour's time a plump Gutenberg Bible.'

The sheets of the morning surf at my own feet would have been pushed to produce a breviary, let alone a Bible. There was no wind and the low sun bounced off the water as if from a mirror. The pebbles crunched beneath my feet, and every now and then I had to vault the tendril of a pipe which stretched redundantly out of the lake and up into the birch plantation. To my eyes, the island became more and more artificial.

I pushed on round the southern shore and came across a high fence. In its hey-day it must have been unassailable, pacing Berlin Wall-like over the hump of the island and deep into the water. I followed it up the cliff and managed to get over.

Inside, the gardens were still neat and well tended. There were cherry trees and mountain shrubs, and wagtails flitted between them. One or two women in white coats swished at the paths with knobbly handled brooms. I said 'Good morning' (in Armenian, literally 'Good light'), and they let me go unchallenged. This was a rest home, but not the Writers' Rest Home. It was the Party Rest Home – hence the high fence to keep out the people. Built on the lakeside rocks, in the best spot of the island, which itself was regarded as the jewel of the republic, was the Party rotunda. It looked deserted. But as I walked up to it a fat man in a track suit stepped out. He was chewing pistachios.

'What are you doing?' he grunted. 'You are not allowed here. Where are you from?'

'Britain.'

'Tourist?'

I told him what I was doing and how I'd reached Armenia.

He spat out a pistachio shell. 'You will have to come with me.'

I followed him across the concrete hall of the rotunda and down a passage to his room. A woman lay on the bed, listlessly watching television. The Party chief went into an adjoining room. On Russian breakfast television, a group of heavily made-up children danced precociously; I was beginning to feel faintly repelled by the Russian cult of the child.

The man was smiling when he came back in. The smile hung incongruously on his face. 'Please, will you drink? I would like to drink to your journey. Please tell us about the places you have seen.'

The Party chief knew the Writers' Rest Home and directed me round the shore. There was no missing it. Its separate, glass-fronted refectory was little more than a set of wide windows that hovered above the lake, grinning like the Cheshire Cat. Was it here, I wondered, that Mandelstam had stayed?

I traced a very old lady, one of the island's oldest residents. She said that, as a child, she had helped build this strange edifice. But the year had been 1932, two years after Mandelstam's visit. This woman must have been one of the children who disturbed his peace on the island, who spent their time chasing an old mad ram, capturing toads and snakes, and climbing over the *khachkars* with which the island was 'literally paved'. I asked her if she knew the poet's name or his connection with Sevan, but she shrugged. He was yet to be resurrected from the Soviet black-list. But the authorities, in 1932, had soon found these idle youngsters a useful role in the building of the State. For half a loaf of black bread per day, this woman was instructed to carry stone to the site of the new Writers' Rest Home. The stone came from a seventeenth-century church which had been pulled down. The *khachkars*, useless old gravestones, they threw in the lake.

Intourist groups were still coming to peer at the remaining churches as 'historical monuments'. A coach stood near the seminary when I returned and I found the priest nervously fingering his ring of keys outside the chapel of Arakelots. The Russian girls, he said, they make trouble; always they come and see the seminary boys and they want to make trouble, asking the boys to pick them flowers, asking for special tour, saying why do you want to be a priest, making trouble with their deep-blue Russian eyes . . .

I walked back along the isthmus to the mainland and around the top of the lake. Three or four sails criss-crossed the water around the island. The easterly breeze had dropped suddenly and the wind was now driving them from the west. The priest had told me of a cemetery of old *khachkars* on my route south, so I hitched down Sevan's western shore and found a forest of headstones in the village of Noradouz. In the late afternoon the far shore of the lake looked scrubbed, polished by the clear air; both the *khachkars* and the distant mountains appeared in the same microscopic detail.

I had grown to love the webs and patterns of these stone monuments. Each one was as intricate and distinctive as the Armenians themselves. Here at Noradouz there were hundreds. Their chiselled surfaces were flecked with lichen and age had tilted the plinths so that each now had a comic, animated gait. I wandered among them, and felt that *I* was the ghost, stumbling through groups of chattering families, humbled with admiration for stern old matriarchs.

Crouching to look closer at one weathered sarcophagus, I made out two figures carved in low relief on the stone. They were man and wife, clutching between them the same symbol of perpetuity that I'd seen at the museum at Dilijan. This Aryan patera, with its spinning segments, seems as much a part of Armenian iconography as the cross; somehow every manifestation of Armenia's pagan heart delighted me.

'No meat, no fuel, no food! You Russians have taken it all.'

I turned to face a fierce-looking woman with three sheep. 'I am not Russian.'

'Now I have only my sheep. Have you come to take my sheep?'

I assured her I had not.

'Thief! Russian!'

'Look, I'm not Russian and I do not want your sheep.'

She cocked her head quizzically. 'Why do you speak Armenian, Russian man?'

In another corner of the graveyard was a grey shed. A strange six-noted mechanical dirge rang from it; inside was a lathe with six blades which spun slowly around a stone block. There was slate dust everywhere; it covered the floor and mossed the eyebrows of the operator, who was heaving another large block from the store. On

211

seeing me he waded through the dust to flick a switch and the machine wound down. He showed me some of his finished *khach-kars*, but they were too mechanical, too perfect; they had none of the skewed symmetry of the medieval versions outside. Yet there was no denying that this small shed was the most industrious place I'd seen in the whole republic: fuel shortages, blockades, economic collapse could not keep the Armenians from honouring their dead.

I asked him how much they were.

'Is it for your mother, or maybe your father?'

'No, no. I'm just curious.'

'This one, maybe twenty thousand. For the special ones, more.'

On average, I calculated, someone would have to wait about five years before earning that.

I walked from the cemetery out to the lake. The evening had brought with it an even sharper clarity and I gazed at the mountains and the strips of cloud above them. Here, after a month in Armenia and halfway down the shores of Lake Sevan, I was halfway down the country itself. To the south lay the province of Zangezour, funnelled between Nakhijevan and Azerbaijan, between enemies. The people of those mountains had never given in. The Persians, when they ruled there, simply washed their hands of this troublesome region, lumping it together with Karabagh as a semi-autonomous satrapy. In a few days I would reach Zangezour, but en route I was keen to find the family of Paruir Sevak who was Armenia's greatest modern poet.


On the bus south I met a man travelling to market. At his feet were stacked three boxes of cherries; another box sat on his lap. He had several days of stubble on his chin and his teeth had been whittled down to yellowy stumps. He pushed up his cap and, scratching his forehead, told me that he had fled Baku a few years ago.

'After the pogroms?'

He nodded. 'Yes, many Armenians died. My cousin died. I fled. I lost many things. Many books.'

'Books?'

'One thousand books. Dumas, Galsworthy, Hugo. I liked Victor Hugo best.'

'You must have been sad to lose them.'

'Yes, it was sad. But Victor Hugo escaped with me!' He tore off a strip of newspaper, sprinkled some tobacco in it and rolled it into a cigarette. He smiled broadly and the smoke rose around his face. 'Now I am going to Yerevan to sell my cherries. Then three days in Yerevan. Many women.'

'You're not married?'

'My wife, she is at home. In Armenia we say "If you go to the forest, why take wood?"'

# 20

Already 10 years, 110 years, 1010 years
that I fear
the multiple and blunt believer,
the multifaced and vain believer.

Paruir Sevak, from 'Let There Be Light'

Paruir Sevak is now the most widely read of the modern Armenian poets; more than anyone else he articulates the current struggle for belief. Born in 1924, he lived out and wrote out the phases of Armenia's dark century, cutting his teeth on the great medieval scholars, moulding his first verses like a Persian bard out of doughy patriotism and love, moving to Moscow and turning to the Armenian genocide with a seven-thousand-line epic published in 1959, only to return to Armenia as a modernist, shaking off all poetic traditions, living in the mountain village of his birth. There he wrote the lines of his last work 'Let there be Light', which was then cut to pieces by the censors. He died shortly afterwards, in 1971, and there were rumours it was the KGB.

The priest at Sevan, it had turned out, was related to Sevak. He had scribbled a note for another cousin in Shiraz, down in the Ararat Valley. She was, he said, still close to the poet's family. I found her in the early afternoon holding court beneath the vines of her garden. She was a homely, dark-skinned woman with long black hair. She sat with her family at a table spread with bowls of cherries and peaches, and white cheeses and slabs of lavash and wine bottles and brandy bottles. She read the note and smiled, urging me to join them; tomorrow they would be going to Sovetashen to visit the house of the poet . . .

How long we spent at that table, in the green, sleepy heat, I don't know. But when I rose to walk around the town, the bottles were empty and the sun almost level with the peak of Ararat. I wandered past the houses and into open country. Beneath Ararat's snow-browed gaze (forty miles away, ten thousand feet up) fruit trees and power lines crossed the valley floor in neat rows. It was still hot. I slept off the brandy beneath a walnut tree and woke to the shouts of children collecting loganberries. I took a handful as I passed and re-entered the town.

There were few people about, yet the whole place was bursting with life. Houses were lost behind thick foliage; vines snaked on high trellises over the roads, which themselves were bordered by culverts of dashing water. What wasn't green was gold, or red, or yellow, or purple. But one old woman wasn't impressed. She sat on a wooden chair beside a patch of lilies. Her hands were buried to the wrist in a bowl of muddy potatoes.

'Shiraz,' she said without looking up. 'It is nothing.'

'It looks good to me.'

'To you it may look good, but I come from a better place.'

'Where is that?'

'Many miles.'

'Lori? Zangezour?'

She laughed mockingly, and shook her head.

'Well, where?'

'You would not know it. It is in Syria.'

But I did know it. I remembered the abandoned property on the Turkish border. I remembered the story of Stalin's invitation, the thousands of Armenians he lured to the republic with promises of 'repatriation', and those who soon saw his utopia for what it was, and those for whom Siberia was deemed more suitable than Armenia.

'Kessab?' I said.

She eyed me suspiciously. 'You know Kessab?'

I said I'd been there and I'd seen Bedros Demyrdjian and old Hajji Babook and Norees Berdirian.

'Oh.' She looked at me blankly. She seemed unable to comprehend. 'And . . . the village, the apples – it is beautiful still?'

'It was winter,' I said. 'It was cold and wet.'

She looked away and shook her head. She didn't believe me. Nothing would convince her now that in Kessab it was not always spring with the apple trees perpetually in blossom; what she saw around her was little more than a drab Russian colony. But for me, after the chill Soviet towns of the north, Shiraz was different. That night was warm and I slept on a carpeted divan in the house of Sevak's cousin. For the first time I felt Persia closer than the jagged skylines of the Caucasus.

It was mid-morning by the time Sevak's cousin had cut roses and carnations and prepared to leave Shiraz for Sovetashen. Driving south beside the Turkish frontier, the Araxes river wound along the wrong side of the border and the sun reflected Ararat in its languid tributaries. Over there, in old Armenia, there was little sign of life – neither town nor farm nor creeping tractor. But here every spare corner was planted and the villages pressed their concrete limbs right up to the wire.

Pulling up out of the Ararat valley, we stopped by a squat, carved stone. Here, on 17 June 1971, en route to Yerevan by car, Paruir Sevak had spun off the road and died. He was forty-seven.

His cousin knelt to kiss the memorial and spread the flowers on its flanged base. We stood for a moment in silence. A warm wind blew up out of Nakhijevan. On the stone was chiselled one of Sevak's couplets: *yeghetsi luis, yeghetsi khaver* (it was light, it was dark). Underneath the words was that whirligig symbol again, the assurance of regeneration. Looking at the road, I could understand the suspicion surrounding Sevak's death. There were no obstacles or bends; it was a straight, wide-open bit of road, an empty place. I don't suppose the truth of Sevak's death will ever be known.

We climbed back into the Niva. Near the breach in the mountains, the only approach to southern Armenia, was the new village of Sevakavan, named after the poet. One night a couple of weeks earlier the Azeris had crossed the border and killed two of the pioneer residents.

At Sovetashen, less than half an hour from the place Sevak died, we pulled up off the main road and found his house and his two sons working in the garden. There was a small museum and along the inside of one wall his life was played out in a strange iconic panorama. His peasant birth looked suspiciously Christ-like, complete with straw and manger and lowing cattle. At his wedding his father was painted off to one side, dancing like an Ashkenazi Jew. And there was a telling scene of the Poet's Apprenticeship: Sevak sitting beneath the mythical tutelage of Mesrop Mashtots, Movses Khoranetsi, Narek, late at night, a cigarette dangling from his sausage lips.

His face was always a marvel to me. At least once in his verse he calls it ugly – and so it was. But it is also one of the most expressive faces I have ever seen. It has the ripe overflowing quality of Armenia's villages with its wide, post-box mouth, huge teeth, broad nose and bitter-sweet eyes. It has something of Pushkin's hybrid fullness, and there is a strange and circuitous link between the two poets.

In the seventeenth century the family of Sevak had been exiled to Persia along with hundreds of thousands of Armenians. The Safavid emperor Shah Abbas had tried simply to empty Armenia. It was the Russians who, in the 1820s, enabled about ninety thousand to return. Out of these faceless numbers, the figure of one unfortunate Russian emerges with a kind of pathetic dignity. Like many Tsarist civil servants, Griboyedev was also a writer. One hot summer in leafy Tiflis (at that time also the hub of Armenian letters), he wrote his play *Woe through Wit; or the misfortunes of being clever*. It was an acute satire and found little favour with St Petersburg's nervous censors, who banned it. It was, however, staged in Yerevan, and money from it helped four or five hundred Armenian families to return from Tabriz in 1826; Sevak's family packed up their Persian home after two hundred years, crossed the Araxes and resettled in the village of Sovetashen.

But poor old Griboyedev paid dearly for his irreverent play. He was removed from St Petersburg and packed off far from harm's way, to Persia. There he was put in charge of overseeing the Turkmen-chai treaty, the agreement that saw the end of direct Persian influence in Armenian affairs, and the beginning of Russian. (It is easy to forget now, after the deadening effect of seventy years of Moscow dictatorship, and the shadow of the Turks before that, that for more than two millennia, Persia has been much the most consistent outside player in Armenia.)

Under the terms of the Turkmen-chai treaty all Armenians were to be allowed free passage back to Russian Armenia and Griboyedev travelled to Tehran to arrange it. His arrival was ill-fated. It coincided with the annual commemoration of the death of Imam Hussein, Mohammed's sainted grandson. At that time in the Muslim capital the Shiites would hammer their chests with knotted fists and wear clothes stained with their own blood; they would cry 'Ya Hussein!', leap about, prostrate themselves and pour hot coals on each other's heads. It was bad luck that Griboyedev chose to arrive on a black stallion, the mount favoured by Hussein's killer.

So rather than an honorary reception, Griboyedev had to run for his life, spurring his horse in through the gates of the Russian legation. Cossack guards kept the mob at bay. But the faithful maintained a vigil outside the gates, cursing the Russian infidel, stabbing and mutilating themselves to show their displeasure. The crisis reached a head when three Armenians crept into the legation, awaiting the chance to return to Armenia. One of them had been a eunuch in the Shah's harem and with him went all the intimate secrets of the seraglio.

So now the mob had the tacit backing of the Shah. They burst through the gates. The Armenians were slaughtered and Griboyedev died, cornered in an upper room, vainly fighting off the Shiites with his sword. A kebab-seller sharpened his knives and cut off the envoy's head, displaying it loyally above his brazier to attract custom. An arm was severed for a diamond ring. The mob tied the rest of the body to a team of dogs and pulled it around the city. Then it was tossed on a dung-heap. For a week it lay in Tehran's Armenian church before being released for burial.

Alexander Pushkin did not know of his friend's death when he rode down to Russia's Armenian front. Trotting alone down a rocky Caucasian path, he encountered an ox-cart grinding along in the opposite direction.

'What is on the cart?' he asked.

The carter muttered, 'Griboyedev.'

Pushkin's reaction was odd. He wrote of the jealousy he felt for his headless friend: 'I know of nothing happier, or more enviable, than the last days of his storm-filled life. Death, coming to him in the heat of a brave and unequal battle, was neither terrible nor wearisome, but, on the contrary, sudden and beautiful.'

Pushkin was to die some years later in a duel, giving these words an added poignance. Griboyedev and Sevak left similarly portentous comments before their own, violent deaths. Just before he left for Persia, Griboyedev had said to Pushkin: 'You don't know those

people down there. You will see it is necessary to play with knives.'
And Sevak in one of his last poems, 'Transiency', wrote these lines:

> Once again I become naive
> Once more I believe in justice
> And it seems to me
> I shall die a natural death.

Sevak's grave was marked by a vast rock, a massive lump of the mountains. It lay like a recumbent whale among the shrubs and flowers of his garden. The apple trees and cherry trees that he had planted were in blossom. If it is true that his life was an occasionally lucid stumble through the murk of the twentieth century, the Soviet murk, the Armenian murk, which ended back in his native village with his devotion to the land, it is appropriate, then, that his most fitting memorial is not the roadside plaque nor even the volcanic boulder, but his spade. On the day he died, Sevak had been digging potatoes. He tapped the spade against his boot to remove the soil and put it against a tree. Then he went inside to scrub his hands and prepare for the drive to Yerevan. Twenty years on, discreetly fixed with wire to the gnarled bole, the spade is still where he left it.

Sevak's cousin was not keen for me to continue south: the fighting, the Turks, it is not safe . . . Not for the first time on the journey, I had to be firm: south for me was the heart of Armenia, I had crossed twenty borders to be here, I'd spent months and months with Armenians in exile. In the southern mountains were the real Armenian villages, the places Armenians had survived for hundreds of years; it was, for me, the final piece in the Armenian jigsaw; that's why I'd come all this way.

After such a speech, she could not prevent me. But I felt a little guilty about having to make it. She left me in a deep gorge and I watched the Niva head up to the pass, burrowing between the high cliffs like a beetle.

# 21

Comrades, respect the power of Armenian brandy!
It is easier to climb up to heaven than to get out of
here when you have taken too much on board.

Inscribed on the cellar wall of Yerevan Cognac Factory by Maxim
Gorky and Mayakovsky

I turned and headed down the gorge towards Goris. The river murmured beside me, whispering through deep pools, arguing over
rapids. On one side the cliffs were a bright wine-yellow, on the other
they were in shadow; I crossed the road to be in the sun. I would
try and reach Goris tonight. I imagined it was about three or four
hours' drive, but there was no sign of any traffic.

Some way on, I came across three men cooking meat over a fire.
They wore shiny black shirts and had deeply weathered faces. I asked
them about getting to Goris.

'You cannot go to Goris. Gunfight.'

'Oh?'

'No, Khatchik,' said another. 'Goris is good, but Djermuk is not.'

'No Levon-*djan*. You can go to Djermuk, but not to Ghapan and
not to Goris.'

'Ghapan is fine, Raffi-*djan*.'

'No, I was there yesterday and . . .'

I said, 'I just need to know about Goris. Is it OK?'

'Yes.'

'No, Raffi-*djan*!'

'Look only last week . . .'

'You are wrong!'

'Silence!' The one called Khatchik stood and held up a glass of vodka. 'To Karabagh, to Zangezour!'

'Karabagh!'

'Zangezour!'

They then, each of them, kissed each other on the lips and subsided into a muttering, laughing lament. They were very drunk. The sun had dipped behind the ridge, see-sawing the shadows up the opposite cliff. It was suddenly cold and I felt uneasy about the coming night, making no progress here among these merry patriots. Just then, from far up the gorge, came the sound of a truck, coughing its way through the gears. As I walked off to flag it down, I could still hear them arguing:

'Goris . . .'

'Not Goris . . .'

'Djermuk tank . . .'

'Soviet mortar bomb . . .'

'Helicopter . . .'

'Turk . . .'

The truck, driven by another leathery man named Khatchik, was going to Goris. I hauled myself up into the cab. There were already two other passengers, a girl in a flouncy dress and her husband who was a mining engineer. They were on their way back to his mine, having just got married in Yerevan. The engineer clasped his bride's hand and stared ahead, smiling at the mountains. We ate cherries and bobbed along beside the river. The lorry was hopelessly slow. Freewheeling between gears, it would nudge thirty miles an hour only to gnash against another worn sprocket and slow to twenty. When we started the long climb up to the border with Zangezour, with the evening sky behind us torn open and blood-red, the machine eased to the pace of a trotting mule. Then a walking mule. Then a sick walking mule.

I kept my eyes on the darker skyline ahead, willing the pass closer. I knew that a night out here, so close to the border, would be a risk, and I knew too that once over the pass we would be in Zangezour. Then I imagined it was downhill all the way. Khatchik wore a deep frown. I really thought we might not make it.

We didn't. He fought valiantly to find first gear for the last time but it just wasn't there. He climbed down and lay beneath the cab while I shook the gear stick and pressed the throttle but it was no good. The gear-box, itself salvaged from another truck for the trip south, had had it. Khatchik stood defeated in the dim beam of the headlamps, wiping his fingers on a rag.

I opened the door and jumped down into the darkness. We would walk to the mine of the engineer, just over the pass. At eight thousand feet the sudden cold was piercing. The four of us set a good pace and there was a bright moon; patches of snow shone on the mountains like flaking paint. We walked in silence but near the border came the sound of bells. Zangezour means 'ringing bells' in Armenian and a skeletal campanile had been erected to mark its border.

Passing them, the engineer gripped my elbow. He thrust a finger at the broad moonlit valley below, pointing at the two or three winking lights of the mine, pointing up at each of the two ridges and saying: 'Turks there, and Turks over there. Always between Turks.'

'Do they make trouble?'

He nodded grimly. 'Last week, one night they come over the mountain and kill three.'

I was glad when we splashed through the mud at the mine entrance and through the door of his wooden hut. His bride lit the paraffin stove and spread a torn white cloth on the table. She put the remains of the cherries on the cloth and a loaf of bread on a board. She hummed and half smiled as she bustled around, oblivious it seemed to any Azeri threat. I felt suddenly a consuming affection for this couple, bolstered no doubt by my relief. When the engineer brought the vodka, I toasted their marriage with such gusto that they were quite taken aback.

The engineer's father also lived with them at the mine. His wife had just died and he kept coming in and out of the hut. He had a pig and a car, and was constantly on his way to see one or the other. I wasn't sure which he loved most. He spent more time tinkering with the car, but last thing at night, wearing a miner's lamp, it was his pig he went to see.

In the morning the engineer said, 'Come, I will show you down the mine.'

'What is it you mine here?'

'Water.'

He found me a helmet with a rubber flap that fanned out over the neck. In the pump room he produced a boiler-suit and I pulled it on over my clothes. Someone had chalked on the wall the familiar profile of Ararat's twin peaks. On the main peak was written: ARMENIA; on the smaller one: AMERICA. What did it mean? That Armenia was greater than America? That the two were now inseparable? And I remembered a scheme I'd heard about on Sevan. It was so fantastic I'd assumed it was just part of the never-never land of Soviet conspiracies and fissure-bombs. A water mine – of course.

I followed the engineer on to the elevator platform. Everything was black and wet and oily. I gripped a stanchion and a bell rang twice. The platform jolted and slipped below the surface. From my helmet a cone of light picked out jewelled strings of water that hung down the thousand-foot shaft. Ever since the communists had taken over in Armenia, the level of the water in Lake Sevan had sunk. Their progressive industrial schemes sucked it out at such a rate that the lake had contracted by more than four hundred square kilometres. In its wake, some interesting things appeared, vast new tracts of valuable land, an isthmus for Sevan island, ancient Urartian sites and finally the *khachkars* that the communists themselves had ditched into the water in 1932.

But now that the old order had collapsed, and with it most of their industrial schemes, the level was rising again. It was creeping back like the lifeblood of independence, bringing with it all the concomitant problems of flooding – the fluvial equivalent of the *fedayi's* swollen nationalism.

What could be done to save the land and buildings that had been built on the borrowed foreshore? The lake was besieged by mountains; there was no natural drainage. The only solution was to drill a hole through the rock and bleed the thing like that – forty-eight kilometres of tunnel hacked out of the mountains, from Sevan to Zangezour. I was dropping down through the mountain to meet it. The platform was painfully slow. It creaked and clanked past the rusting hoops that made up the shaft. I felt an uneasy parallel with last night's straining truck. That had failed. I had seen nothing in the republic that worked properly; why should I trust the sophisticated mechanics of a mine? The truth was that I didn't. If this was reaching the heart of Armenia, then so be it. But let it be over soon . . .

We emerged through the ceiling of the loading bay and dim lights replaced the semi-darkness of the descent. Trucks of waste queued up to be taken to the surface; a couple of miners leaned against them and their milky breath rose in the cool air.

We boarded a battery-charged wagon that hummed along the rails and into the tunnel. A couple of feet of copper-coloured water covered the tunnel floor. After four kilometres the rails ended. A pile of scooped-out rubble rose out of the water, blocking the tunnel ahead. The engineer reached out to the wall and took a screwdriver to a stump of loose circuitry.

Climbing out of the car, I stepped down into the water. Near the wall it was only ankle-deep and I headed out towards the rock-pile. Just beyond, was the rock-face. The face itself was wet and I ran my hand over it. There was a piece of loose rock and prising it loose, I put it in to my pocket. It seemed an appropriate bit of Armenia to take away with me.

Back at the surface the engineer's bride stood at the door of their hut. She had laid out bread and cheese on the table and had picked a few sprigs of campion and yellow vetch. These were in a vase. Having eaten, I said goodbye and walked back to the main road.

The Goris bus came over the pass and I flagged it down. They wouldn't let me on until I proved I was not Russian. Then they wouldn't let me pay. In Goris, they insisted on finding me a taxi to the town's hotel and the taxi-driver wouldn't let me pay either. In fact, he tried to pay *me* and I had to be quite fierce about refusing a twenty-five-rouble note.

The government hotel in Goris was no longer really a hotel. It had been taken over by refugees, from Baku and Karabagh. Its balconies were a gallery of washing, hung with the blank canvasses of bed linen and towels. The garden had become a wasteland where children were hounding a punctured football through the shrubs. In one corner a group of men lay beside a fire, with anonymous bottles, twisting a lump of lamb on a spit; in another corner stood a battered military ambulance. But they found me a room; a family had just left for Yerevan. Closing the door, I felt a sudden surge of relief; it was the first time in about a month I'd had a room of my own. I tried to wash, but the water was only a trickle. So I kicked off my boots and lay on the bed. I closed my eyes and when I woke the low sun was slanting across the red lino floor.

I switched on the radio: reports of fighting in Ethiopia. Addis Ababa was surrounded and was falling. There were tanks in the street. On one report I heard them firing on the old palace. I thought of the first Armenians I'd known there – the few that were left, the mechanics, the son of Haile Selassie's tailor, and the evenings on Lake Langano and in Castellis with the good wine Castelli had kept from before the revolution . . .

I switched off the radio and went on a hunt for food. In the hotel buffet, a woman sat with a hairy chin propped in her palm. She raised her eyes just enough to ask: 'What do you want?'

'What do you have?' I couldn't see a trace of any food.

She shrugged.

'Meat?'

'None.'

'Cheese?'

A shake of the head.

'Bread?'

She shuffled into her store, but came back empty-handed.

I managed to get a cup of tea and was sitting stirring it and listening to my stomach grumble, when a group of hirsute *fedayi* burst in and placed four bottles of arak on a table in the corner. They eyed me suspiciously.

I'd been through this routine so often before. 'I'm not Russian,' I said, in Armenian.

One of them urged me to join them. Soon the whiskery woman was bringing food out of nowhere – plates of cooked lamb and cheese and bread and bowls of herbs. Then the toasts started and the songs and they continued long into the evening. I don't even remember how I reached my bed. Getting food on my own seemed impossible. I had two options: starve, or accept the hospitality and the relentless vodka that went with it.


I was trying to get to Tatev, a village some way out of Goris in the mountains. Its tenth-century monastery I had had described to me by one poet in the diaspora as 'the most moving of them all'. From Tatev I would push south again, over the high pass to the Iranian border and the Araxes gorge. The next morning I put a call through to the Bishop of Goris, whose see included all of Zangezour. I asked him if I could come to his office to get a letter of introduction for the villages. Without the right letters they would take me for a Russian and down here any visiting Russians were spies.

The bishop rolled up outside the hotel in a shining black,

chauffeur-driven Volga. I had not wanted him to come, to take up his time – but time, it seemed, was not a problem. He took off his dark glasses and smiled. 'Let us go for breakfast with my friend the philosopher.'

The philosopher had a lazy face and his flat said 'Party' louder than 'Scholar'. It was all chrome and thick carpets and shields of merit on the bookless shelves. Synchronized swimmers dolphined their way across the TV screen.

'I am learning English,' announced the philosopher. 'Listen: remember me to your wife . . . can you recommend a hotel . . . the hens are laying well . . . I want to see the prig.'

'Pig, I think.'

His wife brought canapes of salami and Caspian caviar, and a bottle of Armenian brandy.

'Will you be wanting a shower . . . the dog is brown . . .'

The bishop wiped his beard and said, 'My friend speaks well, doesn't he?'

Outside the apartment block the bishop leaned on the roof of his Volga and wrote a note for Tatev. I thanked him and went to the bus station. Waiting there, squatting against a wall in the dust, I fielded the normal barrage of hateful stares. I thought of all the multi-ethnic towns from the Adriatic to Irkutsk and how the currency of hateful stares was gaining value. Armenians were used to such chauvinism but here they were dishing it out.

I was pleased when Goris was behind me. Zangezour's mountains were refreshingly uncomplicated – smooth and green and treeless. Across their slopes parties of stooping peasants gathered herbs, moving like skiffs in a wide bay. We stopped in a village and from the bus window I watched a group of girls dancing in the square. Near them danced a group of boys. By the time we pulled away the boys were fighting and the girls were sitting on a wall, exasperated. The road wound across the plateau and then dropped into a vast chasm. On the other side, the cliff was a jumble of trees and rock, and a grey haze rose from the river. Far upstream, beside the gorge's drooping lip, was the tower of Tatev's monastery. The church seemed dwarfed by its mythical setting. The Jerusalem poet had been right. It was astonishingly beautiful; land like this seemed worth fighting for.

The sun was well down behind the snowy peaks before the bus made it to the top. In the semi-darkness, I found the house of

Roupen, the monastery's clerk of works. He gave me a room and took me to see his home-made still; watching the spirit innocently bubble away, and Roupen's proud grin, I knew the evening would not pass without having to drink a large amount of this stuff.

Roupen said, 'Later we go to the village assembly. It is Armenian Republic Day and we must go to the house of my friend. He is a capitalist.'

'A capitalist?'

'Before, he was communist so now he must be capitalist.'

I couldn't argue with that.

From the darkness of the garden I could see their red faces through the windows – they sat around a long table in the ground-floor cellar. Roupen pushed open the door and the sound of their gruff voices enveloped us as we entered. Over the table had been spread a red-and-white check tablecloth, almost hidden beneath a cornucopia of cheese and mutton and bread and wild herbs and arak. Behind the benches and the rounded backs of the men, one or two rifles leaned against the walls. We sat down and were at once buffeted with food and drink.

At the far end the council leader – the capitalist – pushed back his chair and stood up. Behind his head a bare bulb hung from the wooden rafters, haloing the grey tufts of his hair.

'On this the day that the republic of Hayastan was declared more than seventy years ago [*cheers from the table*], let us remember those times and those who fought . . .' and he puffed the memory of the heroes who had rescued a corner of the land from the Turks in 1918, '. . . and the great leader Andranik [*grunts of consent*], and now Armenia is once again independent we should all arm and guard against the Turks to protect the homeland and . . . and . . .' He raised his glass. 'To Hayastan!'

'Hayastan!'

Beside me a giant of a man slopped the home-distilled arak into a glass and pushed it along the cloth in front of me. It was full.

'Drink, English!'

The table was suddenly turned towards me, a sea of bobbing bloodshot eyes.

'Drink!'

I threw it back, now quite used to such things. But the ferocity of that mountain hooch was something new. I felt a flame-thrower had been jammed down my throat; the hot, viscous liquid jetted into my chest. My mouth was ablaze. My eyes watered. I took some bread, smiled weakly and wheezed: 'Benzine.'

The eyes around me squeezed into laughter. 'Yes, English! It is like benzine!'

The giant refilled my glass. Fighting cries echoed around the walls and hung like pennants in the smoky air. The gathering became a little quicker; women bustled up and down the table clearing empty dishes, putting full ones in their place.

The giant turned to me and said, 'In Tatev we have two donkeys.'

I nodded. Was this something to pity or admire?

'Two donkeys!'

'Good.'

'No! Not good. One donkey he is called Mutalibov.'

'The Azeri leader?'

'The other donkey, he is Gorbachev!'

He guffawed with laughter. Then, suddenly quite earnest, he looked down at his glass and shook his head. 'They are like donkey these men, Mutalibov and Gorbachev. Like donkey . . .'

An argument started at one end and the capitalist rose again. His henchmen bellowed down the table, 'Silence!'

He directed his gaze, statesman-like, slightly above the group, towards one of the cellar's oak-bole beams. 'As our land which has been ours since before the days of the kings of Bagratouni and the time of Ani is being routed once again by Turk and Mussulman we pray for victory to Christos who we accepted the first of all the world in the year 301.'

'To Christos! To victory!'

He waved his glass in my direction. 'And now we look to Europe and the Christian countries of the West, to our brothers in America and Britain and Finland to help us from the Azeri and Mussulman who are our enemy and the . . .'

'Victory!' The cries of the group were now cranked-up, pitiless. 'Death to Mussulman!'

'Death to Mussulman!' Fists banged on table. 'Death to Mussulman!'

The tone had switched instantly and I felt the sudden undirected threat of bloodlust.

'No.'

I was astonished to hear a voice of dissent in that group. Astonished too to find it was my own. There was silence. Again eyes were turned on me – now more bloodshot, less friendly. 'No,' I repeated. I could not back down. 'The Mussulman is not your enemy. This is not a battle between Christian and Muslim. In the Middle East many Muslims have long been friends of the Armenians. Armenians were sheltered by Arabs in 1915. This is not even a battle with the Turks. It is with the Soviet generals. Is it not them who are now stirring up this hatred between Azeri and Armenian?'

One or two shook their heads and muttered and looked into their glasses. But others said: 'Yes, he is right.' They raised their glasses. 'Come on. More benzine for English!' And then there was another speech about Mesrop Mashtots and Byron and Sevak, and more hooch and music, and the women were spilling out of the kitchen and we were all dancing, kicking up the dirt on the store-room floor.

# 22

Armenia never had peace, but always war.

Sir John Mandeville

I awoke soon after dawn, on the sofa of Tatev's clerk of works. For the first time I could trace a gully scoured down the inside of my throat. When I swallowed, a stream of saliva scorched down it. This spirit-soaked journey was taking its toll. How did they cope with such drinking? They must have caught it from the Russians, the world's heaviest drinkers. Maybe that's the only real legacy of the old Tsarist empire: vodka – a cosh to the masses, more enduring than Marxist-Leninism and, so it's proved, more exportable.

I did the only thing I could and accepted a large glass from the home-still for breakfast. It soothed the scar and numbed my aching limbs. I said goodbye to the clerk of works and headed through his garden to the monastery.

Around each of the houses, every inch of space was planted with something edible. There were rows of sprouting potato and cabbage plants and gauntlets of hazel poles waiting for the beans; almond trees and walnut trees hovered over them, between cherry and apple trees. The soil itself was black and sticky, peeled back from the seed-trenches like asphalt. This black soil and its properties are honoured in the name of Karabagh – a Farsi-Turkic compound meaning 'Black garden'. It has made these mountain villages into little Edens, and some of its fecundity has rubbed off on to the villagers themselves, helping to swell their high spirits.

The spirit of Tatev's monastery was more measured. At its centre was the church of Peter and Paul, built at the end of the ninth century. It had the usual genius of form and proportion – the grey flanks of its drum curving with elephantine grace, the threads of its interlacing perfectly spun. I climbed some stone steps and followed the upper walkway out to a grassy rooftop. Dozens of *khachkars* paraded in the undergrowth; others leaned against each other by the walls, stacked like gifts at the feet of some fabulous potentate. At the edge of the rooftop, the monastery fell away into space. The whole place had been built straight up from the cliff.

I imagined the first monks here, choosing the site. Here they had water and the sound of water from the falls; they had distant mountains – not so much mountains as peaks; there were rocks and bands of rocks, cliffs, outcrops, pinnacles and crags, and where there were no rocks there were scrub trees and wide shelves of high grass and the scars of red poppies. This was Armenia, the essential Armenia; it did my hangover no end of good.

At the foot of the cliffs, perhaps seven, eight hundred feet below, amidst the jumble of rocks, I could make out the rectangular compound of another church. Walking down there, on an old path that swung back and forth across the steep slope, it became gradually hotter and more humid, the grass grew higher and the flowers brighter and even more exotic. The air thickened and filled with fat, drowsy bees, and dancing fritillaries flitted among them. Dragonflies hovered over the brooks like airborne crosses. Jays screeched from the elder bushes. The purring of the cicadas became a clamour. Tiny frogs hopped away at my approach, splashing into mossy pools. At one point a metre or so of yellow-green snake flashed across the path, as surprised at my footfalls as I was by its legless wriggling. A few old *khachkars* were propped up to back on to the gorge, and snails crawled around their weathered fretwork. I took off my coat and carried on.

The church inside was cool and musty. It was deserted and clearly hadn't been used for years. The sun fell through the slit windows in a series of silvery shafts. The walls were maculated with mould, and ferns sprouted from damp crevices. Outside I found a man squatting on a piece of broken cornice. A long grass stem arced from his mouth.

I asked him for water and he spun the grass stem but did not move. I told him who I was and what I was doing, and that I was not Russian and that I needed water. He smiled, then jumped down and led me back through the church.

This man lived alone in the old narthex. His only possession was a broken trunk. From this he produced lavash bread and cheese, and some water and a small bottle of arak. He had fifty hives scattered over the grassy roofs of the monastery, and we ate honey on the lavash that was full of insects and small sticks.

I thanked him and pushed on into the gorge. To get to the road, I had to wade through the river. I walked barefoot down to the bridge and there sat watching the point far above where the road dipped suddenly from the plateau and started its long, hairpinning descent. A black dot appeared and it took another fifteen minutes before it reached the bridge. The door opened and there in the back, in dark glasses and a perfectly pressed cassock, was the Bishop of Goris.

The bishop gave me a lift up out of the gorge and dropped me off on the main road south. I waited an hour before the next car came through. The Papazian family, or at least a part of it, was on its way home to Ghapan. They had been to a wedding. Baron Papazian drove with intense concentration; his breath smelt of arak and he had difficulty focussing on the road. Mother and daughter wore their smartest frocks, one a black and yellow print, the other black and mauve; when we stopped at a spring in the forest, they tottered through the mud like a pair of tropical birds.

These springs were a part of every Armenian journey. I had been on buses which had stopped simply so that people could visit a certain spring, filing up like liturgants to take the water. Many of the churches were built near water, no doubt replacing earlier sites of worship. Water held a peculiar significance for Armenians. (And I thought suddenly of the marches and the desert and no water, and those other springs at Ras ul-Ain and the desert cisterns choked with corpses . . .) Here the water was channelled into a pipe which pushed through a large stone. At the foot of the stone was a trough and the water slopped constantly over the rim of the trough to drain away down a gully. Above the pipe was chiselled, as at so many springs I had seen, the now familiar circle of spinning segments. The two Papazian ladies dabbed water on their rouged cheeks before returning to the car.

But as we pulled up out of the shadows of the forest, refreshed and watered, another car flashed past us. We all saw its shattered rear window and the man lolling across the back seat. Baron Papazian tightened his lips. 'Last night they killed a man on this road. I think maybe we will not get through.'

Sure enough, cresting a hill, we came across two or three cars and a bus stopped on the road. A crowd milled around, dwarfed by the presence of some anxious-looking *fedayi*. They propped their Kalashnikovs against their hips. There'd been an ambush on the road ahead. But in their excitement no one could tell me more. All I could make out was: 'Russian! Mussulman!' The Papazian family said they could not risk it and would head back to Goris. I thanked them and said I'd wait. Maybe the bus would get through later; this was the only road south.

The forest here was set back from the road and there was a meadow of poppies and high grass. The poppies looked like spots of blood in the glade. In the distance, beneath the southern sky was a line of dusty grey peaks, the last peaks of Armenia.

I paced up and down the road. Ever since I'd first plotted my journey, poring over maps in Jerusalem, I'd assumed that the Araxes river and the Iranian border would be its end. Getting to the bottom of Armenia was the journey's motif, its pattern and, physically at least, the bottom of Armenia was the southern border and the river. But what could the maps tell me of this?

The *fedayi* advised people to return to Goris. But I waited, unable to believe I would be thwarted here. Several hours later a truck pulled into the clearing; it would be going through. I hauled myself up into the cab.

The road to Ghapan was paved with past incursions. Strange burnt-out buildings stood among the trees. The airport on the edge of the town was a wreck. Approaching the narrow end of the republic, the far end of Armenia, I had the sense of something frayed, like the sleeve of an old shirt or a flag left out too long in the wind. Ghapan itself was a confused and broken town. An abandoned fun-fair lay rusting in its centre. The streets were full of swaying Armenians. Their faces would loom out of the dusk. The government hotel was still just about functioning. Having gone through the well-rehearsed routine of explaining that I was not Russian, and how I'd got to Armenia, and the countries I'd been through, the Armenians I'd met, they awarded me the Party Suite. There was no question of payment.

With the door closed I fell exhausted into one of the tobacco-brown armchairs. Guiltily I thought of all the communists who'd lolled in this seat before me. I thought of their good intentions, and their fat, shiny-suited behinds, their moustachioed self-importance. Then I fell asleep. Shortly before midnight I woke and pushed open the bathroom door. Something green-and-white slithered across the tiled floor. It disappeared into a large hole in the wall before I could make out what it was. Throughout the night there was a series of bangs that reverberated faintly through the walls. I was awake a long time trying to decide whether it was the green-and-white beast, the plumbing, or artillery raining from the hills.

In the morning I phoned the local priest. He said he had benzine and would be going south that day and could give me a lift. We met in the hotel café and he said that yes, there had been a mortar attack in the night. Father Vasken had the beard and grey eyes of the *fedayi*. He had only just been ordained and was the first priest they'd had down there since 1921.

When the waitress saw him, she abandoned her queue of customers. 'Oh, Kahana!' she cried and slapped a hand to her mouth. She sat down and, lighting a cigarette, started a long monologue about the old days. She could never cross herself or take mass, or baptise her children, and all her life she had wanted to go to Tatev to light candles for them, and her daughter who'd died and now he had come – like a saint! like an apostle! – she had no need to worry.

'Thank you, Kahana. Thank God you have come.' She gripped his hand. 'Look, I have carved a *khachkar*, in secret. It is for Karabagh. Can I bring it, Father? Can I bring it to the church?'

He said he'd be pleased, and we left the hotel and Ghapan and drove up towards the pass.

'You see how the people are hungry for God. Last week, some *fedayi* saw me in the hotel. "Come, Kahana!" they said. I could not say no to the *fedayi*. They took me to their room. On the bed were six guns in a row. The leader points at the guns. "You must say mass, Kahana! You must bless our guns!"'

'What did you do?'

'I did not know. They did not teach me in the seminary. So I said prayers and put some water on the guns as if for baptism.'

We came over the pass in cloud, but by the time we reached Meghri it was hot and dry. The town is squashed up against the Iranian border, which runs along inside the Araxes river. It was unlike any of the other Armenian towns. Father Vasken had not yet seen one of Meghri's older churches and we went to get the key from the toothless guardian; he'd lost it. He handed us instead a pair of pincers and we ripped off the padlock. Inside Vasken turned up his nose at the ogee arches and the Persian details of the frescoes. 'Mussulman,' he whispered.

Later he returned to Ghapan and I waved him off up the gorge. I then crossed the main square. Old men sat beneath the plane trees and spat cherry stones at my feet. I was bored of explaining I wasn't Russian. I returned their chill stares.

Meghri was an oppressive place. Not a moment went by when I wasn't aware of some sense of encroachment. On all sides the mountains loomed over the town – bare, treeless mountains with sharp ridges which were either in shadow or else a constantly changing backdrop of blues and yellows and reds. There was an unfamiliar dryness to the place. Looking across the gorge, across the wire, to the dragon's-teeth ridges of Iran, I felt the vastness of the east and, by contrast, the last squashed-up corner of Armenia. But it was, as ever, the unseen, human threat that weighed heaviest on Meghri. Azerbaijan lay ten miles away, both to the east and to the west. Soviet tanks were dotted along the frontier and to the north, between the people of Meghri and their compatriots, lay nine thousand feet of mountain. Meghri is Armenia in miniature, isolated and exposed: Armenia on the border, between Iranian Shiites, Turkish Sunnis and the rags of Soviet communism, between three worlds and an adherent of none.

I headed up out of the square and through the town's network of alleys. There was something I wanted to do. I climbed for half an hour, an hour, two hours. I rested at the foot of a cliff. The town's dark houses were scattered below in the dry valley; they looked like something stuck to the bottom of a pan.

Carrying on over the ridge I dropped down and rejoined the Araxes gorge. It was narrower here and the river came quite close to the border. On the same river, only a couple of hundred miles north, were the ruins of Ani where my journey had begun four years before. It was a circle of sorts. In my pocket was the small lump of rock I had picked up a few days earlier, from the depths of the Sevan tunnel. I had intended to keep it, but instead I took it out and pitched it over the fence. It cleared the barbed wire and followed a low arc over no man's land, before falling into the twisting eddies of the river Araxes.

# 23

For the mountain man there is no life save high in
the mountains.
When fate casts him into the valleys, he soon
perishes from longing.

From 'The Red Belt', Polish folk song

I stayed that night with Meghri's local governor. It was hot, hotter
than any night I'd spent in all those months. I slept on his balcony
beneath a bright moon. The whole gorge was lit up in its silvery
light. In the morning I prepared to return to Yerevan. There was a
bus up over the hills to Ghapan. But the road to Goris was blocked.
There'd been another ambush and again the passengers stood on
the road in threat-tightened groups, eyeing me suspiciously, exclud-
ing me. I took refuge in a *chai*-shack. There I met a man named
Ashot, also waiting for the road to clear. He was sitting on his own
with a glass of vodka. His face looked dangerously red.

He asked me to join him and I ordered cheese and lavash and more
vodka. I toasted peace and when we had drunk to peace, Ashot toasted
victory. When we had drunk to victory, I toasted all the Armenians
who had helped me on my route. And when we had drunk to them,
Ashot put down his glass and became suddenly quite maudlin.

Long ago, he explained, he had lived in a village like these ones.
Then he'd gone to Yerevan and things were good for a while. 'I had
a place at college and was the best in my class at English. But afterwards the Party did not give me a job. They did not like me. I could

have been a good teacher or a translator. Instead my life is nothing.'
'But there is no Party now,' I said.
'Now my country needs me to fight, not to teach. I would like to
be *fedayi* but . . .'
'But what?'
He looked beyond me. 'It is difficult. If I could have the chance
to fight, I would . . .'
Just then a *fedayi* swaggered into the hut. He hitched his rifle over
his back and looked around the room. When he saw me, he came
straight over and grunted in Russian: 'You must come outside.'
'I am not Russian,' I said.
'Come!' he repeated.
Ashot attempted an expansive introduction – said I'd been with
Armenians in Beirut and many far places and how far I had come
and that I was a good friend . . . The *fedayi* looked at me again and
I said it was true.
He tugged at his moustache and left. Shortly afterwards he
returned and said, 'Look, the road will not open today. You will
have to go back to Ghapan.'
I asked if I could wait here.
The *fedayi* again pinched his moustache. 'Yes, why not stay, both
of you. You can come to our village.'
I looked at Ashot. His face had become even redder. 'No, no. For
me, it is problem . . .'
As I climbed into the *fedayi*'s beaten-up jeep, Ashot gripped my
hand in both of his. He seemed painfully confused and the drink
had nudged him close to tears. 'Do not be afraid. You must go. I
cannot. I am afraid. I am sorry. No, it is not possible for me . . .'

The *fedayi*'s village spread over the hill towards a wide valley and
the distant Araxes plain. Above the plain the sky was fringed a paler
blue. We dropped down through the outer homesteads of the village
and a warm wind blew in through the flaps of the jeep. The *fedayi*
was called Hamlet, and the village, a familiar series of dust tracks
and green gardens, bore the name of another heroic prince, David
Beg. Briefly, in the early eighteenth century, David Beg had managed
to unite Armenia's mountain chieftains against the Persians. But like
Joseph Emin and so many others, he had failed in his bid to sustain
an independent Armenia.

I stayed a couple of days with the *fedayi* in David Beg. The Armenians here were about as far from the first ones I'd known, behind the barred windows of Jerusalem, as could be imagined. The men wore quick, wide smiles, and looked old before their time. The women had proud, faraway expressions and wild locks of raven-black hair. It was the women who really ran the village. They trailed the children behind their aprons, kept house, swept the leafy courtyards, fed the animals, and spent much of the day in the forest working the strips of land that had been cleared for planting. The men spent the nights on guard and the day dozing by the fields. They had reverted to their traditional role, that of vigilante, mountain warrior, protector of the hearth.

At about noon of the following day, Hamlet and I picked up three trussed chickens and drove through the forest to the fields. We cut hazel stakes and cooked the chickens, and then with a dozen or so others sat out the long, lazy hours of the afternoon, talking in the shade while the water pattered through its channels to irrigate the fields. A little later, leading the horses back to the village with a few of the *fedayi*, we came to an abandoned chapel in the forest. A *khachkar* was propped against its ivy-clad walls, and candle-wax hung down its face. One of the *fidaee* produced a stump of a candle from his pocket and, lighting it, placed it on top of the *khachkar*. Hamlet broke some bread, and someone else pulled a bottle of arak from the saddle-bags, which was passed from hand to hand.

All the *fedayi* wore crosses round their necks and had them tattooed on their forearms. They kept saying to me, 'We are Christian, *they* are Mussulman.' But the whole casual liturgy was enacted with a clumsy bravado. In these warring villages religion had become more a waving of colours than a statement of faith.

It was early evening when we reached the village again. We tethered the horses and looked in on Hamlet's cousin. He stood in the shade of a walnut tree, salting the skin of a bear. The bear's death was discussed and re-enacted at length. He thought it an Azeri at first, as it pushed out of the trees one night and across a clearing in front of his position. When he saw it was only a bear he'd smiled and uncocked his rifle. Then he changed his mind and shot it anyway.

He threw a mocking smile in my direction.

'You think English would like the bear?'

'Keep the bear,' I said.

'Maybe he finds our nights too cold!'

'The Armenian nights are fine.'

He chuckled and wiped his hands and we all went inside and sat around his sitting room. A few rifles stood beside a piano in one corner and a couple of babies crawled around on a woollen blanket. Another infant clawed and fed at the breast of a girl who looked no more than seventeen. The talk was easy and relaxed. I listened to the hard guttural consonants and the throaty laughs. I watched the movements, fluent and expressive, and sensed that here, where the threat was greatest, the Armenian spirit was at its strongest. It was the same spirit that had driven the Armenians through the vast improbability of their history, that in its oddly inverted form ensured their survival in exile. It was here raw and untempered. It confirmed what I'd suspected all along – that these villages, with their perpetual patterns of fertility and fighting, were the fount of that spirit, where it bubbled like a spring from the high Caucasian rock.

A woman brought in a tray of vodka and glasses and Hamlet sat at the piano. One of the *fedayi* leaned on the piano-lid and raised his chin before launching into a song called 'Hay Aghdjik', Armenian Girl.

'Hay aghdjik.' He gripped the piano-lid tightly. '. . . Sinoon aghdjik, chega kes bes sirounik, Hayastani sirouni aghdjik.'

The *fedayi* stood and pressed a clenched fist to his forehead and, when he looked up again, his eyes were filled with tears. 'Hay aghcheek . . . Hay aghcheek . . .'

A little later I went with Hamlet to the village hall. In one corner were groups of boys playing table tennis and carambole. Around the flaking walls were photographs of neck-tied worthies from better days. There was also a theatre beyond the hall, and about thirty or forty people were scattered among its seats, watching a futurist cartoon that flickered against a makeshift screen. Hamlet took me into a side-room which was markedly better decorated. Red velvet banquettes ran around the walls and behind the bar was a rack of electronic equipment. Hamlet slid in a cassette of synthetic Soviet rock. This had been the private room for the Party, but was now in disrepair.

For the moment though it provided the *fedayi* with an appropriate sense of opulence. Hamlet spread his arms and grinned. 'It is good, yes?'

One or two of the other *fedayi* drifted in and flopped on to the banquettes.

Hamlet asked me: 'You want to see video?'

'What video do you have?'

'We have video of ladies, or video of fighting.'

'You choose,' I said.

'OK. We have fighting.' He laughed, but more from good spirits than any sense of irony.

It was an appallingly tacky American film, dubbed into Russian. The dubbing was not synchronised and the tape had been played so often that all the colours had become yellowed. The story, such as it was, involved the training of a unit of crack commandos. They were placed, unarmed, on a small hillock while strange bands of theme-fighters took it in turns to attack them. There were Primitive types with bows and arrows, Roman types with spears, even a couple of tilting knights. And at one point a group of Mongoloid karate experts yelled and high-kicked their way up the slope. Some of the recruits were frankly not up to it, and soon lay groaning or dead on the ground, but the crackest of the crack defenders survived. They then had to leave the hill and jog sweatily across some sort of parched semi-desert. I was just thinking what a good parody it made of Armenian history, when a boy pulled aside the black velvet curtain in front of the door and cried:

'Hos ah!'

The *fedayi* jumped up and grabbed their weapons. I ran out with them into the hall. Others were spilling from the theatre and the boys abandoned their games; a ping-pong ball bounced across the floor.

Out on the terrace it was dark. There was a clamour of expectancy. Then a burst of automatic fire came from the forest below the village. After a few seconds of quiet, a trail of red tracer flashed overhead. Cries of fury rose from the small crowd.

Hamlet thrust his hand up towards the sky. 'Look! Now you see what the Turk does to us!'

I nodded, though in fact the tracer came from behind us, from an Armenian position.

We left the club in Hamlet's jeep. In the darkness I could hear the stutter of light gunfire and now one or two shells. We drove to Hamlet's home. His wife was already standing at the door and the light seeped out around her. She handed him his Kalashnikov and a plastic bag full of spare rounds; his daughter stepped out and coyly gave him the gun's sling, which he clipped on to the stock and barrel. He reached down and touched the girl's head. No one spoke. We picked up the others. At each of their homes a woman stood on the threshold with a gun and bags of ammunition. Then again into the darkness and the lanes, unsure quite what was going on.

I turned to Hamlet, and asked, 'What is happening?'

He shrugged and shook his head.

We took up position on the downward edge of the village, sitting in a line against the bunker of the old milk co-operative. The night was clear and cool and there was a bright scattering of stars. Down in the valley, I could make out the lights of one or two of the Azeri villages. Somewhere above us a dog was barking, but the gunfire had stopped.

Hamlet crawled a few yards around the building to where it faced up the valley. He spoke into a two-way radio. I heard him ask what was happening. 'Chegitem,' crackled the reply. 'I don't know.'

Then from below us there came a burst of automatic fire. Hamlet fired blindly into the trees and waited. The gunfire was returned and I heard one or two rounds tear harmlessly through the birch leaves beside the shed. Overhead trailed more dotted lines of tracer and more shells, and from far off up the valley came shouting and more shooting. Hamlet's radio hissed and someone asked him what was happening. He said he didn't know.

Silence again. The dog barked. Hamlet tried his radio but now it wouldn't work. He crawled back to us and, shaking his head, lit a cigarette.

We sat there four or five hours. At times there was the rattle of gunfire, but it was all a long way away. Sometime before midnight, a force of half a dozen men came out of the trees. Hamlet prepared to fire, but they turned out to be Armenians. We were joined briefly by a messenger from one of the other groups. He was trying to find out what was happening. He sat down against the wall of the hut and lit a cigarette. The match lit his face briefly before he shook it out. Hamlet passed him the bottle and he told some joke about the Azeris which I could not understand. Then he disappeared into the night.

All the while across the yard, a hurricane-lamp swung its milky light backwards and forwards against the barn door. It traced a slow, hypnotic path in the breeze and I thought of how every one of the Armenian evenings had contained in them this – these men, this village, and all that inherited fear of lost land.

# SOME REFERENCES

Christopher J. Walker, *Armenia: The Survival of a Nation*, second edition, Routledge 1990, London.

David Marshall Lang, *The Armenians: A People in Exile*, Unwin 1988, London.

Sirarpie der Nersessian, *The Armenians*, Thames and Hudson 1969, London.

H. F. B. Lynch, *Armenia: Travels and Studies*, two volumes, Longmans 1901, London.

Leslie A. Davis, *The Slaughterhouse Province: An American Diplomat's Report on the Armenian Genocide 1915–17*, ed. by Susan Blair, Aristide D. Caratzas 1989, New York.

A. J. Toynbee (ed.), 'The Treatment of Armenians in the Ottoman Empire', Parliamentary Papers, Miscellaneous no. 31 (1916), reprinted with decoding appendix 1972, Beirut.

Francis P. Hyland, *Armenian Terrorism: The Past, the Present, the Prospects*, Westview Press 1991, Colorado.

Vartkes Yeghiayan (trans.), The Case of Soghomon Tehlirian, Armenian Political Trials, Proceedings 1, ARF Varantian Gomideh 1985, Los Angeles.

Joseph Strzygowski, *Origins of Christian Church Art*, Clarendon Press 1923, Oxford.

Richard Krautheimer, *Early Christian and Byzantine Architecture*, Pelican History of Art 1965, London.

Pars Tuglaci, *Osmanli mimarliginda batililasma donemi ve Balyan Ailesi*, 1981, Istanbul.

Steven Runciman, *The Medieval Manichee: A Study of the Christian Dualist Heresy*, Cambridge University Press 1947.

F. C. Conybeare, *The Key of Truth: A Manual of the Paulician Church of Armenia*, Clarendon Press 1898, Oxford.

K. S. Papazian, *Merchants from Ararat*, ed. and revised by P. M. Manuelian, Ararat Press 1979, New York.

Joseph Emin, *The Life and Adventures of Joseph Emin: An Armenian*, second edition, 1918, Calcutta.

James R. Russell, *Zoroastrianism in Armenia*, Harvard University Press 1987.

*Documenti di Architettura Armena, volumes 1–20*, ed. by Agopik and Armen Manoukian, OEMME Edizioni, Milan.

Osip Mandelstam, *Journey to Armenia*, trans. by Clarence Brown, Redstone Press, London.

Paruir Sevak, *Selected Poems*, trans. and with an introduction by Garig Basmadjian, St James's Press 1973, Jerusalem.

The lines quoted from Aram Arman's 'The Chant of the Returned Poet' are reprinted from *Armenian Poetry Old and New* by permission of Wayne State University Press.

# INDEX

# INDEX

# KODANSHA GLOBE

International in scope, this series offers distinguished books that explore the lives, customs, and mindsets of peoples and cultures around the world.

**MAN MEETS DOG**
Konrad Lorenz
Illustrated by Konrad Lorenz
and Annie Eisenmenger
New introduction by
Donald McCaig
Translated by
Marjorie Kerr Wilson
1-56836-051-7

**SARAJEVO, EXODUS OF A CITY**
Dzevad Karahasan
Afterword by
Slavenka Drakulić
Translated by
Slobodan Drakulić
1-56836-057-6

**MERCHANT PRINCES**
*An Intimate History of Jewish Families Who Built Great Department Stores*
Leon Harris
New introduction by
Kenneth Libo
New foreword by
Oscar Handlin
1-56836-044-4

**THE FORBIDDEN EXPERIMENT**
*The Story of the Wild Boy of Aveyron*
Roger Shattuck
New introduction by
Douglas Keith Candland
1-56836-048-7

**TURKESTAN REUNION**
Eleanor Holgate
Lattimore
Illustrations by Eleanor
Frances Lattimore
1-56836-053-3

**HIGH TARTARY**
Owen Lattimore
Original photographs by
Owen Lattimore
New introduction by
Orville Schell
1-56836-054-1

**GOD'S LAUGHTER**
*Physics, Religion, and the Cosmos*
Gerhard Staguhn
1-56836-045-2

**THE FOUR-CORNERED FALCON**
*Essays on the Interior West and the Natural Scene*
Reg Saner
1-56836-049-5

**THE CROSSING PLACE**
*A Journey Among the Armenians*
Philip Marsden
New introduction by
Peter Sourian
1-56836-052-5

**TRACING IT HOME**
*A Chinese Journey*
Lynn Pan
1-56836-043-6

**TRESPASSERS ON THE ROOF OF THE WORLD**
*The Secret Exploration of Tibet*
Peter Hopkirk
1-56836-050-9

To order, contact your local bookseller or call 1-800-788-6262 (mention code G1). For a complete listing of titles, please contact the Kodansha Editorial Department at Kodansha America, Inc., 114 Fifth Avenue, New York, NY 10011.